Aufgabe

Number 8

"Thing 06." by Kim Beck

"reach / hand" and "No List (no list)" by Diane Ward first appeared in a chapbook published by Seeing Eye Books. The author thanks Guy Bennett for his support.

Aufgabe is published annually by Litmus Press. Single issues are $12, a subscription for two issues is $20. For institutional subscriptions rates and for information about individual subscriptions, contact the publisher directly.

Litmus Press is the publishing program of Ether Sea Projects, Inc., a 501(c)(3) nonprofit literature and arts organization dedicated to supporting innovative, cross-genre writing with an emphasis on poetry and international works in translation.

Litmus Press/*Aufgabe*
P.O. Box 25526
Brooklyn, NY 11202-5526
www.litmuspress.org

All Litmus Press publications are distributed by
Small Press Distribution
1341 Seventh St.
Berkeley, CA 94710
www.spdbooks.org

ISSN: 1532-5539
ISBN: 978-1-933959-09-2

Aufgabe is made possible, in part, by public funds from the New York State Council on the Arts, a state agency, as well as an award from the National Endowment for the Arts. Litmus Press is also supported by grants from the Council of Literary Magazines and Presses, our members, subscribers, and individual donors. All contributions are tax-deductible to the extent allowed by law.

Contents

feature

Russian poetry & poetics
guest edited by Matvei Yankelevich

"Thing 12," by Kim Beck

What's Going On in Russian Poetry?

Matvei Yankelevich

What is *contemporary* in, or about, contemporary Russian poetry? When, about a year and a half ago, Tracy Grinnell of *Aufgabe* and Litmus Press asked me to curate a Russian portfolio for this issue, I was presented not only with the problem of selecting poets in an anthologist's manner, but also with the more salient question of the contemporary.

The contemporary — as is too clear in the formulation of the typical anthology — is always fleeting. There have been several Russian poetry anthologies of various stripes and colors in recent memory[1], but this is not one of them, first of all because I am afraid of anthologies. With every anthology I've contributed to, I have experienced at least a tinge of disappointment, if not a minor bout of rage. After all, just look at those thick tomes with their zealous titles! How long and how inclusive must an anthology be to ward off the suspicion of incompleteness? Who is left out, and why? How do you figure the expiration date on an anthology of "contemporary" poetry? Can we trust either a lone-star translator or a translators' posse and its lurking personalities? The questions whirl, raising the dust — you have to turn away.

And so, in imagining this Russian portfolio for *Aufgabe* #8, I wondered if a smaller selection of poems and essays by a modest number of presently active poets could produce the sensation of knowing, or at least glimpsing, *what's going on* — a sensation so often lacking in anthologies? What follows, then, is an admittedly subjective and (therefore) arbitrary selection of essays and poems from a variety of Russian writers who were chosen by some similarly arbitrary parameters: I decided to limit the scope to poets who (a) live in Russia; (b) write in Russian; (c) are about my age, or a little older, but not as old as my parents; (d) are writing poetry actively and in a public way, and seem to be participating in some way in the literary culture; (e) are accessible through my personal connections; (f) seem relatively translatable (an interesting idea!). Also, I had a page limit — which, as generous as it was, I of course exceeded — and a desire to include essays or artistic statements by as many of the poets as wanted to offer such. For the most part, the selection of the poems to be translated was dictated by the poets themselves, submitted in the spirit of periodical publications. I am grateful to the translators, my willing friends and colleagues, but not only for their selfless labors. In effect, and as it always really is, the translators also acted as curators: They further narrowed the sets of poems that I had received or, in some cases, opted to translate other poems, thus taking some more of the selection process out of my hands. Through this experimental process I have had the luck of finding a group of works that somehow provides an array of answers to the question about the contemporary moment in Russian poetry, at least for myself.

The notion of page count only partially motivated my decision to print only the English translations. For a variety of socioeconomic reasons, the internet has been a primary medium for the dissemination of contemporary poetry in post-Soviet Russia. So much so that a large number of authors published on paper in the last 20 years have also made their books and/or individual poems available for free on the web, and still more poems are only available electronically. It therefore seemed to me redundant to print the Russian originals of these texts side by side with the translations. The online component to this issue (www.litmuspress.org) will post links to the Russian originals, or — in the few cases where such are not already available — will provide the texts themselves.

I should first disclose that the poets I am most familiar with in the younger Russian scene are those whom I met through happenstance in the late 1990s (thanks to the Summer Literary Seminars in Saint Petersburg), and later came to publish in the Eastern European Poets Series for Ugly Duckling Presse. Aleksandr Skidan and Dmitry Golynko (and later Elena Fanailova) were my guides into the Russian poetry of the new century, just as it was beginning. Through them I heard of more poets, met some, read others (many of whom I could not include here). Another key resource was Dmitry Kuzmin's intrepid website, Vavilon.ru, which permitted me to read almost everyone I'd ever heard of. In addition, CEC Artslink commissioned me on several occasions to translate a sampling of poems by several of the visiting poets in their Open World program, which pointed me in still other directions.

Formal verse (rhymed and metered to a lesser or greater degree) still dominates the landscape of Russian poetry, and free verse is seen by mainstream critics and editors as an anomaly at best. (Dmitry Kuzmin's publishing projects run against the grain in this respect.) This selection is unrepresentative for its emphasis on (what in the Russian context would be) more experimental trends, although, to the readers of this journal, the experimental label will seem odd-fitting when applied, for example, to Kuzmin's straightforward confessional lyrics about gay relationships or Tatiana Zima's unrhymed and unhinged rants. In today's culturally conservative Russia, free verse is as marginalized as queer politics.

Just as the dichotomy of traditional form vs. free verse is still a central one in Russian poetry, so is the long-standing division between Moscow poets and Petersburg poets, even when comparing similarly progressive (free-verse) poetics within one generation. (This divide is sometimes felt so strongly that some recent anthologies have for the most part excluded one in favor of the other.) Of course, there is a long history of mapping the mind-body problem onto the geographical space of Russia, where Petersburg is the cold, controlling intellect, and Moscow the warm-blooded and chaotic heart of the land. Reductively speaking, the difference could be said to be one of modernist difficulty (Petersburg) vs. avant-garde accessibility (Moscow). The three Petersburg poets presented in this issue (Golynko, Skidan, Sergey Zavyalov) often use found language or existing discourse — conceived in widely varying ways — as source, or at least as integral to their practice, and are typically more Western-leaning in their philosophical underpinnings. Whereas, Moscow's most coherent new stylistic movement has, at its base, the more homegrown straightforward utterance — seemingly born out of the esthetics of Moscow's 1990s spoken-word scene — which Dmitry Vodennikov has dubbed the New Sincerity (a term also used in the late 90s, to different ends, by the Moscow Conceptualist Dmitri Prigov). (Poets associated to some degree with this esthetic might include such vastly different poets as Linor Goralik, Zhenya Lavut, Ilya Kukulin, Dmitry Kuzmin, Stanislav Lvovsky, Kirill Medvedev, Slava Mogutin, Andrei Rodionov, and many younger writers). The perceived schism being performed along these lines is a rift that recalls the American poetry wars of the 1980s.

The American reader of this Brooklyn-based journal will be intrigued to find just how much the Russians are influenced by American poetry (an indication of which might be Zavyalov's use of a poem by Ezra Pound as the final word to support his essay's claims). Moreover, many of the poets presented here translate American poetry: Medvedev has translated most of Charles Bukowski; Skidan has brought Michael Palmer, Susan Howe, Eileen Myles, and various Language poets into Russian; Kuzmin translates mostly New York School poets. I wouldn't hesitate to say that American poetry has become the most prevalent foreign model for the contemporary Russian poet, replacing the European models of the past (German and British Romanticism for the Golden Age of Pushkin's time, and French Symbolism for Russia's early 20th-century Silver Age). I would argue that this has something to do with an anxiety over the place of poetry in contemporary Russia.

The poet in Russia has only recently suffered the blow dealt to poetry by the introduction of a free market and the loss of traditional cultural values. For the Russian poet, a crisis of identity has ensued which Soviet publishing practices and that culture's valorization of poetry (whether by the official structures or the dissenting intelligentsia) successfully warded off until the 1990s. Thus, it should be no surprise that the place of poetry — of the poet and the reader — in the post-Soviet (and arguably post-Putin) society is central to several of the essays and, indeed, at least peripheral to many of the poems included here. The poet in Russia now has to deal with the fact that the poet is no longer a hero, a reality that American poets are long used to.

Anxiety over the audience for poetry seems to form a cornerstone of American modernism: "If anything of moment results — so much the better. And so much the more likely will it be that no one will want to see it." So begins William Carlos Williams' *Spring and All*, pairing the lack of audience and the contemporary in poetry in a kind of mathematically reciprocal relationship. And it's not that no one will see it, but that no one will "want to." The critiques inveighed by Williams' hypothetical readers of the early 1920s — "Is this what you call poetry?" and the like — are the same ones that contemporary Russian poets feel they must defend poetry against.

As it happened, in organizing the material alphabetically, Elena Fanailova's poem, "Lena, or The Poet and the People," sets the stage. (The title seems to echo Alexander Pushkin's *The Poet and the Crowd*, anchoring the poem to a history of Romantic defenses of poetry on Russian soil.) Echoing the voices that confront Williams, the cashier Lena, at the store where Fanailova (the other Lena) likes to go, expresses bemusement about the book of poems that the poet — somewhat apologetically — gifts to her. Fanailova's anxiety over whether Lena will like the poems and, later, why she doesn't like them, becomes the shaky ground on which she builds her "defense." The defense of poetry is the task at hand for many of the poets in this selection; it seems poetry is threatened in a way it never was in the Russian context[2]. As the title of one of Skidan's essay collections suggests — *The Resistance to/of Poetry* — poetry resists the mainstream as much as it is resisted by its intended audience. Moreover, the official culture virulently resists most poetry that is "of moment," mounting its own defense against what it perceives as a threat to Russia's poetic tradition. Kirill Medvedev's provocatory claim that his poetry is mainstream poetry — perhaps a Whitmanesque, or maybe Beat, but definitely American move — is a reversal that only serves to prove the same point.

I think that from the conscious appraisal of this crisis stems much of what is contemporary in Russian poetry; only the poetry of the past and the future can avoid it. This crisis of confidence is the invisible impetus for the assertion of new lyric and epic modes, by Maria Stepanova and Sergey Kruglov, respectively. It is the implicit subtext of Skidan's analysis of poetry's place in a media-saturated world, and the explicit topic of Zavyalov's thoughts on the place of Russian poetry in a globalized culture. ("How will the poet survive in the coming century? What will he live on and for? What kind of relationship will there be between poet and reader?") The globalized referentiality of an Igor Zhukov or an Andrey Sen-Senkov confirms this anxiety, which also serves to jump-start the vehement reaffirmation of the "I" in Vodennikov's New Sincerity, or its problematization in the transgressions between pronouns in the poems of Anton Ochirov, and the redemptive approach to the poet's voice in Golynko's post-Language *defamiliarization* of everyday Russian speech. The same crisis may also effect a kind of return to a (neo-)folk poetry in the intonations of Stepanova and Linor Goralik, as well as Kruglov's resurrection of religious poetry in its peculiar Russian Orthodox form.

Furthermore, the institutional mediation of the relationship between poet and audience has itself become an object for serious scrutiny, which prompts Medvedev, for instance, to step out of the game completely by forbidding publication of his work and simultaneously refusing his own intellectual property rights. On the other hand, seeking to reinstate the poet-hero, Vodennikov seems to have embraced institutional support and publishes his poems (and commentary on contemporary poetry) in "glossy" magazines, and his five-star website (vodennikov.ru) may be what it takes to return celebrity status to the poet in the 21st-century.

The poet writes toward the future rather than the present, as Sasha Skidan once convinced me in a more elegant formulation. So, it remains to be seen what stance will be taken by poets coming of age after the fall of the Soviet Union. Of particular interest are those poets who will have no cultural memory of what was the traditional role of the poet in Russia for several centuries. One assumes that poetry will still be written, and perhaps it will even flourish after the anxiety over poetry's lost cultural relevance is, as the Russians like to say, *perezhyto* — lived through, survived. Will they demand a return to order (as Eliot and Pound had in their different ways)? Will they become content with isolation, retreating into their local status, their poetry becoming a kind of an untranslatable heirloom product? Will they value global trade over national identity, the epic over the lyric? Or — what is most difficult for a country so vast and yet so centralized to apprehend, much less accept — perhaps they will become absolutely various, at which time the editors, translators and publishers of anthologies will focus only on smaller groups, towns, virtual communities, neighborhoods, or even... just the unique specimens: individual poets. Poets who do not write with the anthology in mind.

The directions poetry will take, it seems to me, are largely being determined by the fierce and friendly debates taking place in the present, on the margins of the entrenched and inert Russian culture, and in the poems that follow. What's going on over there will hopefully have some resonance with what has been going on over here.

— *Matvei Yankelevich*
Summer 2009, Brooklyn, NY

NOTES

1 For those curious, here's a list of recent anthologies of (more or less) contemporary Russian poetry in English translation, going back ten years:

New Russian Poetry, edited by Peter Golub (*Jacket*, #36, 2008. http://jacketmagazine.com/36/)
Contemporary Russian Poetry, edited by Evgeny Bunimovich and J. Kates (Dalkey Archive, 2008)
A Night in the Nabokov Hotel: 20 Contemporary Poets from Russia, edited by Anatoly Kudryavitsky (Dedalus Press, 2006)
An Anthology of Contemporary Russian Women Poets, edited by Valentina Polukhina and Daniel Weissbort (University of Iowa Press, 2005)
Crossing Centuries: The New Generation in Russian Poetry, edited by John High, et al. (Talisman House, 2000)
In the Grip of Strange Thoughts: Russian Poetry in a New Era, edited by J. Kates (Zephyr Press, 1999)

2 During Russian Modernism, what's called the Silver Age, poets — whether Symbolist, Acmeist, or Futurist — were at the forefront of public debate on modern art. They rarely seemed anxious about a lack of interest in poetry, and therefore never needed to defend it. In the Soviet era, stadiums filled to capacity for Mayakovsky, and later for Pasternak and Evtushenko. (Had Brodsky ever returned, I'm sure the same fate would have awaited him, much to his chagrin.) Soviet culture, perhaps by virtue of the hero-worship implicit in totalitarian propaganda, swallowed whole the trope of poet as national hero. At the same time, the intellectual opposition believed in the poet's potential to be conscience and voice of the people. Thus, poets like Akhmatova and Mandelstam were feared by the regime — one must assume, because of their potential heroism — and therefore persecuted.

Poem

Elena Fanailova

Lena, or The Poet and the People

Translated by Stephanie Sandler

There's a clerk in the all-night store
Where I stop after work
To buy food and drinks
(I hate that word, *drinks*).
One time she said to me, "I saw you on TV
On the culture channel
I liked what you were saying.
Are you a poet? Let me read your book.
I'll give it back, I promise."
I say, "I don't have a spare copy right now,
But when I get one,
I promise I'll bring it to you."

I wasn't at all sure
She'd like the poems.
That actor's urge to be liked
Is astonishing, whorish,
It disappeared after Sasha d–d,
But now it secretly returned.

Eventually an extra copy of my book
The Russian Version turned up
A poet has to get involved
Distributing books, after all
Publishers don't do much on this front.
I handed it over. Right there, as I was paying for the food and drinks.
(Kefir for in the morning, one gin and tonic, a second gin and tonic,
Plus a little vodka,
And farewell, cruel world,
To quote Lvovsky's version

Of two Nizhny Novgorod boys' conversation.
No question, I remain a provincial teenager.)

It turned out that Lena and I were namesakes.
I hate that word, *namesakes*
And even more I hate the word *connect*
It arouses physiological spasms in me
Possibly because
The word has echoes of *coitus* and *sex*,
But I prefer fucking, pure and simple.
After all, I am my own highest judge.

"Could you autograph it," she says.
To Elena, I write, *from Elena*.
I hand it over nervously.
For a few days she doesn't look me in the eye.
Then one day there aren't many other people,
She says, "So, I read your book.
I didn't understand a word of it.
Too many names of people no one knows.
I had the feeling that you write
For a narrow circle. For friends. For an in-group.
Who are these people, who are they, Elena?
The ones you name?
I gave it to my girlfriends to read,
One of them knows a little bit about literature.
She felt the same way:
It's for a narrow circle."

I say, "Well, the part about St. Tikhon of Zadonsk,
You didn't get that?"
She says, "No, I got the part about Tikhon."
I say, "What about Seryozha the drunk, did you get that?"
She says, "I got that."
I say, "And the essays, you didn't get them?"
"I got the prose," she says.
"I even wanted to read more
About the people you were writing about."
So I say, "Lena, believe me, I didn't do it on purpose.
I don't want it to be hard to figure out.

It just turns out that way."
She looks at me sympathetically
And says, "Okay."
I keep on justifying myself, "You know,
I write plenty of articles,
And if you understand the ones in the book,
Then you'd get the other ones too, right?"
She says, "Okay, I get it.
So, do you want two beers and menthol cigarettes?"
"Yes," I say, "Lena,
I'm going to work on myself.
The balloon came back, a sign of wealth.
Look, that's almost a rhyme."

Why in the world do I care if she gets it?
Why am I trying to justify myself?
Why do I have this furtive sense of unease?
This forgotten
Wish that she like me?
Do I want to be loved by the people,
Like Vodennikov (poet or pianist)?
Am I conducting a purely sociocultural experiment
Like D. A. Prigov?
I already conducted one experiment
In his memory
At the election of a king of poets
At the Polytechnic Institute
(I read an anti-Putin ditty
At a festival sponsored by his Administration.
The pure wave of icy hatred
That rushed at me from the audience —
Students from provincial theater institutes —

Was more than I had felt in a lifetime.
That's a useful experiment.)

I always used to say:
Never show your poems
To your children or relatives
To workers or peasants

Instead, show factories and production plants,
To the poor — other people's problems, to the rich as well
But I
Show the work of native speech
In a country of natural resources
I am not fucking anyone over,
Like that poetess, Jakhan Pollyeva

Obviously, this is an unthinkable claim
And an illegitimate assertion of power
My father was right to be angry
When he read in my adolescent diary:
I would not want to pretend
That I am the same as everyone else.
("What, do you think you're above the rest?"
He asked me with a passion
That bordered on sado-masochism.)
I was fifteen
And depressed for the first time
My parents didn't notice a thing
I wasn't a complainer
And wasn't used to asking for attention

I don't think I'm better
My claim is tougher than that
I think I'm different — male, female, other, the others
Like in the movie by that name
With Nicole Kidman in the lead

I don't get why
On New Year's Eve
People run around looking for a tree
And for gifts
I don't get the dumb tradition
Of waiting around
For the President's speech on TV
Before the drinking and eating

I spent this New Year's Eve
On a train
From Moscow to Voronezh

With Chinese workers
Their Year of the Rat begins in February
And they went to sleep at eleven
And I fell asleep with them
As opposed to my usual habit
Of staying up until four

I like to look into
Windows all lit up
Aquarium fish
Live there among the seaweed
This is all terribly interesting
But I do not understand how it works
Who thought up the idea
Of drinking champagne
At the Metropolitan Opera?
On the other side of the world
It could have been entirely otherwise

In short
I can't pretend any longer
I walk home thinking:
Who is she, this Lena,
A clerk in an all-night store
Heavyset, fifty years old, with glasses
I love the word *heavyset*
She is plump, not all flabby, tall
A solid bleached blonde
She watches the Culture channel
When she's not working around the clock
Coming out to smoke on the stoop
And joke with the security guard
Who was she in that previous life?
An engineer? A librarian?
I have to remember to ask next time
If there aren't too many people around

And of course, she's right:
It's a complicated text,
Even when it pretends to be simple,
Like now

EDITOR'S NOTES

Stanislav Lvovsky (1972-) is a Moscow poet, translator, and prose writer.

Nizhny Novgorod is a provincial Russian City, northeast of Moscow. During the Soviet era it was called Gorky.

"I am my own highest judge" — Fanailova is quoting a line from Alexander Pushkin's 1830 sonnet "To the Poet." Fanailova also echoes the line in "Don't return: the KGB is back" above.

"The balloon came back, it's a sign of wealth" comes from a song by the popular bard Bulat Okudzhava (1924-1997). The original words are: "The balloon came back, it's blue," changed in translation to produce a near rhyme.

Dmitry Vodennikov (1968-) is a Moscow poet, and author of a review of Fanailova's poetry that referred to her as "a pianist." His own poems are included in this issue.

Dmitri Alexandrovich Prigov (1940-2007) was a premier Moscow poet and performance artist, whose work extended to visual arts and sculpture.

Jakhan Pollyeva is a staff member in the highest levels of the current Russian government. She worked closely with Vladimir Putin as a member of his cabinet. She is also widely known as a songwriter and performer of pop music.

An earlier version of this translation was published online in *Jacket* magazine. This version is part of Fanailova's first English-language collection, *The Russian Version* (Ugly Duckling Presse, 2009).

Essay & Poem

Dmitry Golynko

On Myself, the Optimism of Defeat and the Difficulties of Dialogue

Translated by Thomas Epstein

I belong to a generation of Russian poets whose coming of age coincided with the breakup of the Soviet Union and the (symbolic) crash of perestroika, with ineffective democratic reforms and effectively catastrophic economic instability. Not surprisingly, in my now twenty years of active literary life I have come to consider poetry a form (and an overcoming) of a catastrophic sociohistorical experience. Perhaps this claim sounds excessively solemn. But it must not be forgotten that my generation, which had been raised in the hothouse of Soviet literary life where the poet was simultaneously prophet, messiah, dissident, and Byronic demon, suddenly "vanished" in the whirlwind of the epochal 1990s. Poetry as "exalted" or "sublime" activity ceased to be part of the social fabric and our feverish poets' lives were subordinated without a second thought to the dictates of frontier capitalism and the mass media or simply to the laws of day-to-day survival.

Over these last two post-Soviet decades poetry has not regained its former place of prestige (and even sacrality) in Russian culture, but has rather remained the domain of a non-commercial elite serving a small group of experts and professionals (or at least this is how it is seen in the popular imagination). Yet paradoxically the majority of texts produced during this period have failed to build on the experimental spirit and avant-garde ethos one would have expected. On the contrary, there has been a conscious and growing tendency to work toward lowering the grand symbolic codes of poetry, to reduce poetic utterance to an easily accessible and digestible cultural product. Certainly this paradox can be explained when analyzed in light of the perfectly logical process of commodification of the poetic text (and, in general, of works of art) that occurred with the sudden rise of finance capitalism in Russia.

The alliance between Russian poetry and market economics, however, has spectacularly failed to stick; and it is not only because almost none of the central literary and intellectual magazines of the 1990s have survived, nor that there are alarmingly few interesting cultural projects currently underway.

The greater problem is that during the Putin era, the poetic community was virtually unable to produce any persons or institutions whose high cultural status was universally recognized, not only by the community of his or her fellows but even by the wider reading public. Moreover, in the second half of the present decade certain right-wing tendencies have grown stronger and revealed themselves explicitly in the cultural process. Parallel to this, there has been increased activity from left-wing groups, who equate the poetic text either with direct action or to an instrumental critique of the social order. Under such conditions poetry (at least as it exists in the social sphere) has ceased to be a form of visionary communion with a metaphysical beyond or a subjective investigation of existential questions, but only a tool of self-defense and resistance. The question remains: resistance to what and affirmation of what?

As I see it, the primary challenge for contemporary Russian poetry is to provide active resistance to the devaluation of elevated poetic discourse brought about by decades of excessive devotion to the postmodern esthetic strategies of play and profanation. Paradoxically, the lyrical voice that I have in mind emerges precisely at the moment — at the very point — of its *absolute unimaginability and impossibility*, that is to say, when parodic clichés and cultural stereotypes would appear to have definitively replaced authentic individual experience. In other words, the inspiration for the new lyric voice lies in the cognizance of its exhaustion and in the rejection of the traditional lyric as the vehicle for the expression of the sublime. In this process the lyrical subject itself is treated as an object of intense socio-critical analysis. Contemporary poetic lyricism also functions as a locus for sustained inquiry into the historico-psychological conditions that radically undermined 20th century Russia's dominant myth of poetic speech as a sacrificial and prophetic destiny.

Much of today's poetry has a tendency to claim for itself the right to intervene directly in political discussion, in reform and protest movements. This has naturally intensified discussions over the esthetic autonomy and social function of poetic utterance. On the one hand, contemporary poetry gravitates toward emotional clarity and a distinctly discernible intellectual content; on the other, it draws on the traditions — frequently hermetic and elitist — of modernist linguistic experimentation in order to resist the primacy of glib theatricality and immediate response required by the mediatized systems of success and consumption. In other words, for me what is of primary importance is the sociocultural aspect of contemporary poetry, whose richest results are achieved not by exclusive attentiveness to passing matters of the moment but by a return to modernist esthetic values of innovation and breakthrough, and on understanding inner experience as extreme encounters with the real.

Civic and ethical concepts (such as those of nation, people, association, justice, equality, etc.), which by the end of the 20th century had been largely delegitimized by their assimilation to the rhetoric of party hacks, are now discussed in all seriousness and sobriety in contemporary poetry; indeed these concepts are treated not as abstractions but as completely concrete categories and are even used as the basis for calls to immediate transformative action. Linked to this phenomenon is the fact that during the period of capital expansion, Russian literature — admittedly, less so than Russian art — became the property of cultural institutions and their administrator-experts who judged works of literary art without any consideration for the likes and dislikes of real readers. To give these cultural entities their due, they also provided a much-needed material lifeline, via grants and awards, to many poets (and others) who found themselves marginalized in the greater cultural processes. Unfortunately, much of the cultural production of the period that was deemed significant and even extraordinary appears in retrospect to have been the result of the inventions of an emerging political technology dedicated to the creation of institutions of cultural leadership (it is no secret that nearly all the mechanisms of sociocultural governance in Russia of this period were subject to politico-technological manipulation).

Interestingly, it is (and once more we will have recourse to a solemn tone) by working with Enlightenment concepts and modernist principles of universal human meaning that much of contemporary poetry stakes its claim to "truth value." At the same time, the authenticity of a poetic utterance is defined by its participation in its own national and ethnocultural context and in its ability to become an "event" in that culture by releasing a latently explosive potential. In its form and content much of contemporary Russian poetry owes its radicalism to postrevolutionary Soviet-Russian Futurism and to the "man of the 60s" associated with the Krushchev Thaw. However, instead of the utopian exaltation of its forerunners, this brand of contemporary Russian poetry is marked by pessimism and a sense of doom, a defeatist complex. Yet this esthetic does not lead to apathy; instead it encourages constructive resistance, in other words to optimism in defeat. This is what makes it an international phenomenon, that is to say an inventory of the agitation and bewilderment experienced by the contemporary human person confronted by the postindustrial profusion of goods and services (which has now morphed into global crisis, whether useful or dangerous for culture is yet to be seen).

Contemporary Russian poetry (which, by the way, shares many of the concerns and esthetic explorations of other world poetries, especially German and American) has several controversial and complicated tendencies that are of special interest to me. The first is the change or more precisely the broadening, vast in scale and in consequence, of poetic vocabulary and lexical means as compared to the norms that characterized the canonic literary language of the Soviet period. Literary language back then was still expected to operate in a fundamentally different way from both the crude government-bureaucratic newspeak and from the zealously colloquial language of everyday speech, with which an intellectual at home or a drunk in a bar (often one and the same person) could express himself. Soviet society, with its bookish imperial consciousness and essentially bourgeois mentality, naturally put a much higher value on a pure literary language than on popular spoken speech. The post-Soviet socium, by contrast, rejected the norms and purism of all refined artistic language, opting instead for a barbarous pig-Latin comprised of a jumble of colloquialisms, indiscriminately used foreign expressions, and a consciously debased, non-normative vocabulary.

This artificial and unmistakably semiliterate jargon appealed to the tastes of the cutting edge of the 1990s Russian poetry scene. Not only did it reflect the general enthusiasm for the esthetics of a postmodernism that operated without distinguishing among shades and nuances but it also conveyed, with almost surgical precision, the turmoil produced by ongoing social change. Indeed during this decade, in spite of the celebrated "stabilization" of Russia, there was a marked increase both in the disharmony among the various social dialects and in the individual styles that reacted so violently to them. Poetic language, achieving an almost limitless freedom, made frequent use of maximally expressive and, until then, taboo colloquial expressions. Without a doubt this headlong and chaotic process of broadening the poetic vocabulary possessed possibilities for modernization (especially as it made poetic language more plastic and adaptable to contemporary concerns); but it also concealed the clear danger of turning the poetic text into a slick entertainment or a rakish, nihilistic game.

The language of contemporary Russian poetry (and this also includes fiction, essays and highbrow journalism) is a dense — at times to the point of indiscernability — amalgam of criminal and prison jargon, drawn less from Hollywood blockbusters than generic street scenes out of the real-life megalopolises of the Russian 1990s; from so-called computer slang, produced by a process of mangling everyday words and basic expressions to the point of unrecognizability and then using them as a means of communication in chat rooms and in text messages; from the maximally explicit language of the "yellow press" that addresses the (supposedly) unchangeable lower instincts of the collective unconscious; and also from very specialized linguistic practices, learned by watching television (especially certain soap operas), that attempt to inculcate new norms for "average good taste." Such a language is utterly ungainly and even traumatic for its user, since one constantly "hovers" between incompatible poles of ideology and value, or simply "drowns" in all the informationally indecipherable noise. Under such circumstances poetry, working with a multitude of socially conditioned masks, neither disentangles nor isolates separate elements of the real (in this sense contemporary Russian poetry has left the Conceptualist 1980s far behind), but instead presents a brutal linguistic flood in which elevated metaphors, technical terms, and devalued personal expressions are treated as equally organic.

At the heart of this poetic labor with various socially or culturally conditioned linguistic codes lies an aleatoric principle of composition, governed by the random selection of this or that element of everyday or literary discourse. The extent to which this selection is accidental or intentional depends not only on the poet's mastery of his craft but on the state of the language itself; on its stability or mobility, the dynamism or inertia of the processes taking place within it. Given that one of the primary characters of my poetry is post-Soviet language itself, we must note its essentially dual status in that such a language is simultaneously subject and object of poetic discourse, undergoing a ceaseless process of self-reinterpretation. Being a typical and almost trivial "hero of its time," this language is destined to processes of endless invention and permanent stagnation; in other words, its accidental and compulsory elements are virtually indiscernible. Perhaps the term that best describes such a poetics is decontextualization, which consists of a logical and methodical transposition of linguistic figures (or, more precisely, their parts or fragments) from their natural or habitual contexts to other, hostile or indifferent ones. The unanticipated result of these processes is language as a caustic critic of itself.

At the center of my poetics lies the principle of seriality and a kind of sliding or gliding — as in surfing — across linguistic folds and surfaces. Yet the serial multiplication in which I engage testifies rather to the *impossibility of recurrence*, just as my kind of linguistic surfing inventories the *enclosure* of language and its *ceaseless resistance* to itself. The poem thus becomes a subtle and supersensible ear clogged with the echoes of alien, parasitic, and not fully assimilated speech of others. Such a poem ceases to fulfill the traditional, sonar-like role of capturing meanings and separating their sense but instead mechanically tosses back and forth random fragments of language snatched from the surrounding linguistic background. Is this background hostile or indifferent to us? perhaps passionately concerned? is this background meaningful or meaningless? naturally eroded or does the process itself produce the erasure of everything around it? human or inhuman? can it be heard or does it merely produce the illusion of audibility? All these and many other questions hang "suspended" in a state of irresolvability in my poetry.

Another tendency with innovatory potential in contemporary Russian poetry is its growing narrativity. The defining feature of this poetry is a strict physiological naturalism combined with a somewhat estranged and skeptical Romanticism, doubting itself and everything around it. Cold and calculated descriptions of reality are associated today with a cynical and dispassionate view of reality. This passionlessness derives both from the surfeit of available attractions, sensations and services, and from a desperate fear of showing true emotions since they prove so defenseless when inserted into the web of universal consumerism.

From this state of affairs another noticeable tendency emerges: the intimate emotional life of the contemporary person can only be communicated within the network of those social configurations in which these emotions are constructed and which either promote or obstruct their expression. In other words, the most intense and, so to speak, individual experiences of things such as love and physical attraction, desire and despair, are suddenly experienced as the product of contradictory social conditions, of suggestions and prohibitions that seek to program every aspect of human emotional and sensual behavior. Thus one of contemporary poetry's functions is to provide objective verification of this dependency of emotional life on the surrounding environment and to offer therapeutic treatment for its cure or at least mitigation. Contemporary poetry, by deforming and fragmenting these imposed sociolinguistic codes, helps to identify zones of autonomy and freedom that are otherwise hidden, and makes possible an encounter with one's own emotional experiences. The emotional content of contemporary poetry is thus a product of the crisis and breakdown of that traditional poetic language whose task it was to express the inimitable quality of individual sensual experience. In other words, the uniqueness and authenticity of contemporary poetic discourse can only manifest itself amidst the ruins of canonic poetic material or — what amounts to the same thing — in the process of stringing together or scattering the fragments of overhead speech, whether of highbrow culture or the indecipherable "mutterings" of the mass.

As I see it, contemporary Russian poetry is confronted with an urgent and long overdue task; that of overcoming the dialectic between Russian Conceptualism and Post-Conceptualism, two movements whose intellectual and cultural roots go back to the 1970s if not earlier. Conceptualism carried out a parodic critique of the totalitarian and deadening language of Communist power; Post-Conceptualism engaged in a playful and at times conformist critique of the capitalist language of money and media — but it could not avoid the trap of "sticking" to these languages, that is, of becoming their faithful transmitter. The only way for contemporary poetry to escape this dialectic is by rejecting the language of critical distance while affirmatively acknowledging the indestructible yet conditional nature of all languages of power. Affirmation rather than critique — this may be one of the key strategic tasks for today's innovative Russian poetics.

Another, no less inspiring task is the prospect of freeing ourselves from thematic and content-based isolation, which is inevitable for all national poetries because of their (potential) non-translatability — a fact that distressingly hinders poetry from becoming a truly relevant international phenomenon. Russian poetry — which sets high standards for itself and lies in what is now a semi-peripheral region of the landscape of late capitalism — emphasizes the same amalgam of psychosocial problems that with lesser or greater explicitness, is manifest in world poetry. This is why I and other representatives of my generation of Russian poets are prepared to enter into dialogue both with the realities of post-Soviet culture and with those themes that currently predominate on the global, information-driven stage. As I see it, one of the most promising avenues of potential development for Russian poetry in its dialogic interaction with other cultural configurations is to strive to express universal experience through linguistic reworking of individual experience.

For the Checkmark or For

Translated by Simona Schneider with Eugene Ostashevsky

STIFLING TUNES

stifling tunes in the smoky room
sister ninny flips through photos
past joy is moving in a zigzag
towards a new one, a worse one, but with a killer

figure, eau de cologne on skin
like Monica on Clinton, a Dutchman
flies about aimlessly, a voracious look
accompanies the "virgin," drool ejected to float freely

YELLOW POST-IT NOTE

what does the post-it note recall, yellow
on a white wall? that a dead
battery wants replacement? or some bullshit
obligation to take care of? that suddenly in one

of the sections of the department store
scarce goods were delivered? or that an inhumane act
invokes a reaction? the numbers
dating someone's life? or other thingies

THE COLLECTIVE OF THE UNEATEN

overslept, the meatball, a close relation to rot,
on the bottom of the pot winces its slimy pupil
against the impending cover, remembers what the diners
were ejaculating about, won't have to wait long

to join the collective of the uneaten, frost over with shameful
mold, start stinking, decompose on the fateful
wall of the garbage bag, in keeping with the DOL's rules
get compensation for its dutiful discharge

A CIAO TO NO ONE

who is the ciao addressed to? to the female worker
at the weaving mill, picked up downtown in nocturnal Shanghai
for tourist rates, or to a half-wit German intern
for some reason rejected, it seems her legs

not quite the right shape, or to the spiteful lady gym teacher
from those school years, who taught how to spring
over the vault, who taught, while coming, how to squeeze
the limbs around bars, what a pain in the

HELD UNDER PRESSURE

what meanness, tricked in her loftiest
she repeats, how mean, the polished off nip
clatters, the cry to watch out
incites the look-outs to tense up and slink

backwards, ratted out, the accomplice
denies everything, report filed
stews under a paperweight, victims of the jihad
make the front page, can't chase 'em off

NOT OUT OF DESPERATION

a pizza slice of chinese make
is taken out of the refrigerator
freezer crystals flow all over the frying pan
but not out of love, likewise two chicken

cutlets lie together on the bed of a griddle
out of desperation, having imagined
the continuation of their union, we'll have
to hold our nose, we're not savages after all

LOUD PROMISES

loud promise twittering quietly in the ear
a word kind of like truth, the tang of Chanel
out of yawning pores, table-dance girl totally trashed
shows her cards and the liquid tenderness

of seduction drips along the chin as viscous
syrup, the knee, smeared with green antiseptic
nudges the palm to grab it with a free and easy
motion by the kneecap minx

UNDER THE DO NOT ENTER SIGN

hanging do not enter sign blocks the highway
in its most congested place, a huge jam
allows drivers to relax, to break loose
from the chain of events, in spacious static

to experience the dynamic of diet cola
sloshing in the stomach, decaffeinated coffee
warms up the innards, even crawling out of your skin
it's a problem to get caught up in yourself

DELIBERATELY OR NOT

diving into the menu, the wild thang
gets her paws on it, taken to the restaurant
for the sake of sex, to escape the parabola
of a bummer, she's prevailed upon with every

effort closer to home, she asks for it sliced
thinner, considers the pros and cons of
compliance, if she moans when taking it doggy-style,
she overdoes it, as if deliberately

UNDER SAND

in the sandbox fervently working the shovel
the tender-aged tot is burying something
in the soil, maybe a squashed tube of penny
toothpaste, maybe a gutted condom wrapper

long past its expiration date, maybe
the bowel movement of the pooch
from the sixth floor balcony, maybe ketchup dropped
by a hot dog, not everything can fit in the sand

JUST FOR THE CHECKMARK

task performed just to check it off
bares the behind, letting the breeches down
touches inflamed tonsils with tongue
and crinkles the face, no matter where you cast

your heavy gaze everywhere depraved vision
of past experience, and behind it an inventory
of boxes, checked in order to make it easier
to work out who's bottom dog and who's boss

Ten Poems

Linor Goralik

On the Abrogation of Purgatory in the Roman Catholic Church

Translated by Peter Golub

It makes no difference, no difference Alyenka.
Yours are dead, mine have been killed by sorrow
you feel no pain, I can't stand it
you're twelve, I'm just over three
and here we are sharing an apple
on this two-minute break
an apple core, hard as rock
but sweeter than commissioned naive masses
(your Catholics, my morons).
The last day, but we don't care
although, it seems, like we should be praying
augur, shake, and tally up our sins
die and rise by word of ear
about who'll be transferred where
but you and I left for the balcony
you fidget, I hold you with my sweaty hand
by the gray collar
trying not fall from your lap
we suck our cigarette
I blow the smoke into your ear
into the indent from the rail.
When you shot at them, mom and dad —
When later you rose up to the window —
When I walked where I was forbidden —
When Alyosha went out with no scarf —
When Jerome jumped under the wheels —
When Natasha was a smartass to her grandma —
When Asim set off his heavy weight —
When Ezhen crept toward his brother with a pillow —
When Ilya followed that creep —
When Ellen with a lighter played —

When Bartholomew a kitten caught —
and suddenly the air was filled with padus berries:
Ezhen, Tanya, me, Bartholomew
Irina, Ada, and imagine, Ilya
who that creep had had right in the bushes
right in the padus bush, but even he
through rags and blood recognized the smell.
Well, that's the kind of minute it turned out.
The kind of moment in the padus history.

[untitled]

The milk brother pinched the milk sister
by the milk arm
so hard he leaves a bluish yolk
a blot of butter on milk soup
a faint birthmark
the only one for the entire daycare.
He who is our age, is our milk brother:
we're fed from the same milk kitchen...

Jesus what are you on about Sasha, what Pepsi-Cola?
What homeland, which, what are you on about?

[untitled]

Dark blue turns into light blue.
Pale crawls and slowly heats to white.
Green, still in June turned yellow
now turns brown
casts off almost mauve
for black
metallic.

Ash-pale melts into red.
Two pied watch a continuous yellow.
Quickly, one to two, delicate milk white
blends with scarlet
and everything brightens a bit more,

especially green and blue.
How simple it was when reds chased whites,
and greens chased browns.

Ash-pale still stares
into unimaginable light blue
reds from pain and insomnia,
suddenly silver appears
with a blinding rumbling violence
or gold
illuminated by murmuring wings.
Two pied
throw oily black.

Everything could be simpler
if the colorless made the flow static.
Did gradually not turn reds into browns
blues and grays into greens
all together into pied
hastening
one to two
until light blue gradually turns navy
until white pales and crawls to unending yellow's corners
filling it with red
dripping from small black
a bit below the stuck-together auburns.

Two pied drink haze
from darkened metal.
Blues quickly blacken.
They walk slowly
One of them suddenly pukes brown.

God's vines ripen
his wine flows beneath the sand.
Red does not part.
White remains dead.
Dead is too saline.
Black is gray.

[untitled]

A Mortal Thing buys a fan carries it home,
A Mortal Thing works like a horse doesn't drink and barely makes it,
A Mortal Thing eats a dumpling shows the little one the trick it
promised,
A Mortal Thing has a stomach ache drinks Maalox scary pancreatitis
cancer ulcer AIDS bitch Christ please no more I promise I won't,
A Mortal Thing washed a shirt good job the deed is done,
A Mortal Thing lies counting mom dad Natasha there remains Volodya
grandma Lena Sergey Misha,
five to three our lead that is of course if Misha on Saturday the
operation and all that,
pray to God because we're about to inherit the Earth,
with such a bad mathematical imbalance,
while so-and-so still glues gum under theater seats,
so-and-so forgets to pick them up from school from the rink from after
school daycare,
so-and-so speaks nonsense on the TV,
while so-and-so watches and gorges at night.
And all in all how much of that Earth is there and you promised it'd
help what's there to be afraid of?

That is of course if Misha Friday I mean tomorrow surgery and all that.

[untitled]

Nowhere to turn.
In the evenings
they gather at Chistye Prudy
at the windowless wall.
At first they mull miscellany over:
everything hurts
the heat
the indefatigable eye of the State.
More and more of them.
They slowly plaster the wall.
Press, push, try to displace each other
sit on their heels
or stand on tip toe
so as to weasel
cram into the fray
among the millions and billions
to spread against the wall
and put an ear to it
closer
closer still
and stand like that for hours

listening

how on the other side
the living
cough and trample
waiting for each other
at Chistye Prudy
at the windowless wall.

TRANSLATOR'S NOTE
Chistye Prudy — "Clean Ponds," the name of a neighborhood in central Moscow along the Boulevard Ring; also the name of the Metro station at one end of this part of the boulevard, not far from the man made ponds themselves, which are the source of the name. The area has been known, at least since the late 1980s, as a gathering place for alternative youth (punks, goths, hippies, etc.).

[untitled]

So one of them says to the other:
"I don't want to work, I'm staying home.
Won't leave you, I can't, I won't."

And the other says: "Quit it Alyesha
(or who will you be there — Seryezha, Sasha).
Quit it, you aren't a little boy, this is how things turned out.

Besides what has this to do with you? Sometimes this is
how it is.
Sometimes, the weak do not swim ashore
but this still leaves the work.
Watch how the water leaves from under our feet
come get ready or they will start to panic.

All in all I'm happy that all this happened
although it is a pity we had so little time.
I remain your brother, though you're such a prick,
shithead, asshole — kidding kidding, sorry.
Get out of here Andrei (or maybe Vova)
and plod along for yourself and the rest.
Go on, don't torture mama, enough with this farewell."

And no water, no air, no shelter.

One manages to cross himself
the other manages to turn around
to prepare
to regroup.

[untitled]

How they lay in the burrow together
the hare on his side, the little wolf face down
          and in the sky a star ascended.
The hare pet the little wolf, saying, "It's time,"
the little wolf grumbled, something about leaving later —
as if it were a game
as if nothing were happening —
          as if the star had never ascended.

Time to get up and get the gifts
and wander through December's thickets
and drop crowns into its snows
go blind in the blizzard while chewing scurvy
and carry their souls to the other shore
at night freeze to one another
(so, here, the Jordan would freeze to its shores)
sleep in snow and drink graupel —
simply because this was occurring:
          because in the sky a star was ascending
But they kept lying there, sides touching:
the hare awake while the little wolf soundly slept,
          and in his dream a star ascended —
that vexed and nagged him in his sleep
and in his dream led him away with it:
the little wolf walked, and the hare slept riding his back
and in his sleep spoke to the little wolf of everything:
  "This and that," he said, "with you
  the depth of hellish burrows doesn't scare me.
  And what do I need His gifts for,
  when here in the burrow,
  I lie between your ears?
  And why should I care about the soul?
  Between your teeth my soul is the most immortal."

And so they lay, and their crowns lay nearby
moving their ears, they hoped and did not breathe
walked nowhere, carried nothing, proclaimed to no one
and dreamed that time was still,

that nothing ever happened —
but in the sky a star ascended.

But that damned star ascended.

[untitled]

He flies up and looks: this one also has a stripe on his sleeve,
hard to tell what kind.
He flies up, the other smiles and makes a hand gesture:
"Yurochka, come again, remember: love, compassion."
And he flies up, stares into the porthole, and the other laughs.
And he of course keeps staring, can't turn away.
And the other thinks: "Poor Yurochka, I won't give you away,
won't tell anyone that I saw you,
not Peter, not Paul, not Senechka, not Andryusha,
no one, that is, none of us.
And they'll of course say: "Sure, old man,
if he really flew then why didn't you see him?"
But I'm not proud Yurochka, I won't give you away.
Don't want to scare my boys, that tender brood.
Come when you want Yurochka, get in line, peek in later.
After all I like guests, and they come so rarely.
Don't forget, that is, 'til next time; it'll be great."
He asks: "Soon?"
And the other's like: "Knock on wood, Yurochka, don't even say it."

[untitled]

And on the fifth how do they die?
And on the third how do they?
How do they die on the first Monday?
Lie thinking: "Today all the museums
Are closed for maintenance.
All that inert stuff wants cleansing,
the taxidermied animal looks into eternity more calmly,
when the month's dust has been swept away."
How do they die closer to four,
around a daycare's tea time?
Or how about around the evening news? Or six past
ten? Or five? Or three?
Or what about *right now?*
What kind of menology would it take
to tally each and every one of us?

[untitled]

Upon returning from the cemetery,
Death walks past the dinner on the table
and without taking off its shoes falls into bed,
exhausted, it quickly falls asleep.
You hold the fork still in the air,
need about five-six seconds
for the wave of frustration
to be surpassed by appetite —

like in the morning, when she piles on top
and commences squirming, rubbing
and kissing.

Essay & Three Poems

Sergey Kruglov

New Epic, Old Lyric

Translated by Peter Golub

In recent years the term "new epic" has been circulating in a certain sector of Russian poetry. The term "new epic" — rather arbitrary in my opinion — originated from the quick pen of the Moscow poet Fyodor Svarovsky, who applied it to a rather diverse list of poets, which included (in addition to himself): Arseny Rovinsky, Pavel Goldin, Dmitry Shkarin, Linor Goralik, Boris Khersonsky, Sergei Timofeev, Anastasia Afanasyeva, Renat Gilfanov, Pavel Nastin, Kanat Omar, Maria Glushkova, and Marina Astina. This list could of course be corrected and continued; for the sake of simplicity one could look at the forty-fourth issue of the internet magazine *РЕЦ*[1] (RETs) published in June 2007, and dedicated to the "new epic." The editors — Svarovsky and Rovinsky — modestly omitted their own poems from the issue. However, Svarovsky did include an introduction, which is essentially an attempt at a manifesto. In short, Svarovsky thinks that the term "new epic" can be used to describe both an existing poetic current and a renewed interest among readers in epic poetry, i.e. poetry that tells stories. *(According to Svarovsky, "nonlinear systemic utterance" — his programmatic formulation — signifies the author's rejection of subjective lyric perception; the return of the author's earnestness (destroyed — seemingly — by postmodernism) in relation to the world and to meaning, which comes about through the epic depiction/unveiling of the EVENT; something else about the difference between the new epic and the old; and, finally, summing it all up, the notorious resurrection of narrative/s.)* My personal interest in this topic only partly stems from the fact that my own texts are "hooked in" to the current of the "new epic." More importantly, the topic attracts me because, apart from writing poetry, I serve as a Russian Orthodox priest, and in discussing the above-mentioned notions, it is impossible to avoid touching upon the religious component of poetry. But let me apologize ahead of time, for this essay does not at all aspire to be a systematic article; it is rather a collection of cursory impressions.

"Poetry in the time of the end of the world." Do we have the right to voice such an audacious slogan, in addition to that of the "new epic"? And if we don't have that right, can we at least dream of a justification for the continued existence of poetry — in opposition to Adorno's no less audacious slogan about the impossibility of poetry after Auschwitz (a proposition that has grown metastatically into diverse areas of civilization adjacent to poetry)? Does the phenomenon of the "new epic," perceived and named by Svarovsky, actually exist? And with it hope? Or is it really just something not-new under the sun, not a new narrative (or, rather, a string of old, fainted narratives coming to), but something phosphorescent, bacterially decomposing, and thus REMINISCENT of life: the decay of narratives, and with that natural process of decay comes the opportunity to partake in the ultimate task: to take poetry to the bathhouse for the final time, dress it in clean garments, lay its arms across its chest, and position it in a reverent pose to await the end?

Those wishing to nourish their faith in the continuation of poetry, and in poetry's return to its proper place as the backbone of humanity (or even just one disc in the spine); those wishing to declare the end of the epoch of the "swooning narrative," desiring to breathe invigorating smelling salts; in a word, all those who hope for the motion of water, may — among other things — calm themselves even with these optimistic speculations:

The world is old. It is divided, according to the Gospel (and the entire Christian eschatological tradition) in TWAIN: God's & not God's; destined for salvation & destined for fire: the transcendental & the not transcendental; the healthy & the decaying; the sheep & the goat. In the number of other dichotomies, the epic is to the sheep as the lyric is to the goat. *(The epic, like sacred poetry, is a first-order derivative of the activity of the Logos in the human, the conscious verbal creature. To wit: the possibility of communication between God and Adam; the naming of animals; the possibility to glorify the Creator while still in paradise, before the Fall, although the Bible only suggests this indirectly; sacred poetry, its development, fall and resurrection; the liturgical poetry of the world; the language of mysticism and metaphysics; Dada, Futurism, Khlebnikov; the Charismatic movement and the Pentecostals "speaking in tongues"; etc., etc. The topic of sacred poetry is an enormous can of worms. Let's not touch it. And who hasn't touched it already!... I find much more interesting one of its subtopics: WHOSE language? God's language or the language of the abyss? Is it cosmic or chthonic? What feeds this or that author?)* The epic is the story of the Other / of contact with the Other (as corroborated by the Buber-Levinas paradigms), presented to the human as a possibility or as a given even BEFORE the fall, during Adam's the paradisal state. *(Forgive me, I know this is all rather muddled, "the incommensurable and only fog ahead," it runs, head before hand, wheezes, hangs by the string of the leash: one moment it jerks toward a trash can, the next moment it's pouncing on a passerby, then barking at a stray. One may only hope not to lose both glasses and galoshes in this mad race!)*

So, the lyric seems to me the corollary of "leather chasubles," evidence of the singular state of the human soul, which has spent its ability of direct communion. *("Paradise, my paradise!" Archpriest Stephan Lyashevsky's book* The Bible and the Science of Creating the World *contains entertaining speculations on the topic of what activities Adam took up after the Fall, including the story of his appeal to God. Here it is, the first the mixing of wine and hemlock, of sacred poetry and lyric!)* Let us then connect the epic to the eternal, and the lyric to the present. The lyric always belongs to the author. *(Individuality in detriment to personhood, which follows upon the the corruption of nature?... Bottomless abyss of quotations!)* Whereas, the epic is not so much anonymous as it is BEYOND INDIVIDUALISM, para-personal: the golden cloud of the epic hangs over EVERYONE'S space, nourishing each of us with primeval life-giving juices. *(Intention, having stuck out its tongue, rushes to piss on the sign post that says "myth," but we won't let that domesticated hound mark the post with his dirty thoughts!... And as for Losev — let us only mention "The Dialectics of Myth.")*

The lyric today is drinking the dregs from the bottom of individuality's barrel. The wine of the epic (possibly even the "new epic") still inebriates completely and utterly; it's nearly impossible to find anyone indifferent to it. Mass-media news, the success of biographical prose, documentaries and photojournalism, the "live" transmission of the internet, and all the rest, can be seen as a tendency toward the epic, as a need for an immediate response to the EVENT, which after all does happen, because the world is ending though it has not yet ended. And we hope that the EVENT will live on in eternity, i.e. in a world that's not completely cancelled out, but radically transformed. *(Here we could expand on the comparison of pre- and postnatal episodes of the human life, the life of the womb and the life of the external, their difference and the depth of reality's connections...)* Perhaps, who knows, maybe the lyric won't end, but will simply melt with epic and sacred poetry?! *(Here again is a place for myriad quotations and battles of the mind... dementia?.. haha; sorry, please forgive me. Of course, heeding Swedenborg and Fyodorov won't save you, but there is SOMETHING in their prayers, isn't there...?)*

In conclusion, all this new attention devoted to the epic appears to me as an inspiring and worrying sensory perception, with which humanity perceives *eschatos*. So, Yeats was probably wrong: It's not that "the centre cannot hold," but rather that the leather chasuble is slipping off our shoulders, and will soon separate from us... it's the end of "Old Human"! *(It's no accident that, according to church tradition, the BEGINNING OF THE END is counted from the Incarnation, and these "last days" have been going on for over 2008 years, and counting....)* And the end of the lyric, as it is akin to the gold filigree on these leather chasubles. Parousia[2] will shine, filling the heavens, and true to the covenant that says "stand fast; and hold the traditions which you have learned," we will greet it, with the remains of our hands clutching to our chests editions of *The Iliad*, *Gilgamesh*, *The Encyclopedia Britannica*, and an anthology of poems by the "New Epic Russians."

NOTES

1 The online journal *РЕЦ* (RETs) can be found at: http://polutona.ru/?show=rets

2 Parousia (ϖαρουσία) is a term used in the original Greek of the New Testament for the Second Coming of Christ; literally it means 'presence' or 'arrival'.)

Dictation in Russian with Examples from Manyoshu

Translated by Peter Golub

Squeak, ballpoint, squeak!...
And now let us begin:
"Life bores me and death is unnecessary.
The emperor's sickness, the wars, the names of friends,
The snow and leaves in the small courtyard of the church, while raking..."
Fall sees clear through to the bottom of the land, like through
Thin tea: bare groves, the village.
Across the lilac postmarked field
A tractor purrs, turning
Soil clean, blank side up.
The crows, their black markings, compile
Someone's unknown address.
The harvestman — a cloud hangs an arachnid message in the sky.
Write, write, don't get distracted! Where were we now?
What's next? "The art of living
Yet another autumn day," last year's
Public transportation schedule.
The sun sets; it is Thursday; tomorrow
The carrier from the regional post office
Will bring us Friday. And, maybe
A letter from you will arrive.

Litany

The day evaporates inside the censer
Of the brass afternoon.
In the off-white soap of mountain sky,
A kite lifts his orarion stole like a deacon.

Chased by the vacillating sandy heat
Life came in benzene fumes,
From the city, via the freeways,
Pumping out moronic tunes.

And the city lies down like a tired corpse,
Swimming in the sweat of rays,
Nearing the judgment and the light,
Majestic and enlightened.

Sing faster during the sixth echos
At the beginning of the Menippeah
And with benediction
Accompany all this decay and memory;

The tin of garages, piebald from the sun,
The butts of faith, not quite burnt through,
Slate, shrunk during its escape
To size forty-three.

October 20, 1943:
Closing Night at the Jewish Theater in the Vilnius Ghetto

when the wind picks up
we see
the will of wordless leaves

(willing to will — blown into will
subtract them
prematurely   from the world:
world - will = a show, a presentation)
world [minus] will

that is what is left: a performance, a show

a peripheral inhuman
theater
cosmetics glycerin a studied text but
painted cardboard is good enough to open veins
and one can smash one's head against the coarse fabric
of the stage flats as if a ghetto wall

(peruse through the herbarium
of photos in the foyer: travesty tragedian
noble father
of six million children)

with the maple blush of David's shield
falling fall
onto the ramp —

(hands up come out
for your bow
applause from the audience in black)

— this is us willing toward God
our backs to the wind —
leaves

blowing burning autumn smoke
(the street sweeper sweeps)

(life! what life: fool's gold
we borrowed from frightened Egyptian women
now we return the props
we no longer need them
"Shemot" has had its run and closed for good
the director's satisfied)

we will not leave anyone in october's
branches
on this shore: our prophet
our bumbling prompter
will cross the burning river
of Paneriai with us
and walk into the audience

we move in a straight line
from flame to light: we are
no more
who will judge us?

EDITOR'S NOTE
Paneriai — A town near Vilnius, Lithuania, also knows as Ponery; site of the mass murder of Jews, Poles and Lithuanians (approximately 100,000 victims) during World War II.

Five Poems

Dmitry Kuzmin

[untitled]

Translated by Peter Golub

for Vasily Chepelev

I missed out on a lot when I was a kid. I had no one
with whom to play doctor; I never
held a stethoscope in my hands.
It is awkward
to hold the cool metal object
with warm hands
and touch it to another's, also warm skin —
you are both warm, between you the cool
metal (only once
when I was brought by one of my boys
to an expensive clinic
did I see how they preheat it —
the stethoscope, the metal spoon to check the throat —
they even had a special hotpad for it).
Now it is different: it is easier
to use the fingers,
even if they are cold,
and press them to your skin,
then lower,
we need no extraneous objects,
we are still young, already naked,
although before, before — when I dared
touch only myself — one could
use a stethoscope, but never the hand;
I missed that as a kid.

[untitled]

I dreamed of a correspondence between two lovers,
high-school seniors, in the mid-eighties,
the same round cursive (one of them made a copy? for me?)
Winter and spring — letters saturated with feelings.
Summer — letters from separate vacations.
September — the last from her, an explanation for the breakup
... *you're always thinking only of your own, about what worries you.*
You wrote that you liked Estonian jazz musicians,
I subscribed to "Estonia Today," to learn a bit about them
(of course such a magazine couldn't exist, let alone about jazz)
You wrote of your love for trolleys and buses —
I had nothing to say in reply...
Perhaps, she should have attached an epigraph to the letter:
If only you were cold or fiery!
If only someone would send me letters about trolleys and Estonian jazz.
The reasons given by the one leaving, mind already made up,
always seem to miss the mark.
I read everything in the train, in the empty car, and miss my station,
my backpack gets jammed inside a compartment,
the emergency break is nowhere to be seen,
behind the window the inexpressive yellow landscape picks up speed,
and I was supposed to meet you somewhere here,
the picture falls apart, the wave ebbs, no one to fix the vernier,
time to wake up, *Sesame Street* on the neighbor's television,
the neck and chest ache — maybe from the-day-before-yesterday's hickeys,
maybe early symptoms of the flu,
and I'll never be seventeen again.

Last Year's Photos from Lake Seliger

The lake retreated, the boats were left tied to the shore.
Long sharp grass grows everywhere.
In the photo you sit on the edge of a boat,
your feet dangling in the wave of grass,
in a bright yellow windbreaker,
your face stained by last night's fire.
The Ostashkov highway murmurs small cars,
howls trucks behind my back,
these are not in the shot. Across the road
an autoshop's abandoned yard —
the rusty shells of ZIL-trucks,
the cabs' blue even lighter in the cheap print.
This was the color of the sky over the pines,
where at the top a woodpecker knocked,
flickering his red hood, too small to catch on film.
Further on begins a wide sandy road
called Communard Street.
This one of you is from the back —
you're walking into the bright future.
A Young Pioneer cabin on the corner
with two funny stone crocodiles placed at the entrance,
one of which has had his tail knocked off.
The pale-pink station with a huge padlock on its door;
you doze on a bench near the entrance,
while a big rooster walks in the background.
The next one is already in Velikie Luki —
against the pattern of a brick tenement
I wash my head under a water pump,
like in the shampoo commercial for "Wash & Go."

I was in Germany this summer, you were in Anapa.

[untitled]

For D.K.

One 27-year-old poet,
in a state of heavy inebriation,
addressed a 38-year-old poet
who went by the diminutive Mit'ka.
At that point one 23-year-old poetess
made an acrimonious comment
to him, something to the extent that
he would probably refer to one 54-year-old poet
as Seryozhka.
The 17-year-old poet
present at the time
looked to her admiringly.
And the 38-year-old poet remembered
a passage in a biographical sketch
by a 62-year-old poet
about a 70-year-old poet
who had died some 25 years ago:
Not long before his death, the older poet
had suggested that the biographer
refer to him informally and without the patronymic,
but the biographer couldn't do it,
which he regrets more and more with each year.
After reading this sketch the 38-year-old poet
had made an effort and, in his correspondence
with that same 62-year-old poet, began to use the addressee's
full name, but without the patronymic,
and still using the formal "you" because the 62-year-old poet
had never suggested anything of the kind, though
he did sign his letters in the diminutive, Grisha.
After this episode the 23-year-old poetess
left to go walk in the rain
with the 17-year-old poet,
the 27-year-old poet fell asleep,
and the 38-year-old poet began to write a poem
wondering to whom he should dedicate it,
his mind stopping

on the 17-year-old poet,
because more than anything else
he wanted to be with him, or be him,
which all in all is the same thing
and also because they both
happened to have the same initials.

[untitled]

Translated by Yuliya Idlis and Matvei Yankelevich

to Slavik

I couldn't take you, though you wanted it so,
begged for it, pulled your butt cheeks apart
with your strong fingers so that it'd be
easier for me to enter you; but I couldn't
get hard any more, exhausted and sleepless,
and afraid it might hurt your first time,
because for the two nights and the day between
we've been making —

— we took a room
on your ID (it's triple the price for Russian visitors),
I thought of pulling the mattresses from both beds
down to the floor — a homemade king size —
this way you, being six feet tall, wouldn't have to
scrunch up your legs during our short bouts of sleep;
and you thought of putting the tacky table lamp
behind the blinds, so that the soft
reddish light —

— I pulled off the useless
condom, all sticky from the camomile hand cream,
kept saying "sorry, it's me, just can't, too tired," and
you smiled at me: "Now you've got something
to come back for," and I flopped on my back,
so that, while giving in to you, I could see your face:
eyes squinted with tense focus, the sharp line
of cheekbones with a three-day stubble, lips trembling
and locked a split-second before the last hoarse —

— check out time:
nine a.m. so I set the alarm on my cell
but couldn't fall asleep, while you,
curled up like a pretzel, pressed your head
to my chest and we dozed off by turns,

and once, when you thought I was asleep,
you whispered: “I don’t want you to go” —

— midnight in Bryansk,
the Russian border, passport control, and for some reason
there’s music at the train station, a trackman’s bar clinks
as he shunts the switch, a streetlamp from the platform
shines light on a fantasy novel for the guy on the lower bunk,
across the aisle an unattractive cadet undressing,
and the pattern of his chest hair repeats yours;
oh now I would —

Two Manifestos & Five Poems

Kirill Medvedev

Communique

Translated by David Hock

This is how I see the contemporary cultural situation.

On the one hand we have an authority that is gradually recognizing itself and its cultural priorities, and — as it often happens — already taking shape, a readiness among active culture-workers to act according to those priorities, or the priorities of a new bourgeoisie, that is also recognizing its needs (in literature among other things).

On the other — "contemporary art," too close to me in its ideas, manifesting itself (at least in the Russian variation) in the form of irresponsible, infantile merrymaking and supposedly independent intellectual utterances taking place in a bounded territory staked out for that purpose.

On the third — a firmly established book business, a handful of publishers who are often half-literate, indiscriminately printing one thing after another and hardly having time to adhere the right label, and who, for purposes of profit take advantage of the most unprincipled devices and provocational strategies, flirting with what are to me the very ugliest and most disgusting ideologies. The inhuman struggle for awards. The endless pre-staged literary pseudo-events. Certain literary lobbies waging a cruel, primitive battle for cultural influence. The nauseating speculations of critics and journalists unabashedly serving their masters; critics who either foist their own cultural world on the reader, unaware of just how underdeveloped and small-minded it is, or preach xenophobia and pseudo-religious obscurantism, cultural or otherwise.

All this crushes and depresses me. I want nothing do with a system that so devalues and banalizes the Word, that so profanes it. In the situation as it stands, it seems impossible to me to participate in literary life, to publish even with those who favor me, to use the welcoming disposition of this or that person or institution, to develop the theatrical principle in contemporary poetry which once interested me.

I'm interested only in the position of the artist waging the "battle for art." However, in our time, it is first and foremost a battle for the position itself. Its meaning lies not in claiming this or that social role but — on the contrary — in vision, undistorted by the social situation, and in freedom from the strictures imposed by the art world. This is the only position for which it's worth fighting at a time when art is becoming increasingly drawn into the sphere of commerce, politics, and social life.

I refuse to participate in literary projects organized and financed by the state as well as through cultural channels. I endorse only books or other mediums put out by my own labor and with my own money or publications on my own site on the internet.

I refuse any and all public readings.

This is not a heroic pose; this is not a PR strategy; nor is this a desire to secure my own publishing business. This is a certain necessary self-restraint. I am convinced that my texts are the real poetic mainstream and for that reason, I hope that if, in my person, the mainstream takes such a half-underground and, as much as possible, independent position, then perhaps in my country there will be a more honest, uncompromising, and truly contemporary art, with no ties to the insufferably vile revanchist (or on the other hand, pseudo-liberal) ideological claims of the cultural, financial, or political powers.

Manifesto on Copyright

I do not have, nor can I claim, copyrights to my texts.

Nonetheless, I forbid my texts to be published in any anthologies, readers, or other collected publications once and for all, considering such publications to be repulsively manipulative actions of one or another cultural power.

As a result, my texts may be published in Russia or abroad, in any language, ONLY IN THE FORM OF AN INDIVIDUAL BOOK, gathered and arranged according to the will and desire of the publisher, to be released in PIRATED FORM, that is, WITHOUT THE PERMISSION OF THE AUTHOR, WITHOUT ANY CONTRACTS OR AGREEMENTS WITH HIM, which must be indicated in the publication data.

I am grateful to those who have published me up to this date.

EDITOR'S NOTE

Kirill Medvedev originally published his "Communique" (on September 22, 2003) and his "Manifesto on Copyright" (on November 30, 2004) directly on his website (http://kirillmedvedev.narod.ru). Medvedev's texts included in this volume have been translated and published without the author's knowledge or permission.

[untitled]

Translated by David Hock

the rowan tree shimmered
there were a whole lot of dogs
all looking for something,
maybe they were looking for acorns or chestnuts,
but mostly they were alive —
dogs,
little old ladies with children,
acorns and chestnuts,
if there were horses here,
the horses would also be alive,
but, ladies, gents,
in a few days there will be cold and ice,
cold and ice,
a salty haze of snow
will paste eyes shut
milk cap mushrooms
will shrivel and wilt,
of things dear to us
all that will remain is the rowan tree
and already, somewhere here —
in the mandarin groves,
in the warm courtyard,
in the pestilent heights,
where darkness rocks a teeter-totter,
and every morning white bread turns into a jagged, icy torture —
there is a
rehearsal;
i went toward the lights;
their brilliance shone before me like a wall;
these weren't hot fires, but cold ones —
the fire of cold, which in an instant turns water into ice;
if even the thought of ice should flash by
everything around freezes over;
that's how Siberia appeared, and the northern lights
are just the last flutters of thought;

there's no other explanation;
the noises of the radio testify to it,
especially between broadcasts;
the TV screen bears witness to it
when the channel is shut off
and the screen flickers with lines and dots;
but we'll put the ashtrays back where they go and sit just right.
men talk about hunting;
a waitress wipes down silverware;
there's a church drawn on the plate...
in 1974 the director W. Herzog arrived on foot from Berlin
to Paris. his woman-friend had got well again
(he had come on foot so that his acquaintance would get well)
and not long before that i was conceived
at that time i already had —
as it says in a brochure against abortions —
at this time a person already has
a skeleton, nerves, a flowing bloodstream, breath,
a child uses its hands to grab, sucks its finger,
and if something hurts, it quickly jerks its hand away, which shows
that it feels pain...
(but there's something he still doesn't know!)
in 1980, the musician Jan Curtis hung himself
after watching Herzog's film *Stroszek*;
there exists a white ovary of the head
and a pearly spittle of the tail
both of them like spittle —
i noticed this in chicken eggs,
in dribbling clots, in the unformed
fetuses of chicks;
turning them out in the morning onto the frying pan;
there was no one to tell it to;
for that one must address oneself to the cold,
must talk of other things,
address the emptiness, a space that is
maximally free from ears and mouths;
address god or i don't know whom —
swallowing this gurgling hell in the mornings.
i can write a brochure against abortions.
i could write a brochure that would

make my readers
lose their fucking minds;
those fighting for
the propagation of our nation
would lose their fucking minds;
God would lose his fucking mind —
the author of many brochures on the evils of abortion
would find himself unemployed
his infinite children
will die of hunger —
maybe
they will die of cold —
they will never find out
how the rowan tree shimmered,
they will not see the milk cap mushrooms —
just like me:
i wanted to be a musician
but turned to a stone;
i'm turning into
a banner,
a bomb,
a rumor;
someone will find someone happy,
someone will become
heavy or tearful, or even mean —
i will become a musician;
my child will see me in the morning
coming out of a café.

[untitled]

i ate, listened to the radio and went to bed, but can't really sleep —
i'm prevented from falling asleep
by a beauty competition among the vegetables
in my dreams;
i'm a fan of the eggplant
... and i see a strange depletion underway —
everything falls from its place.
not everything falls from its place,
but everything turns into some sort of decaying globe of flora —
the end is coming to everything.
something else is coming instead.
speech lies in wait like death
for any old thing;
like a passion, an incredible weakness
defeats the world;
abundance and fragrant morning cream
are watched over by ashes.
emptiness begins to pour out.
every cavity
turns out to be filled in its own way,
in place of emptiness
a surprising intensity appears,
and all the news
turns into its opposites —
each item of news
turns into its opposite.
for example, the news:
an expert in interreligious discord,
unable to find grounds for criminal charges in the works of the accused artists,
was killed with a sawed-off shotgun through the door
to his own apartment —
and i dream that he wasn't killed with a sawed-off shotgun or through the door,
but in another apartment,
and not in his own,
and in my dream he did find grounds for the charges,

and it's as if he were never killed at all —
whatever variations,
whatever news
turns into its opposite
IN THE COMPETITION FOR THE TITLE OF BEST VEGETABLE
THE WINNER IS THE BEET
... i dream of a person walking on the border of a dream,
or more precisely, on the border separating two dreams —
a buddhist one and a christian one.
a person walking on the border of the dreams,
along a certain fringe
separating mountains of words,
all of them damning.
they tell him: "go back,"
and he says: "fuck off."
he's between a desert and a desert.
he says: "i'm between a precipice and a desert."
he walks on ice,
but says he's walking in ice.
then he says that he's on his way down,
they tell him "beat it,"
but for him it's no longer a question of "to beat or not to beat,"
for him it's just the question:
"to beat down or to fall in love"

[untitled]

on the 11th
two years ago
began my worst month ever
it started to seem to me
that i was already gone — it's here;
look, it's here,
but i'm already gone,
they've dragged out my soul and took it away,
it just doesn't belong to me anymore,
actual demons overcame me,
these were
the real thing, actual demons,
they were something unverifiable and invisible to all,
invisible to the eye, but real,
it's the kind of thing after which, it seems,
one can suffer a whole lot
and the very simplest happiness
seems, afterward, a great gift,
and the most simple gift
— after all that — seems
a gift meted out by fate.
i was two steps away
from glory,
two steps from
going and getting baptized into the orthodox faith
or converting to
any-which-one
of the monotheistic
religions,
absolutely no matter which,
it took me the rest of the autumn to recover
but then my soul came back to me,
but only a little at a time —
i think
that souls never come back right away
because a soul is a condition.
conditions don't come back right away

[untitled]

Translated by Keith Gessen

I'm standing here turning the pages
of a book by a young Petersburg poet,
with a funny kind of aggravation,
and sympathy,
with some slight irony.
I watch the things
this city makes,
no one is as close to the source of poetry,
to the world's ice,
attached to it through some special,
if seriously polluted,
pipe.
I didn't think I could still take pleasure
in the cold harmony
of the world,
from the only possible right combination of words.
Standing here, turning over these sweet conservative verses,
which you need to read
over tea, with milk,
in a bathrobe (!) (?),
and imagine yourself
in a hungry city,
a cold city during the war,
with the books of your favorite poets,
wondering which of them to throw
in the stove for heat,
and which to exchange
for some bad herring and a loaf of bread.

And then to find yourself in a hungry
city, in a cold building,
and imagine yourself sitting
with tea, and milk,
in a bathrobe,
turning the pages of your favorite book,
and taking pleasure
from the cold hopeless harmony,

from the gentle melodious word-picture,
from the only possible right combination of words.

In short, everything's all right with this book,
and "Denis Sheremetyev"
is, of course, the only possible right name
for its author.

So everything's all right, but —
but what?

No, no, no, eveyrthing's all right.

But still, maybe,
something's missing?
No, nothing's missing.

Maybe the problem is that
I'm turning the pages of this book
in a store that got blown up a few days ago
and still smells like dried fish,
and everywhere, on the tables, on the shelves,
you can see the edges of burned books?

No, that's not it.

Art, as we know, is higher
than all that.

Actually, I don't believe that,
but for now, so that this poem
works out,
I believe it.

And this book's a little burnt too, actually,
but it's okay — see, it survived.

So everything's all right.
Although, maybe the fact that
everything's all right is the problem? No, that's not a problem.

Or maybe it's that when everything's all right,
that just doesn't sit well with me?
No, it sits well.
...
(Then what the hell?)

[untitled]

I've seen crumbling ridges,
and sea ports, and terrible towns.
but an asshole like you
that's something new.

A man who hires a prostitute
gives her more than he pays for,
and she gives him more
than he pays her.

Then where does the surplus go,
why are they both cheated?

It doesn't go anywhere, actually, it just disappears,
it melts into their mutual kindness,
it burns up
in their feast of kindness and self-sacrifice,
and that's why in the morning there's frustration —
hysterics, anger —
she wants someone who won't
pay anymore,
and he wants someone who will
only take.
And each of them needs some pressure —
egoism or cruelty,
their own or someone else's, it doesn't matter —
but so that one of them would get it,
so that one of them would be satisfied.
This is called: "I need love."
The kind that causes pain,
that causes music.
Music plays
and the one who's going to sell her tomorrow,
that is, in essence, the pimp, the salesman,
he knows her better than anyone, and loves her selflessly.
A pretty girls hands out cigarettes near the metro

but smiles at me just because —
and there's nothing anyone can do about it.
And only me, I'm the only one who thinks
everything's bought and paid for,
I'm the only asshole who thinks that,
even if not everything's bought and paid for yet,
not everything's stamped out,
even if you can still win some kind of prize,
in the end it's still going to turn out to be
a gratuitous boot-full of cash.
...
Oh, I know why I have so many bones to pick with you
my dear friends:
you're naive, and so pure,
you're blameless.
And I wanted to take your sins upon my head
(if only you'd had some).

Four Poems

Anton Ochirov

[untitled]

Translated by Christopher Mattison

death's prolonged aspect
an oil well we're born into
a mostly similar summer approximately seventy times over

(a poem in seventeen words)

Processes

"Atoms and emptiness are the only real truths," said
Satunovsky, I
often appeal to that which in the Russian language is called
"Bog" — by which I mean that word —
"God" — is a customary coding of space, the same
as all the other words.

Some people think that I [who is this "I"?]
am referring to a Christian god,
some
even think they know what he looks like —
sufficiently human, if
you are to believe the European painters.
Others take this to be a discussion of a type of
abstract
essence, or the highest echelon,
where deeds or words are weighed upon the scales, still others
think it's all about the messianic nature of poetry — an occupation

as old as the human world (I know nothing about
the human world) —

which is why — for example — Indian Muslims
read the Koran in the original,
not knowing the language — simply
reciting the words; which is just as much a case of ritual
as those Russians who, in the nineties, infatuated with the East,
recited words in Sanskrit, much like
the aborigines (according to Nastya)
build clay airplanes,
just as it's a ritual for drivers
and front-seat passengers
to strap themselves in with the safety belts.
Clay machine guns suddenly flare out a rhyme.
I always carry a clay machine gun, and am not alone,
a significant number of my friends also carry them,
and it's a good thing they do.

You know
that we are all immortal but you do not
know what that really means —
our friends are infatuated with religion and they read books,
we are infatuated with quantum physics and the cultivation of plants,
with marxism or revolution,
and if I say that everything is connected — then what? We will wait
for the collider or, you say,
may two thousand and twelve.
You know, I think, in a sense, we've
already let it go, long ago.
In other words, there is nothing to wait for. Let's
synchronize the scintillating processes,
that are happening
at the level of our — so far, still human — mugs.

EDITOR'S NOTE

Yan Satunovsky (1913-1982), poet, children's author, and chemical engineer. In his youth, Satunovsky was close to the Constructivist poets in the late 1920s; but he is better known as a member of the Lianozovo group, which he joined in 1961 — an influential but underground arts circle that included the poets Genrikh Sapgir, Vsevolod Nekrasov, Igor Kholin (and sometimes Gennady Aigi) and the painters Lev Kropivnitsky, Olga Potapova, Lydia Masterkova, and Oskar Rabin.

Faith, Hope

I.

what am I to do if
they want hope
when
everything has ended

and I
know
there'll be no hope
and nothing
has ended

it's good, one must say: good
everything's real, as tangibly
real as film
imagination

as thought
as memory

good lord
they even believe in god

how embarrassing
no, not embarrassing

2.

that's how it is
you simply cannot say:
"he is in need of comfort"
[you are in need of comfort]
or "he is frightened"
[you are frightened]
that is, you do not say it to his face:
it's not that it's tactless, it's just that
you don't do it
anyone alone
among strangers

at that moment he'll
push you away in the same
way he pushes himself away
at that moment he simply
catches a glimpse of himself —
don't do it
let him not see
himself

it's a good thing he knows
nothing about himself
[what a pity that you know
nothing about yourself]
but then
he is able to believe (now)
or to hope (now)
or to cry (now)
or — later — to be consoled

and I am able to love him
imperceptibly, unnoticed

Militiaman

blasphemy / mental crime
self-denunciation

(making a spelling mistake, a schoolgirl whacks
herself with a ruler)

"what if Jesus is full of shit?"
"I'll kill you, scum"

"can't you really just laugh it off?"
"this is serious"
"why do you mock me with your laughter?"

(making a spelling mistake, a schoolgirl whacks
herself with a ruler)

:

you vainly believe these words
(schoolgirls don't care about spelling mistakes)
on the other hand
they're into relationships between people:

what are the emotional hooks
we use to hold onto one another

:

and then
everyone
grew up

< *the militiaman remained a midget* >

Four Poems

Andrey Sen-Senkov

Drawings on a Soccer Ball

Translated by Peter Golub

on the german team
the last name of the player
translates into russian as
pig crawling up
blond graceful critter

the polish boys
got lost at the equator
nothing to breathe
the qualifying south american auschwitz
the polish boys will asphyxiate doubly

poplar down
a million white fluffy unofficial balls
and none of them counts

eleven glasses of islam
drown in mexican tequila

they say
that for daniel defoe's novel
the round island of tobago
was an uninhabited soccer schedule

in korea there are only seventeen last names
when a short last name is pronounced
inside it something is quietly specified
a fan of the croatian team
runs out onto the field

kisses the feet of the forward
now there is one more
who knows
that the lips of fingers
are one color with the nails

a five-year-old child
who has just learned his letters
reads as гус
like some sort of animal
that looks like a mangled white ball

the penalty is not called
no need to place the fork
in the slow meal of the tie game

the venous blood of the portuguese jersey
dries into scabs
into red cards

the face of the african fullback
is marked with the goalmouth's white line
forever in overtime

in saudi arabia
the players are forbidden to play for foreign clubs
because they may possibly lose
the round white grains
specifically grown by the soccer desert

in cologne the relics of the magi
who two thousand years ago saw
he who gave hope to the christian halfback
later sold for a good price
who kicked in his goals to the death

the english referee
shows three yellow cards
for a single player
a yellow ellipses

in a moscow sentence
moving across midnight

the two meter crouch:
an emaciated compass —
a tad gulliver

the argentinian trainer
a former taxi driver
stopped at the intersection
of gasoline outlines
in the nonexistent semifinal

mom named him after
the american actor ronald reagan
with the family promise
that he was to forget
that the actor finished as a president

the equador team
has a player named guagua
this is the name of a bus in latin america
the dark skinned bus
stumbles into an eleven-meter crash

the scarred face:
to fly out of the windshield at two years of age
so as to softly land in a french nightmare

the pig did not climb to the top
elegantly perched on the bronze branch
of the german soccer metro

EDITOR'S NOTE
гус is "swan" in Russian, though missing one letter

Family, Do Not Kill Me, Please

Translated by Zachary Schomburg

they wanted a girl
a boy was born
a girl was not born

after this
everybody only watches
the kinds of movies
where the credits
have to say *no animals suffered in the making of this film*

1882: Negative Theology

to Mikhail Iampolski

*

god died with a smile
because he didn't suspect
that he was condemned
to another life sentence

*

in an abyssinian palindromic hex
SATOR AREPO TENET OPERA ROTAS
one must first find the place
where placing a period
might stop the magic
I'm sick of

My 37th Winter

*

the old snowman
wants to make friends
with the new snow
wants the new snow to like him,
even as a quadruped

the snowman gets down on hands and knees
doesn't notice his carrot-nose breaking

the new snow is a cold leash
crumbling, the snowman begins
to crawl

*

"spring is coming — he'll melt"

only such words die, without undressing first

Essay & Poem

Aleksandr Skidan

Poetry in the Age of Total Communication

Translated by Thomas H. Campbell

Let us sing the surface of the song.

—Aleksander Vvedensky

Since the mid-90s, the Riga-based textual group Orbit (*Orbita*) has accompanied its poetic performances with electronic music and video/slide projections. Midway between multimedia installations and techno parties, these performances produce a sensorimotor effect. Listeners (who are also viewers) are plunged not into a lexical-melodic flow, as they would be at a traditional reading, but into a cybernetic-machinic plasma. The group's printed output displays the same tendency. The first issue of the almanac *Orbit* (2000) already gravitated towards synesthesia. It was amply supplied with photographs, which subordinated the texts to their visual logic. The second issue was packaged as a CD-ROM that presented listeners with a "soundscape of Riga in the year 2000"—techno mixes by DJs and fragments of internet acoustic projects. It was telling that when this high-tech product (which requires special equipment for playback) was presented in Petersburg, the venue was not a literary club, but the Pro Arte Institute, a citadel of contemporary art that serves as an incubator for the city's young artists, curators, gallerists, and other art scenesters.

It was around this same time, in the late 90s, that another poetry group that actively uses music and video during its readings, Helter Skelter Drills (*Dreli kuda popalo*), arrived on the Petersburg scene. Although the Drill's stage presence is much more nervy, even aggressive — unlike Orbit's neutral, impassive trance pulsations accompanied by views of sterile urban spaces, the trademarks of the Petersburgers are a deliberate grunginess, brutal gestures, and appropriately jumpy videos — it would seem that their work draws on the same esthetic premise as their Riga colleagues. The premise is that the word as such has become devalued and ineffective and, therefore, needs to be compensated for by an energetic audiovisual supplement. In fact, performances by the Drills, heirs of the post-punk sound, often resemble rock concerts more than poetry readings. Poems are sung into microphones, and the frenzy of real bodies onstage and digital bodies onscreen serve as a peculiar reminder, bequeathed to us by Greek myth, of the fate that befell the first lyric poet, Marsyas.

Similar moods guide such relatively recent collective undertakings as the Listen Up Theater of Poets, the Musical-Poetical Ring, and Asya Nemchenok's Videopoetry project, which combines video art, live music, and poetry readings. It is of less importance that all of these groups favor different formats. For Orbit, this format is the multimedia show. For the Drills, it is the rock concert. For Listen Up, it is the poetry cabaret or poetry theater. What is more important is that all of them strive for a total esthetic effect in the spirit of Wagner's *Gesamtkunstwerk* — for spectacle, for interaction with the audience. We might also mention Dmitry Vodennikov's slams, which by definition aim for direct, "corporeal-familiar" contact (as Bakhtin would have put it) with the audience; or the Musical-Poetical Ring, which stages "battles royal" between musicians and poets. It is, of course, possible to debate the degree of talent and professional merits of the performers in such projects (if such categories are applicable here). We can ask whether they bring something new and meaningful to poetry itself, or instead reduce poetry to the role of an ingredient, a "handmaiden" to other art forms. What I find most interesting, however, is the symptom itself, which is especially clearly manifested in Orbit's high-tech experiments. As Dmitry Golynko notes, the poetics of this group "articulates a radical mistrust of, and a cautious suspicion towards, the conventions of the text-in-itself, showing how unprofitable and useless it is without audiovisual vaccinations and injections."[1] The trajectory of the Nizhny Novgorod duo PROVMYZ (Sergei Provorov and Galina Myzinkova) is telltale in this sense. While they began in the early 90s with scintillating neo-futurist performances, they quickly abandoned poetry for video art. In this medium they have enjoyed indisputable success, as witnessed by their participation in the last Venice Biennale.

The sense that the poetic word is "unprofitable" and "useless" is fueled by a complicated set of problems occasioned by the sociocultural transformations of the last several decades. The turn to new technologies on the part of poets is merely the tip of this iceberg. The "soft" terror of the mass media and the cult of consumerism have replaced ideological control in the post-Soviet space. The everyday experience of the urban dweller is more and more determined by a constant cerebral shock. By virtue of its constancy, this shock is no longer perceived as such, but merely as a rhythmic tickle, the invariable background that follows us everywhere — on the streets, in cafés and supermarkets, on buses and trains, in movie theaters, offices, and airports. The speed with which information is transmitted via electronic and wireless networks has increased so exponentially that our customary (bookish) skills for reading and making sense of it malfunction, yielding to machinic processing and digital surfing.

Television, the internet, mobile telephony, computing, and all the other forms of instantaneous recording and communication form a market of synthetic, simultaneous perception that deepens its industrialization and automation. They lead to the emergence of what Paul Virilio has termed "machinic vision."[2]

As the lived environment mutates, so does language mutate. The center of creative work has shifted. This is apparent in the destinies of philology and (even more so) semiotics. Having achieved its structuralist acme in the 60s thanks to the configuring of linguistics as a hard science (with phonology as its basis), semiotics has ceased to be the frontline of theoretical research, in the same way that philology had, earlier, ceased to be the paradigm of the humanities. Thinkers no longer appeal to linguistic models and poetic language to ground their concepts and procedures, as had been the case with Heidegger's ontological turn, Lévi-Strauss's structural anthropology, Lacan's psychoanalysis, Kristeva's intertextuality or Derrida's deconstruction. On the contrary, their methods have migrated into the analysis of other, nonverbal practices.[3] This situation in many ways resembles the one described by Roman Jakobson in "What Is Poetry?" (1933–34):

> The latter half of the nineteenth century was a period of a sudden, violent inflation of linguistic signs. This thesis can be easily justified from the standpoint of sociology. The most typical cultural phenomenon of the time exhibit a determination to conceal this inflation at any cost and shore up faith in the paper word with all available means. Positivism and naive realism in philosophy, liberalism in politics, the neogrammarian school in linguistics, an assuasive illusionism in literature and on the stage (with illusions of both the naive naturalist and the solipsistic decadent varieties), the atomization of method in literary theory (and in scholarship and science as a whole)—such are the names of the various and sundry expedients that served to bolster the credit of the word and strengthen confidence in its value.[4]

Need I remind you what followed hard on the heels of this late 19th-century crisis?

We will refrain from labeling the current changes a decline or pronouncing a final verdict on them. Such appraisals — "rise" and "fall" — depend on the system of coordinates in which they are made. Take the so-called golden age of Russian poetry, for example. Even the poets of this golden age contemptuously referred to it as an "iron" age. Pushkin: "Our age is a trader; in this age of iron / There is no liberty without money." Baratynsky: "The age proceeds along its own iron path." For the poets of Pushkin's day, the golden age was the time of Shakespeare or Dante, or even of Homer. Baratynsky dates the "infant dreams of poetry" to the prescientific, prehistoric age, thus refusing the contemporary world the gift of "prophecy." What we Russians nowadays call a golden age of poetry, he perceived as an age of cupidity and shamelessly mercantile concerns, of the "impudent cry" of polemical journalism, which was capable of engendering only what is trite and commonplace. At the brink of the Russian Silver Age (at the turn of the 19th and 20th centuries), the poet Nikolai Gumilev made a similar gesture: he compared the fallen state of contemporary language to an "abandoned hive" and referred his readers to the "hosanna" of the divine Word, which could make the sun stand still and raise cities from the dust.

Nevertheless, it would be wrong to yield to the temptation to engage in such (comforting) relativizing. Historical ruptures have indeed taken place, and they have radically altered the situation and function of poetry in society. Perhaps they have altered its essence as well. In Russia, these shifts did not coincide chronologically (chronically?) with the same shifts in the West, and this presents a separate problem. It seems that only here and now are we in Russia fully confronted with Hölderlin's "childish" question: "In meager times what are poets good for?" In meager times or, to put it differently, in "times of adversity" (*in dürftiger Zeit*) — that is, when everything has already been said, all myths debunked, the gods have perished or departed forever, and the work of art has nothing to say. All the artwork can do is *indicate* this exhaustion, this emptiness in which it is lost itself, in order to become, paradoxically and *visibly*, the experience of endless wandering. This is what happens in Andrei Monastyrsky's "Perforated Composition" (1973):

> Where am I?
> In bad weather.
> Life is
> at an end.
>
> Music
> fades,
> speech
> falters.
>
> ———

Speech falters: a line is drawn under it. This is an ending. And this ending (we should not forget) led to Collective Actions (as the Moscow conceptualists came to call their "outings to the countryside").[5]

The current turn of poets to spectacular forms and technologies is, therefore, not simply their means to find a new audience, preferably a bigger one. It is not simply a means for concealing the word's insolvency with a "direct" psychosomatic attack or, on the contrary, for demonstratively flaunting the end of an egregious literature-centrism. Nor does it come down to merely expanding the range of poetry's possibilities. In performance art and multimedia technologies, poetry seeks to reunite with the ground that has been slipping from under it — the sensual reality-cum-irreality at stake in all the artistic revolutions of the 20th century. Apollinaire had already formulated the esthetic program of the future avant-gardes in "On Painting" (1909): "Artists are above all men who want to become inhuman. Painfully they search for traces of inhumanity, traces of which are to be found nowhere in nature. These traces are clues to truth, aside from which there is no reality we can know."[6] Until a certain point in time, this program was held in common by poets and artists. The futurists, Dadaists, LEFists, constructivists, and surrealists wrote joint manifestos and published their works in the same periodicals and books. Moreover, it was the poets (Apollinaire, Tzara, Breton, Khlebnikov, Kruchenykh, Ilyazd, Pound, Marinetti) who acted as the ideologues of the new currents. The situation changed in the 30s, however. This moment is recorded in Paul Valéry's essay "Problems of Poetry" (1935):

> The fate of an art is linked, on the one hand, with that of its material means and, on the other, with that of the minds who are capable of being interested in it and who find in it the satisfaction of a real need. From the remotest antiquity to the present time, reading and writing have been the sole means of exchange and the only methods of developing and preserving expression through language. One can no longer answer for the future. As for minds, one already sees that they are wooed and captured by so much immediate magic, so many direct stimuli, which with no effort provide the most intense sensations and show them life itself and the whole of nature, that one may doubt whether our grandchildren will find the slightest savor in the outdated graces of our most extraordinary poets and of poetry in general.[7]

Valéry doesn't specify what kind of "immediate magic" and "direct stimuli" "show [us] life itself," but in any case it is clear that, compared to them, poetry (and its graces) will seem "outdated."

Valéry, of course, could not have predicted that things "themselves," objects and phenomena, would be replaced by their electronic images; that information flows would replace nature; that the reality principle would be shaken to its foundations by the "reality effect," delivered to one's door by industrial means. He likewise could not have predicted 24-hour music, entertainment, and news channels, which establish a new temporal regime of planetary "real time." He could not have foreseen satellite communications, microprocessors, low-orbit automatic tracking cameras, implanted chips, and other "material means" for increasing the velocity of the "means of exchange" and perception a thousandfold. However, it was in the 30s in Europe and the US that what would be called the "culture industry" (Adorno) and the "society of the spectacle" (Debord) came into their own. Cinema became the most important of the arts, and a total mobilization began to proceed apace (a mobilization of natural and human resources designed to service and prosthetize the rising technosphere). In 1934, finally, media technologies were used for mass propaganda purposes for the first time: Leni Riefenstahl's *Triumph of the Will* captured the NSDAP (Nazi) Nuremberg Rally on film, and Hitler's speeches in the Reichstag were broadcast over the radio.

In this same year, Ernst Jünger published the essay "On Pain." In it he addresses the possibility of repeatedly experiencing an event in all its immediacy from a distance via instantaneous electronic transmission. He sees in this the potential to transform any socially significant event into the simple object of a news broadcast:

> Today any event worthy of notice is surrounded by a circle of lenses and microphones and lit up by the flaming explosions of flashbulbs. In many cases, the event itself is completely subordinated to its transmission; to a great degree, it has been turned into an object. Thus we have already experienced political trials, parliamentary meetings, and contests whose whole purpose is to be the object of a planetary broadcast. The event is bound neither to its particular space nor to its particular time, since it can be mirrored anywhere and repeated any number of times.[8]

Jünger sings the praises of the technological era's objectivization of events as a new form of esthetic purposelessness whose spellbinding, anesthetic power we can fully appreciate only today, in the age of reality shows and the (preferably slow-motion) live rebroadcast of natural and manmade disasters. (We should recall here Stockhausen's remark about the collapse of the World Trade Center as the most perfect work of art.)

The mobilization potential of media technologies paves the way to the spectacle of a reified, standardized humanity that despises pain insofar as "[h]idden behind the face of entertainment promoted by the all-encompassing media, are special forms of discipline."[9] These forms of discipline differ radically from those we customarily associate with the traditional forms of art. They inculcate in the masses the esthetization of alienation via the phantasmagoria of the image. This esthetization celebrates its triumph using remote-control technologies. They also inure the masses to a new technogenic sensibility whose herald was photography, the first industrial anesthetic:

> The photography stands outside the realm of sensibility. It has something of a telescopic quality: one can tell that the object photographed was seen by an insensitive and invulnerable eye. That eye registers equally well a bullet in

> midair or the moment in which a man is torn apart by an explosion. This is our characteristic way of seeing, and photography is nothing other than an instrument of this new propensity in human nature. It is remarkable that this propensity is still as invisible as it is in other fields, such as literature; but no doubt, if we can expect anything from writing as well as painting, the description of the most minute psychic events will be replaced by a new kind of precise and objective depiction.[10]

Out of fairness we should note that this new form of objective, photographically distanced description already existed in simultaneous poetry, the Merzbau of Kurt Schwitters, and the objectivist montage poems of Blaise Cendrars (e.g., the "Kodak" cycle) and other poets. The problem, however, lies elsewhere: namely, in the fact that the new visual methods can produce the same effect better, more quickly, and, most important, with an impact a thousand times greater than the "outdated" medium of poetry.

After World War II, the paths of contemporary art and poetry diverged ever further. Contemporary art was institutionalized and taken under the wing of governments, museums, foundations, and corporations. It gradually became an inalienable component of the culture industry and the political propaganda machine, as the Moscow Biennale has recently demonstrated with such showy brilliance. Citing the campaign to promote American abstract expressionism, mounted with the direct support of the CIA, some historians argue that the institutionalization of the visual arts undertaken in the west in the postwar period was a farsighted, well-conceived policy to socialize and, thus, domesticate the anti-bourgeois spirit. This policy channeled radicalism into the autonomous buffer zone of the arts.[11] (Clement Greenberg, American abstraction's principal theorist, had been a Trotskyite in the 30s, while the majority of artists had been leftists of one stripe or another.)

This version of events sounds plausible, but it is only a part of the truth. No less significant is another factor: the deterritorialization of art, its escape from the surface of the canvas and traditional easel painting. Its new forms — assemblage, object, happening, body art, land art, installation, process art, relational esthetics, video, and multimedia — conform precisely to the deterritorialization wrought by transnational capital. Two logics encounter and reflect each other here: the immanent logic of art, which seeks to overcome its own limits (the limits of the "human," per Apollinaire), and the logic of the expanded (re)production of goods. Put crudely, if the thing (the painting, the object) has become an item on the market or has been purchased by a museum and exhibited there as "contemporary art," then for me to remain an artist I am now forced to create, for example, ideas or relations, not material things. In turn, these things acquire an exhibition value (a price) — that is, a commodity form. Nowadays, the "universal" of this crisscross logic, the esthetic sign of expanded (re)production, is the "project."

But what kind of "project" could the poet have? Poetry quite quickly, as early as the 1910s and 20s, ran up against the material boundary of deterritorialization: pure phonetic writing (glossolalia, transsense language) and/or the blank page. Mallarmé had already anticipated this dead end in his poem *Un coup de dés jamais n'abolira le hasard* ("A Throw of the Dice," 1897). Here, it is not the word or the line, but the page that functions as the self-standing unit of text. The collages of the Dadaists or the "vacuum" poetry of the Nothingists (*nichevoki*) pushed poetry to the verge of exhaustion or dissolution in the other art forms. (Mallarmé himself described his experiments with terms borrowed from scenography and dance.) Other less radical and notorious practices were even more unable to acquire that disturbing ambivalence constitutive of the commodity. This is what Marx has in mind when he writes of the commodity's "fetish character," of its "metaphysical subtleties" and "theological contrivances." These qualities have been borrowed by the contemporary artwork, even (and especially) in the form of a rejection of the work as such. The dyslexia, aphasia, and speech defects evinced by the OBERIU poets were not only a revolt against normative totalitarian grammar, but also a reaction to this dead end, which reduces the poetic utterance to a mark on the page or a wordless gesture. It is telling that Vvedensky and Kharms turned to genres of dramatic farce, to "processions" and vulgar mystery plays. These forms laid bare the archaic, magical/ritual mechanisms (dating back to spells, incantations, and prayers) that in fact would now form the impossible horizon — the origin and, simultaneously, the limit — of all poetic utterance.[12] The later works of the OBERIU are imbued with a particular sense of horror because these corporeal-linguistic techniques, sacred in their origins, appear in these works as out-of-control automatic writing machines, alienated from the enunciating subject. (Antonin Artaud, a poet who abandoned poetry for the theater and cinema, dreamed in parallel with the OBERIU about a new spiritual automatism rooted in archaic ritual. However, the figure of the automaton has attained its genuine, high-frequency resolution only now that contemporary electronic and digital technologies have fused with biotechnologies.)

Valéry's prediction has been fulfilled in one other way. As the world is integrated via mass communication, the World Wide Web, and porous national frontiers, as it becomes (as they say) globalized, and national cultures mix, lose their strict contours, and more and more often generate a non-national, supranational or international art, poetry, on the contrary, is locked in its local traditions as in ghettoes, unable to overcome its cultural and linguistic barriers. Since the time of the surrealists and, with certain provisos, the beatniks, not a single poetry movement has emerged that could lay claim to true international status or provoke a public response outside its local audience. The influence of the Italian hermeticists, the German-Austrian concretists, the French Lettrists, the American Language poets, the Latin American Neo-Baroque poets, and other current national poetic schools bears no comparison with the influence once exercised by the symbolists, futurists, and Dadaists. (This doesn't mean, of course, that there have been no significant or even great poets after the surrealists and the OBERIU poets. Perhaps the contrary is the case. But this is not my point.)

In other words, the industry of contemporary art has the advantage of upward mobility, as the sociologists put it. This means immediate access to the international market, while poetry is forced to make do with a national symbolic economy. This economy is literally symbolic: it consists of several thousand (or even several hundred) devoted poetry lovers, and most of these are one's fellow poets. It is a closed economy: it corresponds to the hermeticism (and hermetization) of local poetic traditions and poetry itself as a form of creative work within an ever-expanding field of cultural production. "Scratch on, my pen: let's mark the white [paper] the way it marks us" (Joseph Brodsky, "The Fifth Anniversary," 1977.) Today we perceive in these words not the unique experience of an émigré poet, stranded in an alien linguistic and metaphysical landscape and thus deprived of his rightful audience, but a universal statement of how things stand in the poetic economy. Poetry is an anachronism, a natural economy (pen?! paper?!) in an age of permanent industrial revolution. To borrow the late Dmitri Prigov's favorite expression, poetry is a cottage industry.

Let's summarize. The center of creative work has shifted to the visual arts because (1) they immediately reflect, and partly coincide with, the new technogenic environment, (2) which mobilizes the cerebral and sensorimotor resources of human beings along with the earth's natural resources and outer space. (3) The visual arts correspond to the dominant regime of temporality and synthetic perception established by the mass media. (4) They are inscribed in the culture industry and, consequently, (5) in the capitalist machine, which deterritorializes any form of identity based on linguistic competency. This competency has been replaced by (6) an expanded (re)production and consumption of audiovisual images, (7) which now form the primary zone for experiments with the collective unconscious. This unconscious is nowadays not structured like a language (per Lacan), but like an exteriorized sensorium, a screen-projected ectoplasm whose center is nowhere, but whose effects are everywhere. (What are the ontological and neurophysiologic premises of this reconfiguration, in which the audiovisual image is privileged over the written or spoken word? This is a separate question, and the search for an answer to it would lead us far afield.[13]

In the face of this machine, what is poetry's lot? First and foremost (and this is obvious), exclusion from the machine. Is this exclusion something new, however? Hadn't Plato already dreamed of exiling the poets from the Republic? Don't we encounter the very same figure of exclusion throughout the history of poetry, from Ovid to Dante, from Villon ("I'm received by everyone, and everywhere exiled") to Hölderlin ("We are in exile"), from Tasso in chains to Pound behind bars, from Tsvetaeva's "all poets are Yids" to the wanderings of Celan? This is not a romantic figure; it is not an historic *dispositif* summoned into life by particular (transitory) circumstances such as tyranny or a corrupt and arbitrary bureaucracy. In and of itself, the poem is already a form of exile from the world, and the man who gives himself over to the seemingly harmless game of poetry thus testifies to his willingness to dwell outside the law, outside the order of truth and its infrastructures, his willingness to be *thrown* outside, even outside himself. He risks something extreme, something more than madness and death, something more even than the "lawless thrills" of the poetic game itself. In all ages he has lived through "meager times," times of adversity and misfortune. To ignite misfortune round oneself, to admit the hell of nonsense into his head, the hell of wild noises and screams, to devour his head (the rat-eaten head of Orpheus) under fire — this is his success.

But why? How can we call a time of adversity success, moreover, an unprecedented success? And why Hölderlin? Because, at very least for Heidegger (the thinker who thought the essence of the technology and destiny of the West, that sunset land par excellence), as with no other poet we still feel Hölderlin's link to the Greek origins of poetry as *poiesis*, a link that is felt through separation and undoing. Written on the threshold of the new industrial era, his hymns call out to the dawn of dawns when art still bore the name *tekhne* and thus belonged to *poiesis*. This chiasmus, this errant unity-in-separation of art and technology permeates all of Western history. It exposes and makes plain the "placelessness" of poetic locution, which once was the intermediary (the medium) between men and gods, heaven and earth. To persist in this placelessness, this widening gap into which the "surface of the song" has now been sent to wander, apparently means wishing for the impossible. But perhaps the impossible is the only domain and the sole destiny of the poet — that is, of the man who must "take upon himself the weight of the double infidelity and thus keep the two spheres distinct, by living the separation purely, by being the pure life of the separation itself. For this empty and pure place which distinguishes between the spheres is *the sacred*, the intimacy of the breach which is sacred."[14] Poetry must still invent means for dwelling in the heart of this absolute rupture, for delivering and enduring it as an openness to the future. And, perhaps, as an openness to future (absolutely real) collective actions.

NOTES

1 *Novaia Russkaia Kniga* 1 (2001), p. 95.

2 This is a "machine of absolute velocity." It undermines such traditional notions of geometrical optics as "observed" and "unobserved," and it has begun to effect an "intensive blinding." See Paul Virilio, *The Vision Machine* (Indiana University Press, Bloomington, IN, 1994).

3 It is not only the flowering of visual studies that I have in mind here. The "re-qualification" of the leading theorists is symptomatic as well. Thus, near the end of his life, Barthes wrote about photography (*Camera Lucida* is, perhaps, his best book). In the 80s, Deleuze turned his attention to the cinema, while Lyotard and Rancière took up the study of the visual arts. The only exception in this series (by no means complete) is Alain Badiou — but even he has written about the end of the "age of poets."

4 Roman Jakobson, *Language in Literature*, ed. Krystyna Pomorska and Stephen Rudy (Belknap Press, Cambridge, MA, 1987), pp. 376–7.

5 In the preface to "Perforated Composition," Monastyrsky writes that it was "conceived as a performance in which the invited guests (mainly artists) were first supposed to listen to the author perform the text of the composition itself (a kind of *Stimmung*). Then they would be handed pieces of paper. As the author read his "Pictures," they would draw, in any style, the subject that had just been read out. (There was a five-minute pause between the reading-out of each subject.) This performance was realized once, in November or December 1973, for several of my artist friends." Andrei Monastyrsky, *Nebesnomu nosatomu domiku po puti v Pagan* (Moscow, 2001), p. 54. The composition itself is built on the serial principle, whose invariants are children's counting rhymes and love charms, the ür-phenomena of oral poetry.

6 Guillaume Apollinaire, *The Cubist Painters: Aesthetic Meditations, 1913*, trans. Lionel Abel (Wittenborn Schultz, New York, 1949), p. 11.

7 Paul Valéry, *The Art of Poetry*, trans. Denise Folliot (Bollingen Foundation, Princeton, 1985), pp. 95–6.

8 Ernst Jünger, "Photography and the 'Second Consciousness': An Excerpt from 'On Pain,'" *Photography in the Modern Era: European Documents and Critical Writings, 1913–1940* (The Metropolitan Museum of Art/Aperture, New York, 1989), p. 209.

9 Ernst Jünger, "Über den Schmerz"; quoted in Anton Kaes, "The Cold Gaze: Notes on Mobilization and Modernity," *New German Critique* 59 (1993), p. 115.

10 Jünger, "Photography," p. 208.

11 Cf. Serge Guilbaut, *How New York Stole the Idea of Modern Art: Abstract Expressionism, Freedom, and the Cold War* (University of Chicago Press, Chicago, 1983); Taylor D. Littleton and Maltby Sykes, *Advancing American Art: Painting, Politics, and Cultural Confrontation at Mid-Century* (University of Alabama Press, Tuscaloosa, 1989); Frances Stonor Saunders, *Who Paid the Piper? The CIA and the Cultural Cold War* (Granta Books, London, 1999); and Michael L. Krenn, *Fall-Out Shelters for the Human Spirit: American Art and the Cold War* (Chapel Hill, 2005). All these historians concur that art and cultural values (in particular, American abstract expressionism) were weapons in the Cold War and a matter of direct concern to the US State Department. Frances Stonor Saunders offers a particularly detailed account of how the CIA infiltrated and influenced a variety of cultural organizations. To this end they used such friendly intermediaries as the Ford Foundation and the Rockefeller Foundation. Moreover, the CIA did not just openly or secretly fund artists and intellectuals who toed the official Washington line. It also financed arts, literary and opinion journals (in Europe and elsewhere) that adopted a critical stance towards Marxism and revolutionary politics.

12 In "The Kernel of Comparative Slavic Literature," Roman Jakobson reconstructs the general prototype of the Slavic verse, tracing it to folklore — in particular, to laments (keening), to sung and conversational verse. "Even where there is some alien influence, it appears only as an incitement to realize a traditional form of the native lore, which is familiar to the modern poet both from earlier literary adaptations and from the oral tradition which still surrounds and inspires him, and which speaks the same language he does. Thus 'new rhythms' in Czech or Russian or other Slavic poetry of this century are structurally — and often also genetically — closer to certain forms of the native folklore than to the French vers libre." Roman Jakobson, "The Kernel of Comparative Slavic Literature," (*Harvard Slavic Studies*, vol. 1, 1953, p. 35). In another essay ("On Russian Folklore"), Jakobson makes a confession that also sheds a new light on the genesis of structuralist poetics. He talks about how he had occasion to read Alexander Blok's study "The Poetry of Spells and Incantations" (1908) soon after it was published. He was stunned and gladdened by how abruptly the study broke with the notions that he and his Russian contemporaries had been taught in their textbooks on the oral tradition. Among other things, Blok's essay charmed Jakobson with its beautiful example of the strange magical songs, filled with incomprehensible words, that were performed to ward off mermaids.

13 I will limit myself to remarking that one would have to discuss the arrangement of the sense organs and the imagination, which is capable of transporting us through time and space. This function has now been taken over by the media technologies. What philology defined as the word's "inward image" is now being replaced by the exteriorization of "internal" mental and neurophysiologic processes. (Hence, the new "sensorium," which is an electronic version of the cerebral cortex, dissected and turned inside out.) As the philosopher remarks, "As if it were necessary for the world to be broken up and buried for the speech-act to rise up." Gilles Deleuze, *Cinema 2: The Time Image*, trans. Hugh Tomlinson and Robert Galeta (University of Minnesota Press, Minneapolis, 2001), p. 268.

14 Maurice Blanchot, *The Space of Literature*, trans. Ann Smock (University of Nebraska Press, Lincoln, NE, 1982), p. 274.

Objects in Part

Translated by Thomas Epstein

*   *   *

what ought to be thought
amor fati

the form of time and the caesura
ontological difference and the game

deduction
syllogism

quality
inherent property

donc je suis
a passing thought

< who are those men in the black coats? >

the arbitrariness of the sign
the vicious circle

almost exactly similar to
a distant point

*   *   *

universal cognition
a really good mood

contingence
the absolute

the founding of geometry
the four elements

tetrahedron
tetragrammaton

the panic-stricken rituals of theater
law of the father

the dead
letter of authority

< who are those men in the black coats? >

* * *

sun
gold

fire
zenith

< ashes >

the masculine principle
in which each symbol

simultaneously
in turn

constitutes

remains within the framework of

to efface the boundary

gives rise to, and is reflected

in one another

* * *

obsessions
because to influence

though I did finally arrive
defense mechanisms

convulsive beauty

in the sweltering surf
in the corruscating whirlwind of sparks

beyond formalism

< or will not be at all >

the active causal connection
< hit save >

of Satan's celestial mills
Descartes's theory of vortices

fate traded for a whim
regular exceptions

* * *

also
alien to knowledge

to occur

in truth
dissolve in the light of a typical day

you, nightingales, begin
crying too

the name
their names

automatism of repetition
in this part

like a woman expelling corpses

he once said
a primordial scene

a finely tempered expulsion
two-Gods-in-one

the value of metonymy
apophrasis

they're singing
they're singing

the world is the totality of facts

a spasm
an inexplicable shudder

paralyzed anxiety

* * *

a literal translation of the final stanza
exhaustion of the procedure

the superfluous figure of the poet
learning a language

however both movements
are morpho-syntactic unities

besides
so-culled culture

imitation, again
runs to the swing
catches and greases
shakes the glass without breaking it

in accordance with the melancholia of the mountain-dwellers
inner declension

metric system
euphonic condensation

all that remains
of an expired expression

* * *

she brought down from the mountain
a late-night pedestrian

epigraphs
on golden tablets

naked souls above the river

disjunctions
pleonasms

relics of a fanstasy world

frozen forms
fossils

subtlety in the description
of partial objects

this ironic utopia
moribund idyll

ash on an old man's sleeve

< a sudden illumination >

* * *

perhaps
it's a question of degree

to actually appear
would it be too much to ask

in any case
it's esthetically correct

nevertheless

ought we to regret
prepared to believe it

all that he tried to say
you haven't forgotten anything

if my recollections about
art are exact

there's nothing to express
no means of expression

no desire to express
however

to speak logically
none

* * *

while
all the same

in the meantime

in view of the insufficiency
at the same time

in other words
it follows that

in essence

the ultimate dictionary
out of a number of red balls

whatever the nature of
the economic threat

they're speaking
they're speaking

the founding of geometry
semiosis

and so on
similarly

decoded streams
the decentered subject

you try that again and we'll kill you

they're speaking
they're speaking

the crisis of metanarratives
consequently

a passing thought
I'm lost, I'm dying

< who are those men in the black coats? >

the pendular
structure of the phantasm

Essay & Six Poems

Maria Stepanova

Only One, Not Alone, Not I

Translated by Peter Golub

Judging by what poets, and those who know how to read poems, say about poetry's purpose and essence, the activity should not instill any popular or private sympathies; it should not bring its disciples laurels or banknotes — *ni fleurs ni couronnes*. Emily Dickinson wrote that poetry is recognized by a feeling of penetrating cold, that no fire can warm. Something of this is also found in Pushkin when he speaks of the quick cold of inspiration. It is these thermal shifts, jumps, transfers from shadow to light, and other accidental attributes, that appear to constitute the very meaning behind the pleasure of poetry, which for some reason we have been enjoined to experience.

The landscape, which the poetic text presents to the senses, is eremitic (because strangers don't walk here), is strange (because the place of which we are speaking is strange). It promises nothing; it is not heaven or hell, and its sole purpose seems to be the witnessing of the other's existence. What happens to us, if we attempt to master this mode, "this brief, fruitless egress from the world," as one poet called it — does it straighten or warp us, or does it simply leave us on the shore with our mouths open and hands empty? The print runs of poetry collections and journals force the conclusion that the number of those who wish to regularly partcipate in these activities is very small. For instance, in Russia this number is something around 500 to 1,500 people. But it seems that this is plenty: an entire auditorium of extreme athletes, for the serious reading of poetry can certainly be considered such, cannot be too vast.

However, the zone of poetry is not without its verdant fields and damp meadows, where an entire army of poets, mentioned by Mandelstam, find their residence; here the "Sentinels of Love" [a song by Bulat Okudzhava] keep their watch, and *Twenty Sonnets to Mary Queen of Scots* bravely lie with poems written on pink valentines. The love lyric is the only sector of poetic production that from its inception rejected the idea of border expansion. It does not try to widen the scope of poetry, which blindly feels for new resources, but stays within its perimeter, recruiting new "I"s for the continuation of the old "love." The anthologies and collections of love lyrics, released year after year, do not serve some quick cold of inspiration, but a clear and moral function: they service a continually working conveyer facilitating the reproduction of mankind. They offer up mirrors in which it is so pleasant to recognize yourself and your own, and present a whole collection of reflections, a catalogue of stock positions for a psychological Kama Sutra. They effectively complete the pedagogical task begun by family and school. We see that love is possible: "I loved you," and that it passes: "I find no tears, nor interest." We learn the science of separation, the entire scale from "God grant that someone else will find you his beloved" to "God grant that others find you their beloved — but they won't!" We refer to the professionals, and are convinced that the limned sympathies correspond to our own. We pick through the standard selection, craftily disguised as unique, in an attempt to match the contour of our experience to the template, and when the trick works, subsequent existence becomes not only possible, but is justified, illuminated, repeated on a higher plane, in the elevated register of role models and grand examples.

Where simply-poetry offers and promises us nothing except itself, the love lyric leads us by the hand, illuminates dark corners, and shoos away the ghosts from our bedsides. "All of this already happened, do not be afraid, you are not alone," says the love lyric. "You are alone, but you are not here, here is another," says simply-poetry.

The love lyric is a faithful friend, a kind teacher, and a relaible guide. It teaches us to deal with love (happy and hapless), separation, death; for every occasion it has a quote, which makes the reader sigh, "yeah, ain't that the truth" — the reader had come precisely for this sigh. It could be said that the love lyric is to the normal lyric as nonfiction is to fiction: it is a witness to the reality of the real. It shows that even the most dizzying structures of poetry have beneath them a common earthly foundation, which we all share. Its futility provides lyricism with the possibility of utility. It is amusing, that throughout its existence poetry has insisted upon its nonidentity with truth — at least, the juxtaposition of heavenly truth and earthly truth. To which of these sides falls the love lyric? To which is it most contiguous? To the sounds of heaven, or the quotidian sounds of earth? Everything points to the latter.

This is why, when the conversation turns to love, it is so important to know who exactly is speaking. A superlative choir typically proclaims its inimitability — but the three chords, upon which the love song rests, have changed little throughout the hundreds of years of different covers and arrangments — it is more and more important to know whose voice it is possible to make out. Who is singing? A tenor, a child, a deaf man? From where is the voice heard? From the screen, the wall, the train platform? The criteria of authenticity continues to exist, but the interesting stories remind me less and less of my own, and it suddenly becomes clear that the important thing is that this is not "I" — not

"I" but another — that this is the experience that goes beyond our own. That is, simply put, the experience of he who is in more pain. The credulity of the reader begins to correlate directly with the pain of the author. We return to the zone of extreme tourism, and our guides are those who know the laws and customs of the locals. This is an arcane knowledge. The possession of this knowledge is not facilitated by the mere experience of tragic love — or even the inexperience of it.

This knowledge is kept for us by the dead, and this is why the best love poetry of the 20th century — "Unwittingly falls to the empty earth" — is that of Osip Mandelstam, which is not addressed to a woman walking along Voronezh Street eighty years ago, but directly to us, without mirrors and the like, offering direct news of the resurrection. With this knowledge we are presented the humiliated and traduced, with all those who *challenged* or *deprived* (I pronounce these words in the English language where they have a clear and elevated meaning). This experience is possessed by children, and those who are like children. This is probably why the author of these lines considers the height of the love lyric to be a poem by Vera Inber, "The Centipede's Children" — a tender, clumsy, many-worded thing, like love itself.

Song

Translated by Simona Schneider

In a den of calm-iniquity
On an empty bell tower
On the eve of the ninth of May,
On top of the world.
See the summer-home honeycomb
Stalin-era highrises,
Viewing all kinds of views,
But can't see oneself.

The peasant woman turns to the soldier, says:
Who we once were long ago,
On the eve of the ninth of May
I'll never know.
As on a grater, holes
In your old army undershirt,
My quilted work-coat
Has burnt sleeves.

How the planes fly,
How the steamships go,
We meet every stop along the way
At the ship's ladder,
And at every ladder
A new Loss awaits us
And the womb of Loss —
Like a parent's armoire.

... He doesn't answer her,
He keeps silent in reply,
He swings his sleeves,
Jingling his keys,
And, without any pain,
The shadow of victory
Falls on the murdered plain
Left behind by St. George's Day.

[untitled]

In every parkywarky, on any-many boulevard
Pretty-women push strollers forward and back,
Couples stroll, picking out gifts and cards,
Little kaolinite masks.

And kaolinite contains
Clay, clay, clay, clay,
Cells of the body, eternal bread,
Everybody's paternal grave.

By the pond, skypers hunch over their laptops
Chatting it up with the third world
On Myasnitskaya Street: snipers on rooftops,
Their fingers dancing on the trigger.

It's in-aug-goo-goo-ra-tion eve:
On-duty walkie-talkies rustle,
City-citizens hug their posters,
With steely picket-signs they huddle.

A child cries, goo-goo,
Heavenly lights shine, insides purr,
Moscow stands still, Yaroslavna coos,
I'm going now, to buy some curd.

Way too many choices tonight,
As if the city ate up and died out.

[untitled]

In the constant, foil-colored, festive sky, In the burnt, immemorial, foil-like sky, You can see a ladder propped against the clouds, Which words have trampled top to bottom.

And one of them plods along, While another vocalizes songs, And mine is swinging — hanging off a rung,

Barely hanging on,
It's soon to plummet down.
Comrades will run to it with questions, Tongueless, which is to say — in all tongues at once, With a cluck-cluck, and a quack-quack-quack: How is it up there? What's it like? And in answer, like a bell, moos without a tongue:
"What moosic you can hear from the fifth rung!"

[untitled]

Monument — Manument, how many days are you?
Only just now built, only just erected.

Under one leg: what's tender. Under the other: what's needed.
104 train stations in the depths of earth
The lines of Brest — Litovsk, and Labor — South,
And just now they've dug a new one, a final line.

Down there they're playing soccer, and fiddling violins,
Be happy, Be happy,
each and every one!

All the golden idols —
All the different kinds —
One is euro-stylish,
Another's like a beast.

Green walls filled with tarragon soda —
A drink once popular in days gone by —
Carp stroll about, gun cartridges shimmer,
Single-use ladies blow bubbles of hot air.

Lacquered plasma
Glows to the point of orgasm —
Giving out the news
The whole night through.

Red news, blue news,
Sports and cultural and culinary news.
You chose.

[untitled]

Saturday and Sunday burn like the stars.
The elder tree froths and sputters.
At the railroad junction crossing —
A public wall.
Behind it: slabs of dark, damp canvas
And a lunar sour cherry
And crosses, placed side by side, close,
Tighter than embroidery.
It's an easy place for yellow dogs to cower,
For old ladies to babble and squawk,
For huge women to wail and beat their chests
And rub their temples into the rock.
But these are days, identical, as stumps of trees,
Like the pair of my knees:
One glares at the sun, the other rests in the shade,
And the one and the other are the same — decay.
But these are nights when, between the closed gates,
A nation of nettles gathers.
And Tender May ascends into its garden,
Anointing them with tears.
And here, between night and day, hand over fist,
Made of a thousand candles, eternal and inhuman —
Peace.

EDITOR'S NOTE
"Tender May" — the name of a boy-band popular in the 1980s.

[untitled]

Poplar down will grow wings and zoom to the zenith,
Then it'll grow talons — and start climbing the vertical.
He's a crow through and through, but a crazed Nachtigall
rings in his ears, like an alarm.

And there's the self-fueling plane, gaining height.
He sees clearly the curls of your clouds.
Under his wing — ice hangs like ripe grapes,
And the seaside steppe no less than burdock.

You choose a dot — now place a perpendicular,
And climb, under high voltage, like an electrician.
Does the iron drone loud? Does a student sit still?
Does the plant ovary break, or the ide-fish take the bait?

Far up in the firmament, one plane leg says to the other:
We've served well — now we're going south.
And a little higher, the hand says to the hand:
Hold my fingers a while in your icy sack.

And above them, connecting ear with ear,
The smile of the seventh day shields its face.

EDITOR'S NOTE

"One plane leg says to the other..." — a riff on a Soviet-era comic ditty, itself a schoolroom perversion of a serious patriotic song.

Essay & Two Poems

Dmitry Vodennikov

On Poetry

Translated by Peter Golub

Poetry is inappropriate.

When I was young, I read a book by Svetlana Alekseevich, *War Doesn't Have a Woman's Face*. The book contained the eyewitness account of a woman who had survived the German occupation (I quote the account from memory, so please forgive any possible inaccuracy):

During another one of the fascists' brutal games, a group of soldiers sicced a German Shepherd on a five-year-old girl, when the dog began to dismember the child, the soldiers listened to her screams, and laughed. All the soldiers were extraordinarily handsome young men. "Today," remembered the woman, "when I see handsome men laughing (in the café, at the bus stop, or just in the street), I get a feeling of sickening fear."

Now, when I chance to read (which I do less and less) about the WHO, WHAT, AND HOW of contemporary poetry, in the papers, on the internet, or just in someone's LiveJournal, I too feel sick and frightened.

I

It is very easy to live when you personally have to answer for nothing. Then, every private trifle seems interesting; however, this is easily *remedied*.
If a person has a child, she will never joke about a child's death.
When a person has *real cancer*, she of course jokes about it, but not like other people. She will do it a little differently, *for fundamental reasons*.
If an individual **personally answers for her poetry**, one can of course tell her to drink herbal tea and watch more television, but this will change nothing.

I do not wish for anyone to be sick, or to lose their loved ones.
I even do not wish for anyone to read and understand poetry.
Because this *also* takes you beyond the bounds of your personal *not-responsibility*.
And very few people can withstand this.
I simply want to say that chatter is good, because it is easy to disown, while personal responsibility looks ridiculous and comic. This is why the poet today is simultaneously strong and defenseless.

Because she is one of the few who in our time answers for her words. Like a mobster, a small business owner, or a soldier caught in the middle of a war *unleashed by someone else.*

here
no one is going to turn anything
into poetry
this is not a circus
I do not care about
the climax
of iambs, trochees, anapaests
AND SO FORTH
I DO NOT CARE ABOUT
the acquired immunodeficiency syndrome of post-
conceptualism
a poem
is essentially
a cry
no, I am of course crazy, but I
still exist
within the frame of a sufficiently abstract
societal norm
this is
my way of surviving
no more
so
....

2

So, a while ago I was in a car with some friends and the conversation unexpectedly turned to poetry (it was indeed *unexpected* for we usually talk about love or some other trivia). I had gotten into my head that a person who cannot read real contemporary poetry is *late*. This lateness is measured according to how much the person limits herself (due to arrogance, finicality, or an inability or unwillingness to make her own choice, begin her own path). If her zenith is Akhmatova (for instance), then she is about 40 years late; if Sumarokov then about two centuries; if Dementiev then she is forever late.
My friend Sasha Orlov took up my thought (or was it his thought from the beginning) and added:
"Poetry can never be contemporary, because the poet, like an idiot, always runs in front of the train."

This is true. In a strange way, speaking only about themselves (and *they* are always speaking only about themselves), real poems always target something new both in society, and in perception, and in self-perception, something that for journalists, politicians, and regular people will become obvious only in the future, i.e. if it ever becomes obvious.
And of course, this *newness* eventually spends its initial integrity, its real meaning, and becomes superfluous, fuzzy — what is most interesting — *irrelevant*.

For this —*for something to be new* —THERE IS NO NEED to write *vers libre*, to write metrically, to experiment with font, nor not to experiment. All one needs to do is to honestly look inside oneself.
Not to watch oneself (because this is impossible), but precisely to *look*.
I assure you, the result will be monstrous.
But if all is genuinely understood, and **the inner picture** *adequately* expressed **in the form of a poem** (*vers libre*, meter, experimentation, not experimentation), then through it (the monstrous life) will break some strident, all-illuminating light. Despite all the author's, possibly superficial, shamelessness. Because the light is multiplied into shame, and produces, as the final result, poetry.

And in this sense *it is not worth* it to fear shame.
Because poetry is always inappropriate.
Because poems are not written (not one's own nor others), for one's mother.
Poems that can be shown to mom are not poems.
A life that can be related to a stranger on a train is not a life.
Real life is a secret, harrowing, doubling — shameful, painful, sweet.

It is that for which one is willing to give anything.
And if one has given everything for THIS life, then that truly is YOUR LIFE.
Everything turns out to be quite simple in this world.

What has crumbled again will not be restored:
An apple, fished out of a well,
Is no longer an apple, but a different
Sphere — dolorous, pulsating, full...

(e.r.)
....

3

Poetry **always** evens things out.

This is *why* today's poems are so replete with first names and nearly unbearable intimate details.
(In the *best* poems, these names become your own, and the details carried over and continued.)

There are fools who are still debating whether or not direct speech is still possible in poetry.
Ha! It is the only thing possible; there is NOTHING LEFT besides direct speech.

<now
having done some loathsome thing
or abomination
I understand
what
I
have
done
I instantly understand
what
I
have
done
well almost immediately...>

... As one anonymous reader once wrote me, in response to my thought that poetic strategy is the same as life strategy (and also in response to my thought that a poem should always have at least one line that refutes all the above lines, which creates TWO truths, and two truths is always better than one):

"Yes! and even better, if another line appears that refutes the second truth, and so forth, and that the last proposed truth suddenly seems very simple (i.e. it appears thus), like for instance the wish 'to capture the entire sky with one glance' ... but all the previous truths will participate in the last, creating it. If this is a strategy, then it is the most crucial of the known options; today it is the only one that seems possible."

And this *too* is one of the peculiarities of the new poem.
To not stop, without finishing speaking.
It is all in the minuet: in this *almost*.
This WAY every new line refutes the previous one, and in the end, by this strange and painful method, everything folds into one whole truth.

In essence, this is real poetry: a sphere *dolorous, full, pulsating* held by the hands near the solar plexus, clearly conscious of what heroism or abomination one has just committed. Or *nearly* committed.

Take this sphere into your hands. It only seems frightening at first. And then it is ok — you get used to it.

4

And finally...
I would like to return again to that "ridiculous personal responsibility" and to the dog.
Except that now let us return to *our* dog.

Some may find me abrasive. Or pathetic. And those who consider me thus *will be correct*; they will have all the evidence. Exactly as I have mine... Personal and not personal.
Because, while witnessing the very real flowering of contemporary poetry — and parallel to it the absolutely climacteric criticism, which attempts to delineate this flowering — I have for a long time now wanted to call a spade a spade.

Most specifically —
I want to return pathos's right to exist,
to say that poetry *will never end*,
and also to defend these guys before they are attacked.

……

What can be more ridiculous than a dog that snarls while guarding its puppy? That is, if we note that no harm is intended. Perhaps someone *simply wanted to coddle* it. There are many people who simply like to **coddle** — children, puppies, cancer patients — and even ruffle the hair of poems.

I do not know about the first three, but I do not advise the last.

Real poems tend to SNAP.

[untitled]

Translated by Matvei Yankelevich

In a Soviet schoolboy uniform i drank the stilted air
and after twenty years: a rainstorm in July
and i was tearing out — with longing, with the roots —
our names from letters we had sent.

With blood i tore up all that had been between us,
like weeds, when the earth is in your hands:
a violet-yellow vodennikov, and little Alya's cornflower blue,
Lena by the fence, and you, all red and black.

I threw them all at the feet of the rainstorm, in July,
without right of correspondence, as they say:
dad, stepmother, mom, Andrei, Polina, Yulya
(somehow Yulya was especially hard to throw away).

But i said to my sister: don't be afraid, dear
sister of mine and my brother, as i move
into the dark, i bless all those who lived with me,
i bless them with a purple belly, a blue-eyed brim,
with the storm that creeps into the letters and the leaves.

The other way around — through false and broken sleep,
through bouncing balls and shouting in the yard —
i hear it all: you are alive and well,
and planning to live long upon the earth.

But what am i to do with shards and fragments,
with the shred that's torn apart in the lilac gloom,
from Sanya, the boy, my very own:
me, and this stupid love of mine.

WW3

... and now: whatever you want,
not only these *Results*[1],
and not just this politician with the beat-up eyes
and totally not these soldiers,
soldiers in bloody dust,
but who
will forgive them — them! —
for their ugly feet
(and why do i keep butting in, with my feet?)
for their ugly feet,
for their beautiful boots.

You who walk bowlegged,
perspire, sweat, for us,
then lies there, like aspic.
I figured it out, you want it just like this.
But it can't be.

That's not why we were asked not to shout,
why they fed us sugar, but filled us with salt:
neither to degrade,
nor to beat, nor to kill —
none of this will I allow.

O, this crimson, rough, fresh juice —
it flies so, like an appletree in april!
(and we'll think it's just more gunfire...)
"What's that on your soles, mister?"
"Dirt, m-my b-boy."
Oh, really...

Come one, get up already,
Arkharov, Barsukov,
Vodennikov, Ershova,
Sadretdinov,
Khokhlova, Kholomeyzer, Khokhlyakov,
Khmelyova, Yatsuki — I CAN'T STAND IT!

I've had it — up to here — with you,
and I am — in your hands,
you — you're like jelly (Sit!),
and me — I'm like a battery,
you — you're wearing such amazing boots today
(all of you in such amazing boots today!)

and I'm without them,
and I am stronger — thank you

TRANSLATOR'S NOTES

1 *Results* is a translation of *Itogi*, the name of the Russian *Newsweek* magazine.

These two translations were originally commissioned by CEC Artslink.

Essay & Two Poems

Sergey Zavyalov

Est Rebus in Modus[1]

Translated by Thomas Epstein

It has been widely accepted for quite a while now that what we call literature and the arts as a whole, and poetry in particular, is the product of an agreement, that is to say a public consensus that can never be final or absolute, just as total agreement on anything in an advanced society is considered impossible. Certain forces will always be trying to displace the center of gravity either — conventionally speaking — to the "left" or to the "right," and if the participants in the process did not occasionally encounter phenomena seemingly destructive to the "classic" laws of the mechanism that these forces control, then the literary process as a special "problem" could never arise: the governing conservative forces, taking advantage of the universal human tendency to lose interest in change over time, would rely on the less ambitious (but majority) of the population and attempt to transfer governing authority to its more youthful but like-minded counterparts while nonconformist radicals — counting on their inherently greater intellectual mobility and creativity — would lie in wait for some particularly awkward action of the former in order to try to seize power.

However, in more interesting (at least to their descendants and outside observers) times, what is in question is not so much the ownership of the insignia but their meaning, that is to say "what makes a philosopher,"[2] as the Greek saying puts it. When Diogenes, who splashed urine on an opponent as a form of argument, or Herostratus, who burned down the Temple of Artemis, engaged in seemingly mad acts "beyond the limit"[3] of the permissible, they nevertheless made sure (even if the one in the form of a caricature of a philosophical gesture, the other in a self-annihilating esthetic protest[4]) to base their actions on a form of logic that they admittedly took to the limit but nevertheless in obedience to a hierarchical structure. By contrast, the artifacts (and consequently their creators) that are of interest in this essay seek to remake the foundations themselves and to create new boundaries for the basic oppositions between *natura* and *cultura*, sacred and profane, subject and object.

A classic example of such a reformulation can be found in the parallelisms offered by the apostle Paul in his "First Letter to the Corinthians" (1:27-28):

> Yet, to shame the wise, God has chosen what the world counts folly, and to shame what is strong, God has chosen what the world counts weakness. He has chosen things low and contemptible, mere nothings, to overthrow the existing order.

There is no place for argument when the reply to a question no longer takes the form of a performative artifact or even silence but rather, for example, the trivial allegory of a "lukewarm" (to cite another biblical commonplace[5]) man: not the madman's affect nor the idiot's aphasia because intellectual level — or even the presence of mind — is not in play here. Even more radical is the second parallelism because the willpower and strength of mind of the philosopher living in the barrel — versus the "warrior" or "hero" — are opposed to, even the opposite of aristocratic values; but in the end this becomes irrelevant because these values (power and strength) turn out to be of no interest and present no problem because they are opposed by weakness (not only corporeal but weakness of action, thought, spirit). And the final one: for it is the meaning of perfection that led its adepts to Diogenes's philosophy of Cynicism. For his followers it was not a question of the trivialities of life but of posthumous glory; yet the apostle's words give precedence not simply to obscurity and triviality but to what is reviled, beaten down, useless. The social destructiveness of this text is comparable only to the thinking of the Shahids: "You tremble for your life, for you it is the highest value, while we part from it in laughter because it is of no value in a world governed by the faithless." Before turning to out immediate subject let us briefly explore two parallels suggested by the foregoing reflection: between the Cynics and the Romantics (from late Goya and Blake to Baudelaire and Wagner), and between early Christianity and early avant-garde (cubism, atonalism, *dada*).

To start, we must lower expectations: for those of us unblended by the saccharine clichés of the mass media, it is all too easy to see how any fundamentalism (for example, that of early Christianity) is appropriated by "leftist" intellectualism (the era of Constantine) or how revolutionary-avant-gardists (Origen, for example) are marginalized by evolutionary-modernists (such as the Cappodocians). The very spirit of modernism (in contradistinction to the avant-garde) consists in conceiving of the link between the old and the new as a natural, inevitable, and therefore legitimate development.

The same fate awaits the great cultural (or countercultural, it matters not) project of "postmodernism," whether articulated with a conscious avoidance of pretentiousness or as pompously as possible.[6] Postmodernism, which in its first upsurge was as revolutionary as any artistic movement (rejection of the canon, of hierarchy, rejection of all and any isms, "death of the author," etc., expressing itself in such provocative slogans as "Enough of dead white males!") is inevitably subject to a process of *deconstruction* whose result is its social neutralization and intellectual emasculation. However, this radical reconstruction of the hierarchical ladder may be to our benefit (we can perhaps replace the ladder with an elevator!).

Let us now pose a question: is this struggle with the canon thus illegitimate? Or is there also in it the quite legitimate desire of a maturing civilization to avoid repeating the same mistakes over and over again? What value do the endless lists of British Poet Laureates and winners of the prerevolutionary Russian Pushkin Prize have? Can any intellectually honest person support the claim that Sully-Prudhomme, Frederich Mistral, Giosue Carducci, Werner von Heidenstam and Karl Spitteler (the first Nobel Prize winners) constitute central figures of early 20th century culture? And what could be more vulgar than the transformation of a group of brilliant neurotics (*nomina sunt odiosa*) into heroes of state, almost into church fathers? And what of the idea of teaching in the schools only poets of one's own country?

For Russian culture, the key question is the future makeup of a poetic canon for its national *Musaeum* (Temple of the Muses), now that its ceiling has been definitively destroyed (alas, no renovation can save it). What architectural principles will be used to lay its new foundation?

I propose that we begin with the two primary participants in the process: reader and poet. Let us try to draw a sociological portrait of what in the nauseating language of marketing might be called the "poetry consumer." On this count we simultaneously take an extremely optimistic and extremely pessimistic position. On the one hand, poetry will cease to be read, and this time definitively, by those who in various discourses appear as members of "the middle class," "the petite-bourgeoisie," "the *intelligentsia*," etc. As a result, all those projects associated with what I would call the trivialization of culture (memorials, museums, television and radio programs about poets, even mass-market poetic series) will come to an end, become a relic of the past. On the other hand, while the number of readers will surely decrease, the sophistication of these readers will increase.[7] This optimistic (though not, alas, for the reader, as will be seen below) prognosis is based on the experience of the "unofficial culture" of the late-Soviet period (especially the 1970s-80s), when anti-Soviet attitudes, acquired at a rather young age, cast one out of the "normal" socium of "normal" interests, amusements, ambitions, acquaintances, etc. In its stead we found ourselves in a completely different world (and intensity) of questions and questioning (above all of an ethical, philosophical, and esthetic nature), which excluded all the routine processes and codes of the dominant society, simultaneously marginalizing and liberating us.

The second of our prognostications: the reader of Russian poetry will become bi- or trilingual: in the globalized culture[8] what we recognize as the "national" element can no longer be preserved. On the one hand, it will be drowned in the gutters of trash culture, itself inspired by the multinational corporations that more and more squash the state and its institutions; at the same time national cultures will tend to fragment and be subsumed into the escapist mosaic of "local identities" and "group discourses." However, in spite of the apocalyptic coloring of the portrait I am drawing (the primacy of unelected centers of power over elected ones), this circumstance can become the foundation for a vibrant culture capable of inspiring new and creative energies both in our postulated sophisticated reader, and through his or her expectations, in the poet as well: poetry in one's native language will, from the beginning, be constructed *within* the world context, thereby avoiding provincialism.[9]

Digressing for a moment from our central inquiry, let us pose a question: what part of the canon of contemporary Russian poetry, and especially what part of the classic Russian poetic canon, will such a reader abandon? What kind of authorial hierarchy will be constructed in its place? To answer this, we must try to imagine ourselves encountering the Russian poetic corpus for the first time (similar to what we might experience in encountering the Georgian, Armenian, even Finnish corpus for the first time). What would we most likely find *not* of interest? Probably what we already know. What need do we have for an Armenian Alexander Blok if we already have our Russian Blok? Or a Georgian Lermontov? Rather we will be most drawn to that which has no immediate analogy, that which is unique and expresses some national specificity.

Based on such a premise we would expect a drop of interest in Pushkin, Lermontov, Tiutchev, Blok, Akhmatova and Brodsky, and a rise of interest in Nekrasov, Kliuev, Khlebnikov, and Mayakovsky. Also, the synchronic participation (as opposed to epigonic repetition) of Russian-language poets such as Osip Gennady Aigi and Vsevolod Nekrasov in extremely complex, worldwide cultural phenomena should be of great interest to these readers. And, of course, everything exotic. For Russians, this would apply especially to "Soviet" civilization with its seemingly inside-out relationship to "general human values," allowing the reader to see the human being from an unusual and, at times, extremely productive point of view (as, for example, in the poetry of Olga Berggolts).

Let us now turn to the poet. The task before us becomes more complicated: clearly the poet's work has never been reducible to a single social role or a unitary mental outlook. This was obvious to the first theoretician of the phenomenon under discussion, when he divided poets into the "noble" and "ignoble."[10] At many historical junctures there has been a temptation simply to assign the poet's social role to a caste or estate (poet-warriors, poet-priests, poet-fools), attaching them to some social body rather than concentrating on their individual outlook, showing — for example — how a person under the same circumstances orients him or herself in a completely different way (monasticism/bohemianism).

It seems clear that the socioeconomic model of poetry based on grants, prizes and stipends, which dominated the Russian cultural landscape in the first post-Soviet decade, is coming to an end. "The Revolt of the Masses" has been replaced by its dictatorship and there seems little prospect that the putative "Russian middle class" is about to trade in its conformism for "higher values."

Perhaps the unique experience of Russia and Eastern Europe will soon become a model that our formerly more fortunate poet-brethren will have to follow. The experience to which I am referring is one of total resistance to the surrounding socium, because after 1953 there was no need, either in the USSR or in Eastern Europe, for bloody totalitarian dictatorship, and in the majority of the Soviet republics and the nations of the Warsaw Pact "people and party" were indeed united.

Just as during the late Soviet period in Leningrad a parallel "second reality" emerged with its *samizdat* magazines, its apartment-based seminars, art exhibitions and poetry readings, and most importantly a parallel society with its own system of values in which the idea of a Soviet career was no more attractive than were the baths and lupanars to the first Christian "martyrs," so in contemporary Western Europe, in its most comfortable bastions, the threat of total cultural standardization is real and there seems to be no alternative to it on the horizon. Whatever potential support poetry has had has been definitively undermined: high school education has been destroyed and the university is now being drawn and quartered.

How will the poet survive in the coming century? What will he live on and for? What kind of relationship will there be between poet and reader? Beyond modified forms of *samizdat*, beyond recognition of one's cohorts via accidental quotes and slips of the tongue; beyond a shared isolation from so-called "life" — there would be seem to be little. Except for — obviously — political radicalism. And with political radicalism, a radicalization of values.

And now to conclude. It is always nice to have recourse to an authority from the past to provide additional support for one's position. Ezra Pound, who barely escaped a death sentence in the most democratic of countries, seems to have clearly expressed the plight of the poet in the future:

THE REST

O helpless few in my country,
O remnant enslaved!

Artists broken against her,
A-stray, lost in the villages,
Mistrusted, spoken-against,

Lovers of beauty, starved,
Thwarted with systems,
Helpless against the control;

You who can not wear yourselves out
By persisting to successes,
You who can only speak,
Who can not steel yourselves into reiteration;

You of the finer sense,
Broken against false knowledge,
You who can know at first hand,
Hated, shut in, mistrusted:

Take thought:
I have weathered the storm,
I have beaten out my exile.

NOTES

1 "There is a middle course in all things." (Horace).
2 *Pogon philosophon u poiei*. "The beard does not make the philosopher."
3 *Sunt certi denique fines*. "There are fixed limits." (Horace). Continuation of the first Horace quote.
4 The trivialized image we have of Herostratus occults his conscious stride toward death.
5 Revelation, 3: 15-16.
6 How else are we to understand the discussions about the totality of "the situation of the postmodern"?
7 However, the reader (like the poet) can also simply disappear: in this regard, see the history of the Middle Ages.
8 No matter how repugnant it is to the present author.
9 And the discussions that emanate from it: for example, not long ago (in *Druzhba narodov*, 2005, #12) there was a discussion of whether or not unrhymed poetry could be written in Russian or Lithuanian.
10 Aristotle. *Poetics*. 1448b.

FROM **Through The Teeth**

translated by Simona Schneider

I THE FINAL JUDGEMENT OF MR. TERREO
EN HOMMAGE À ZBIGNEW HERBERT

1

leaves the house book dust unwiped printouts with handwritten corrections favorite book-covers photographs of faces dear the kitchen door won't shut all the way: swelled everything said: tomorrow sun high mud on the bottom of puddles nearly dry will he make it there most likely not yes and where and if he buys it — then what the only time being twenty two years ago under different circumstances

And he will be like a sword in the angel's hand.
And his sharp edges will not grow dull.
And the infidel will lose both of his eyes.
As if the flash of His steel affected his vision.

2

still, with his anamnesis, downhill is better leg muscles will hold out all the while ill at ease isn't that how it is: no one is closer and staying was not an option — who would you be afterwards and you can't take it with you before night toppled down scattering lizards weigh what you've done rain will fall — the sun will set can't bother with self-reflection it's not the first day you'll eat through the last of it — sleep through and don't think you're very needed they can recite just as well it all comes back to the one thing yes: no one is closer

And by His will, the womb of the infidel's wife will dry out and become infertile.
And her flow will become putrid.
But the wife of a righteous man is like a fig tree adorned with fruit.
And her bosom is sweet to any who come to know her.

3

and so everything's wrong whereas he imagined having become routine not quite right it will end soon where to is unclear now to take a big detour anyway no one's waiting chorus: it's he that hasn't the strength to live — and they would know better he'll get to it today

And he will appear in the angel's sight having joined His army.
And only he who is worthy of a holy death will perish.
While the cast-off will fall in ashes under the feet of the righteous.
And the infidels will rejoice of their lot as compared to his fate.

4

one good thing: what a view he won't suspect a thing it can even be done in the open hasn't sweat through yet — though he's in first class if they only knew it still, it's possible this is all so so why uphill: why today's the last time to make a call tomorrow the battery will die and what will you say: nothing to say

And the angel trumpeted of His wrath.
For the elders of the tribes have forgotten the hour of prayer.
And their sons do not envy the war with the infidels.
While their daughters partake in disobedience and fornication.

5

he's depressed: doesn't want to kill anybody seems he hasn't lost his nerve same as he was — no new emotions or the heart would ache: and fear I think is a strong emotion on the wall: death to the main Swine-eater and strangely: not an ounce of solidarity but there was so much wrath but for some reason when I see these empty pupils and so what then

I am your Lord and God and I gave you ownership of my land.
From the great river Ra to the Rifaei Mountains the land is mine.
So now are you jealous of my lot?
When it is full of infidels and their wives and the children of their children?

6

went out into the city   reading the signs on the entranceways   the majority are long ago strangers   not to mention the language   he never did learn it properly   he had always planned to, in his youth   and that, too, passed by somehow   and to hell with it anyway   newly renovated walls   enormous stores   young women with well-groomed legs   and them too

And flames fell from the sky of His mighty rage.
And a hurricane of His wrath destroyed their shelter.
And in the holy war the beating of their hearts resounded.
And the righteous reposed in green pastures.

7

in conclusion the character does something such that, afterward, the poet's presence in the text turns out to be unnecessary; then he, frustrated, leaves it and in his stead appear first the EMS workers, next the police, then investigators from the state security service, as well as journalists and film crews; gradually, they will fill the whole space of the page with nothing remaining, and it will become impossible either to reconstruct the sequence of events, or even to go back to the beginning and re-read the entire text.

II TIME OF DESTRUCTION

EN HOMMAGE À CÉSAR VALLEJO

Stall — 2 zł.
Urinal — 1 zł.
Wastebasket and washbasin — additional 50 gr.

— Restroom sign at Osventsim Station

They were all rather unpleasant: they didn't wash often enough; with company they behaved unnaturally, lustily grinning at their own obscenity.

Though, it must be said, each one in his own way. And the fat rude Brokha with gigantic tits always covered with tart crumbs who never did find a husband.

And pimply Herzl, the result of a misalliance (mom — a cellist, dad — a maintenance man), lied improbably that he was studying to be a lawyer.

And then there was the rather spiteful Srool, raised without a father, whose granny, having filled the entire housing block with her shrill voice, didn't know how to speak a single language other than slang; he almost ended up in a correctional facility for stealing at the age of twelve.

His old man then turned up — apparently also having done time — without a leg (at the time, a typical scolding went like this: I'll tear your legs off); it seems I saw his prosthetic leg: a pinkish thing.

And arrogrant Tevl, who smoked and guzzled unbelievable crap, merely to avoid being obliged to borrow from his stepfather, who never did break into the bourgeoisie; the only thing that reconciled him: during get-togethers he scraped away on the violin or tinkered on the piano; actually a fairly vulgar way, i.e., with what's called "soul."

Even lively Rachael (one time when I passed by to see her, she turned out to be without her usual white panties) — who kept a copy of the novel *Stempeniu* in the capacity of a "pillow book," and her little selected Heine, which she read with an accent — was, when you come right down to it, also a complete idiot, not even so pretentious.

Those that were more pretentious (dressed in European clothes and babbled in German without any noticeable accent), hit the road without waiting till the end of the year.

That autumn, the local thugs, who wrote *jebać żydów* on the walls, died on the front or were interned; the Russians executed some, a few disappeared into the woods.

The new organizers of everyday life and times had more perfectly hygenic habits, and those who were in charge of them had all the more reason not to mix up different forms of εἰμί, εἶμι и ἵημι; some could even read the music.

so the author has nothing to add to what's already written

EDITOR'S NOTES

Osventsim — better known as Auschwitz.

Stempeniu — a novel by Sholem Aleichem.

jebać żydów — Polish phrase meaning "Fuck the Jews."

εἰμί, εἶμι и ἵημι — Ancient Greek verbs: "to be" (inf.), to be (first person, singular, present, i.e. "I am"), to send

Poem

Igor Zhukov

Alexander of Macedonia and Legs

Translated by David Hock

For Charles Bronson

Being unique, he is always on the brink of extinction.

—from testimonials on the Marquis de Sade

I

Alexander of Macedonia didn't know how to swim

2

a cat scrutinizes its excrement like Salvador Dalí

3

a slender ballerina age 50
height 162
weight 53
with dark gray-green eyes
an Aquarius
awaits an affluent knight
ready in boon to bring love
attention
concern
preferably Libra

4

in 1974 the fourth-grader Rafik writes a composition:
during recess we played horsies
Igor Zhukov broke his leg
we came to visit him
he galloped on one leg
and the next day he's already walking

5

if I had served as director of the school
would the cops also be breaking my ribs at forty?

6

Alexander of Macedonia was chucking fruit
then he ran a spear through the virtuous Cleitus the Black.

7

when he sleeps with her he has dreams that he's lost
    suitcases with groceries
    pants
    keys
but when he doesn't sleep with her he doesn't find
    suitcases with groceries
    pants
    keys
in his dreams

8

in the province there's an outbreak of fox rabies
the foxes bite cats
in the province there's an outbreak of cat rabies

9

in a camp near Syr Darya, Alexander of Macedonia
suddenly discovers
that he's a cripple
his head's not right
his throat
his leg
his sight
his hearing
his leg

10

in 1915 they cut off Sarah Bernhardt's leg
the impresario of a certain American circus
sends her a letter with the proposition:
10,000 dollars for the cut-off leg in order to
exhibit it in a private museum and guarantee
Bernhardt immortality

11

but look at what the brothers Grimm have done in "Cinderella":
in order to put on the slipper one of the sisters
cuts the big toe off her own left foot
in order to put on the slipper another sister
cuts a slice of heel off her own left foot
in order to put on the slipper

12

a princess ascended in the air
in a hot-air balloon up to happiness
and the fly and the mosquito
flew around singing

the verses of my daughter

13

when Alexander of Macedonia decided
to get married to Roxana
the Macedonians were surprised
because previously he had always
preferred the company of men

14

I want you to teach me something about myself
so far all I've learned is that I am
your grandmother

15

in 2003 some old woman
puts a hit on her neighbor's son
for 10,000 rubles
the dilettante hit man takes the advance —
5,000 rubles —
drinks it all up and goes
to the police
they let him go for lack
of *corpus delicti*

16

Elsa Triolet makes beads out of fish glue
Tatyana Yakovleva makes women's hats
Lilya Brik tries on a slipper falls out of bed and breaks her hip

the married life is going swell

EDITOR'S NOTES

Elsa Triolet (1896-1970), born Elsa Kagan, was responsible for introducing the young Vladimir Mayakovsky to her sister, Lilya Brik. She emigrated to France shortly after the Bolshevik Revolution, where she translated Mayakovsky's poems into French. In France she married Andre Triolet, and later Louis Aragon, with whom she later worked in the French Resistance movement. Her correspondence with Victor Shklovsky in the 1920s served as the start to her literary career — her first books were written in Russian, but in the 1930s she began writing in French; she was the first woman to win the Prix Goncourt.

Lilya Brik (1891-1978), born Lilya Kagan, is best known for being the "muse of the Russian avant garde" (Neruda). She was the wife of critic Osip Brik and the lover of Vladimir Mayakovsky. Her face became iconic in the early Soviet era through Alexander Rodchenko's photomontage posters and book-covers. She worked on several early Soviet films, as an actress and as a director, often collaborating with Mayakovsky, among other writers. Her 1935 letter to Stalin about Mayakovsky's literary legacy (five years after the poet's suicide), precipitated the re-publication of the his ouvre. In the 1930s, she divorced Brik, married a general who was soon executed in Stalin's purges, then married the writer Vasily Katanyan. Suffering from a terminal illness, she committed suicide at the age of 74.

Tatiana Yakovleva (1906-1991) moved to France with her family as refugees from the Bolshevik Revolution. She met and was engaged to Vladimir Mayakovsky in the late 1920s, but they were never married. At the start of World War II, she fled occupied France with her daughter (the writer Francine du Plessix Gray) and moved to New York.

Three Poems

Tatiana Zima

[untitled]

Translated by Max Nemtsov

twenty nine scars unpaid debts and shitty karma
the sea-and-sail in my pocket with no teeth to match the smile
were you close to me it would be the fifth bloody season
I would laugh in the face of this world and you'd be saying
don't go crazy on me anyway it's too funny to cry no?
I would kick at clouds so they'd pour some rain on our heads
I would feed my heart to the dogs it's so useless
and I'd make the world do some fierce blooming
but the doctor comes and says go on weep you're ill there's no hope
he writes up a prescription: Sanguisorba flowers
some Blattidae entrails some pluck and some fetid kernels —
saying summer's coming dear now it's really on us

Letter in a Bottle attn Sasha Belykh re: Moral Nature

> They sat covered with a quilt, not noticing that the village was ablaze,
> and burning pigs squealed in their barns...
> either the pen was heavy, or the heart was empty.
>
> **— Alexander Belykh, "Flaubert's Dreams"**

i wake up in the city with a broken nose and October in my ear
who would dare tell me that it's time to write a requiem
when everything draws to a close i'm tempted to say hi there honey —
and i do

every morning i wake up in the same body i went to sleep in at night
every morning i wake up in the same body in the same country with the
same thoughts
every morning rings out with my animal wails
at my attempts to wake up human every morning

in all my lies there's no lying there are only naked truths
hemorrhoid morphology syntactical paranoia all true
and he has no talents apart from one million dollars
not enough to buy one Van Gogh

my mother says i'm a tomcat brazen and lazy
i don't go after mice i don't give a damn snorting and purring
i don't like kids don't like people at all nor tv nor radio either
but i like roads violins snow and loneliness

but i saw didn't i how she cried with her kerchief in horror
she felt so bad with not a trace of St. Exupéry around i saw it i did
there's some misunderstanding in the fact that i'm still alive
it seems there's something wrong with those who du côté de chez Swann

how she taught me to imitate birds in Mandarin and Russian
i kissed her hands kissed her heart rainy evenings
told her farewell in French and in Spanish
but she left English-style without a word

so we'll go to your beautiful quiet lake Sasha
let it all rot in hell we'll just listen to lotuses blooming
oh i'm damned tired Sasha of waking in the same age and body
with a good view of human misery and sorrow

and you know Vasya Zorin has a soul of an angel and real tears in his eyes
he reads poetry from clouds of the 9th century
Sasha now i know what our Lord had in mind when
he was reckless enough to create us humans

oh i was running in and out books one after another i blush at the thought
anyway i could spoil the look of any book with a torn-out folio… but
this naked beast that's been drinking my blood all these years
i know Sasha it could never quench its thirst with blood

and in his poems fat cicadas look through monocles
and the heart raped with unlove is carried away to die at dawn
he doesn't cry thinking he laughs sweet Jesus he's not aware
that to laugh and to cry is the same thing

so i'm told i'm God's own fool and that such rascals are marked for life
but i keep my love under lock and key to keep the evil eye away
and still it wants to go where no ravens go with their bones Sasha
don't you let it out that it's got wings of cast iron

Sasha there are no people in these bodies knock knock who's there
is it really i who squints into the fall with motley eyes
i see Bashō's frog flopping into the pond and i hear
the rain scraping against the grape leaves

[untitled]

Translated by Matvei Yankelevich

To fanailova

listen
you say words that aren't
take a recount
of the purple leaves
in the half-empty forest
multiply the age of the abyss
by the address-less-ness of prayers
and divide
by a heart

short by one drop of rain
just one
itty bitty one
to make air
into water

the forest lacks both force and foxes
for shameless pageant
song
the throat lacks birds
and ribs
no way to weave it
nor to catcall

look
how circles spread
over the earth
from our cackling and weeping
how the dogs keep
the fierce watchmen
on their leashes
how the earth can't
stand up underfoot
and everything inside

look
how heavy the transparency
of metaphoric figures
on winter's threshold
the snow's already tipsy
december's magic
conceals what's burning
alive without melting

Three Poems

Olga Zondberg

He wasn't here in the morning

Translated by Natasha Randall

A plush, light-brown teddy bear is lying face down on the lid of a trash can, and it looks almost new.

This can only mean one thing: there is a dangerous maniac earning a living in the city, who is used to holding himself in check.

Every time he has the desire to murder, while it's still morning, before it's too late, he goes to the store and chooses a soft toy, he steals it, takes it to one of the outer neighborhoods — it depends on his mood but the farther the better — and he throws it away there.

On the days when the need to murder is especially burning and it isn't mollified by delays or pretenses, he obtains a toy, not from a store but by taking it from the kids for whom he lies in wait in yards and near the playgrounds.

The Legend of the Life and Death of the Stone Alchemist

Two colors — gray and green — defined the landscape of the high mountain platform surrounded with steep, almost vertical stony walls. The dry soil, the sparse vegetation and an old, crooked oak, the roots of which clung to the edge of the platform, and its trunk, branches and leaves hung over the precipice — and that's all the markings of this place. This is where he lived, the stone alchemist, and somewhere below, at the bottom of the precipice, the city where he was born and lived for a bit less than twenty years, led its own life. These years had been long ago erased from the memory of the stone alchemist. He remembered his one and only childhood dream but only vaguely really — to die and give away parts of himself in pieces. He also remembered how he left the city and miraculously scrambled up to where he lives now without falling from the steep wall. The city had been expecting something from him for a long while, considering the young alchemist to be an otherworldly youth, which is why his parents weren't ever surprised by him.

In the following years, the alchemist carried out a business that he conceived of himself, prompted by a drop of syrup which once fell on him. He turned ordinary gray stones into precious ones, impregnating them with the syrup of the crooked oak. Work went slowly, and for half a century the alchemist only just managed to create ten such stones. It was his gift to the city which he intended to dump down on them when death approached.

The stone alchemist would never have known that he was stone, if he hadn't once started to break up. At first it plunged him into despair, but soon the powerlessness was replaced by a fierce thirst for activity. In a week he prepared as many jewels as he had in his whole life until then — and his heart, which the alchemist half in jest named his cornerstone, really became as heavy as a stone.

Meanwhile, the disintegration of the alchemist was accelerating, just as the work of his brain was accelerating. And then, waking up one day, he understood what he needed. With a smile, he looked at the jewels, made with such effort, he raked them into the far corner of the tent, after which he tied himself to the crooked oak, and hanging over the precipice, drank the whole supply of mixture which was prepared from the syrup so that a hailstorm of jewels would be scattered over the city. The cornerstone at last turned over and scratched a sharp edge somewhere deep inside....

The heavy gray stones looked nothing like precious stones, and dropped onto the city from the sky, falling on people's heads and killing them instantly.

[untitled]

No one will be wasted: everyone is able to do life in one way or another. You don't have to know how to build a house in order to survive. You don't have to know how to do anything and you don't even have to pretend, and if something is needed, you just wait as long as you don't mind it. Activity without necessity like that makes as much sense as discussing feelings. Nevertheless you can look at anyone — and you'll see in front of you a possessor of rare skills, sometimes a great many... And even though morality in our circumstances is more important than intensivity and the results of what is done, sometimes these skills are unquestionably useful.

For example, some people are easily able to separate their middle and ring fingers, at the same time squeezing the middle finger to the index finger and the ring finger to the pinkie.

Ilya can bend his fingers fantastically and snap them.

C.K. is able to bend the last phalanx of each of the fingers on his hands, except the thumbs, keeping his fingers straight.

Evgeniya can do the same, and she can also whistle with two fingers.

Igor can portray many complicated figures with his fingers, and besides that, he can breathe with one lung at a time, swaying from side to side with his head in one place, he can wink horizontally, tightening his eyelids towards the bridge of his nose at the same time or in alternate, and upturning his eyeballs in his eyesockets backwards and up.

T. can wiggle her ears, move her toes one by one, and can even make a "goat" out of them.

Sveta can easily lift small objects from the floor with her feet, can write with left and right hands at the same time in mirror-like reflection, she can move her pupils very quickly from right to left, and she can also tap herself on the noggin at the same time as rubbing her stomach in circular motions.

Zhenya and V.G. can fold their tongues in four.

I. can turn his tongue over, 180 degrees.

M. can lift his left eyebrow, and then his right eyebrow, he can compose a text with eyes closed and he can meow like a real cat.

Tanya can read a thick book in one night, and can sew or knit a beautiful thing in a couple of hours.

Olya can give injections to newborn mice.

Pavel can assess a whole person just by looking.

Dmitry can remember telephone numbers well, when he's in the mood.

Vanya P. can sing and whistle at the same time.

V.G. can light a match with one hand as he throws up the matchbox and catches it.

Alexei, travelling on the railroads, can stop the snoring of his fellow travellers with his mind.

Seryozha can make lead sinkers in domestic conditions.

And, well, I can be as offended by a cat as I can by a person.

poetry

Edited by
Julian T. Brolaski,
E. Tracy Grinnell &
Paul Foster Johnson

With contributing editors
Jen Hofer &
Nathalie Stephens

"Thing 01." by Kim Beck

Two Poems

Diane Ward

"... Or a bricked-up door,
Or an echo that still can't be
Still, ..."

— Anna Akhmatova, "Echo"

reach / hand

for Will Alexander

how do you see the wind?
dry-scratch
between whispers
single tap against the volume wall

a bird's worth in the bush
hollow-boned strut
dirt glance
no tracks

no notebook
but unbound ideas
objects fanned out
live all around

flower-coded color
mocks the sunlight
as homage to the sun

and if we're in hell — well
we don't like it
but we'll give it a chance

in our mind
seeing as we can't materialize
in name
wander around the spines
meaning strength
in every direction

an outline, ill-defined
and this is what happens in here:

stay where the water put us
have we lost our head?
it floats away
for the same reason
that anything falls to earth
while its idea remains
suspended

I'm not going to shudder loud enough
to make a difference
but cling above the din

to be peopled-out
means to drift
outside the scale of touch
existence in which each side is different

pin-pricks and -drops
love levels outpace themselves
the echo reaches all the way up
just below the sand

that leaves us:
the space beyond the brush's tip
so sound blows back
to catch all the pieces

No List
(no list)

first word spoken
and last
unfinished

met nowhere
on the narrative grid

we feel sound

had no sound
but meaning, bypassed
you are a stand-up

silence

both sides don't wait
a cumulative love / not love

veins in rocks
map the relative strength
or are a map

of the time strength took
to manifest itself
spooning weakness

sorry for the rat
and for the hand
closing the cage door

(to begin with
open or close
between

I didn't (no phalanxes
one lip is up, one is down
wasting time

fingers through hair
(the path
more than the vehicle

all thoughts are parched
all others quenched
alone, when you're all together

desert oasis sprouts from fault
(the sprung rhythm squeezed
along

now you're a downright
gyrator   now you've gone,
spun out

paths

nothing determined
nothing dreamed — except this:

all the stars started
without any idea
that this goes someplace

that place might be
here
might not

inroads
close callings
lined up separately
finally,

package removed from contents
contiguous voices exchanged
so that what flows is felt
as space between

kept it all within the margin
are you done yet?
is that how you would spell it
if it was it
which it isn't
I guess

is that how you would speak
to me, a person
here
from you,
a person
there

an old fire
cradled within its issuance
the power to stare back at itself
(create its own abrupt image
take it away

I destroyed something fragile
with my eyes closed
I am a fault, myself

I have a current number
but no nominal righteousness
some of my friends have
a lot of friends

that leaves me
as a friend of those guys
but maybe not those guys

things we never needed to know
that water's thoughts are never
to stop
no shape unimagined
nothing unallowed
so all excepted

I dictated a daily protuberance
that extruded itself within each hour
so it's ok to say
'give me some ________'
ok

I am that silhouette that reeks of physicality
not counting the parts that reek
of myself

neither motion nor development
but balance
and its opposite
shaking with my new stranger
gag without reflection
mushrooming

this gray matter
never thinks about
dark matter

brain coral's small black central orifices
look like drains

try to identify every plant
within one standard city block
can't stop it

(nothing gets done alone
what are you watching now?
and is there a record
something being taken away
some unspecified place

the sense
of a ribbon of highway, a stop
a sound that echoes all in one direction
that would be toward you
that would be away from me

heat as the record
of what passes

what's a room without walls —
time?

today's lesson: my footsteps
touch one another
in measurement

Normal
(normal)

Default
(default)

No List
(no list)
:
(:)
.
(.)

Three Poems

Kimberly Lyons

#2 Sonnet

when thoughts staineth it's like this morning
which is foggy, introverted, over Bklyn
as I creep out for coffee
sit in this empty café staring at a cement wall
the surrounding hum of air conditioners condenses thought
to a gray stream in which a few sparkles hide.
I wonder why I dreamed last night of swimming in long grass fields
to come to an edge of a Venetian lagoon and then swam
with monstrous snapping eels
as though the instance of panic
warns of menace or maybe it's the inner part
of my self, a sort of joke
that brings this information from one section to another
that I contain the monstrous eels and it's my own thoughts that staineth.

#2

Dear Elizabeth, today modified yesterday with salted insurgence
Baroque bafflement serving as an arch of wetted hydrangea
The ghazal of the broken TV just lying there smashed
And regions are traversed block to block the roulette
Is sensitive to its immersion and dialect, euphony and utterance
Which is a refracted voice
A tinted spectral horizon
The envisioned you; a location and well.
How she closed her eyes and was positioned in a horizontal
With pockets and wrist bone, lengthening and lighting.
Eventually this rain permeates the experiment
Holsters the air
Deducts a palette, its signals in the field
Not substance or content, ingredient and fix.

Octagon

For Chris

In the black box
Of a kitchen at night
You come to look for something
And find the wrapped enigma of a promise.
Our secret soap, a geometric cipher.
The lure of a beacon
A constructivist rectangle
And a rock-like shine.
Dry water, wet air
The congealed facts, fats,
Fire and pumice of our decade. The Tide
Which extracts every impression.
A kleenex and a crayon
Hidden under your pillow.
The templates of a product
And its inevitable corruption.
Octagon
A secret agent
Of renewal and moderne
Glows under the sink
Unused and unwrapped
and waits for a futuristic future
When everything else in the kitchen
Will have achieved its imagination.

Ten Times My Hand on the Table

François Turcot

Dix fois ma main sur la table **Translated by Nathalie Stephens**

quand tout vit
quand tu vis
et qu'à partir de rien
je n'existe toujours pas
j'approche une chaise de la table

— Martine Audet[1]

I THE WORKROOM

On the coffer of hours

first resistance
encountered   at the trail of waking

the shard calls me back   a diversion
a profile

silting of the sharpened dawn

---

1 when everything lives / when you live / and from nothing / I still don't exist / I bring a chair to the table

2 THE HORIZON OF THE TABLE

What moves
a voice not mine
a hand not yours

placed on the table
the envelope   the seal that attests to you

with the strike of a reed upon a letter
between the hand and the fold
nearby   the palm measures doubt

3 A SQUARE OF LIGHT

The square from which a light unfolds
not as clear as you

on the table I spell what is repeated   I'm coming back to it

from here I call   you won't come
claim your love

the quick of morning renewed

4 A SINGLE PLATFORM

By this open rectangle
where impatience is archived
the hand's arc   emptiness startles

at the edge of the letter
particles of dust in the distance
like ectoplasms

5 A HAND, A TREMOR

Ring of fist on the table
of morning   shattered porcelain

impossible surface   a negation

call of the bent hand
scratching the curve of a question

will I return?

6 CLOISTER

Twelve steps to the cloister
between the seams   stale bread
and the refinement of waiting

the schema of your laugh moves aside

halts your stories   no one revisits
the folds of my face

the silent crumbs of you left behind

7 A WINDOW, AJAR

Before   in truth the window
impervious doesn't tell your story

the small box of the radio
supports a glass pane

a road map striped
by a ballpoint pen lifts

the incomplete list of our initiated gestures

8 A FURROW

Eight times over in morning encounter

an insect a porous flower
leaned against the rampart

a honey circle
interrupted by chance

a furrow prescribed
by a hand withheld

9 AN AMULET

I laid an amulet there
several skins on your name erased

from the table to the hand
from the finger pointing to the the lettering of your name

the eye circulates   rebuilds the thinned image
in capital letters on the wooden body

10 EVER THE TABLE

Begins with a repeated sequence
ten times announces the table and morning again

no   I am not counting
fears I'll return to them

this lateral light envelops your name
doesn't conjugate it   echelons

unfolds it   ever on the table

Two Poems

Karen Weiser

The axis of vision approacheth

Can one fall if the cosmos continually expand?
Come back from far off, darned with the rummaging
of the eye, and our slow eddies will continue
to consume and reproduce in the kitchens of our selves

I turned plantlife in this origin story
nothing more than a run of notes, sad
pricking of elegy. Though the timing is off now,
registering a static, that grain of vanishing pretexts
rewriting the interior music of a body

And a cosmos in its clematis drawing room
wades out to the extra-corporeal promised land
It's the ocean of more everything
We found our underwear swimming
This noise is its own response

like a threshold barking, so momentary
I hardly notice it channeling me, but I can imagine
As far as I can see translucently

Nothing shuffles off our present

Nothing shuffles off our present
but forms form around the flaws
plovers from which the apple strays
venting small movements that tremble with proximity
The channel steadies when I move closer
tempted into artistic sanitation that used to be
called clarity; the kind of Revolution of one body
around another, but inside, kingdom of mere dreaming
There is no outside yet to bleat with unlovely aspect
nor bounties for channels of thought

Horse evils may befall horses
but sounds used to be untethered
as a shape to rest thought upon
Now we pay the sculptor for the dead statesman, and ho(a)rse
inanimate materials say:
dip your watch in the marsh and fail me
so we will not grow moldy:
time will melt the increments
that attach thoughts into sequence

Vacuum

Ari Banias

There is a fake twin brother who's always telling this one old story. And every time he tells it like it's new, and inside his story I think I recognize mine as he talks the sound of a vacuum back and forth, erasing the carpeting. He talks a highway and a dip in its cracked asphalt where some weeds have pushed up, and they seem, somehow, to recognize me; they flap wildly in the gust of passing cars. And he talks us into one of those cars, heading back to the house at the end of the long driveway, *that* house.

If color were a feeling, he talks the carpeting in our stories into the same convincing shade of peach; the same, our walking shoeless on it and how we sink. He says the doors are hollow and if not for the slatted floor-vents hissing air, one could hear everything happening. If not for the television, its hundred cable channels always on. The low garble of that talk. And the lock broken without reason, that stayed broken, so someone would have to hold their foot against the door, the light bulbs blown, the crank-out windows forever closed, every crank missing. He talks about it all — the basement, the pantry, the empty garage. Those thinning woods at the edge of the yard.

But soon his voice, the dark line of highway we ride, will scatter like ash when he swerves too close to an edge; the details sharp, the danger real. The car will have stopped moving — then there won't be a car. So we won't be in it, sucked backwards in time, and the patch of roadside weeds we passed further back, whipped and starved, won't remember. The vacuum will fold into the closet, the buttons find their holes. When the fake twin stops talking, there's no story. The house that throbbed with specificity could be any house, or every.

money order: envío al 5 de enero de 2008, entrega urgente

decirte algo real, un hielo más sublime que todas las mentiras con que te di a beber mi enfermedad, porque soy esa mancha, la más negra de la página, una que jamás volverías a leer, ni siquiera ahí donde duermen mis otras mentiras como hielos hirvientes dándote al puro gozo, aún contra la idea de placer incubada en vos por tantos años y tantos duelos, desde cuando en tus ojos azules como cualquier lugar común para canción o poema, sí, en esos ojos se miró a sí mismo un destino feliz a pura burguesía y televisiones y niños comiendo bien, no mi enfermedad viviéndote, echando la culpa sobre ese cuerpo que dormías, porque sos bella y has sufrido más que yo, decirte algo real y sucio, una mentira en su rayo exacto de verdad, agua por la que me has ido odiando hasta en tus sudores provistos por Deseo, como cuando me tomás sin besarme, como diciéndome "hembra sucia, hoy te toca a vos la humillación," y entonces el camino que penetro es inverso y veo que mi semen se ha convertido en el iris de tus ojos indicando a un cuerpo como el mío que iría volviéndose un azul de pudrimiento cadavérico para hacerte sonreír y cada labio de belleza, sé, fue creado para vos y sabés mostrarlo, esas risas confirman una decisión superior con la que quisieras tensarme los clavos y ser la primera que me agarra a escupidas, ay, derretir mis llamas gélidas como un choque con la situación, no, ya no buscarme más por tus sábanas ni en ninguna mancha sobre la página, ni ningún ojo que hayás visto o tocado después de mí, ni tan siquiera algún ensueño lleno del brillo de ese tu corazón que terminé de hacer mierda

TASTYSCRUMPTIOUSDELI-CIOUSANDDELECTABLE

Alan Mills

<u>RICOSABROSODELICIOSOYEXQUISITO</u> **Translated by Dolores Dorantes and Jen Hofer**

money order: sent january 5, 2008, priority delivery

to say something real to you, an ice cube more sublime than all the lies i fed you about my sickness, because i am that stain, the blackest one on the page, a page you'll never read again, not even there where my other lies sleep like boiling ice cubes giving yourself over to pure pleasure, still against the idea of pleasure incubating in you for so many years and so much violent grief, since in your blue eyes like any cliché in song or poem, yes, in those eyes she saw herself a happy fate of pure bourgeoisie and televisions and kids eating well, not my sickness living you, blaming that body you put to sleep, because you're beautiful and you've suffered more than I have, to say something real and dirty to you, a lie on its exact ray of truth, water for which you've been hating me even in your sweats supplied by Desire, like when you take me without kissing me, like saying to me "dirty girl, today it's your turn to be humiliated," and then the path i penetrate is inverse and i see that my semen has become the iris of your eyes indicating a body like mine that will continue to become a rotting cadaverous blue to make you smile and each lip of beauty, i know, was created for you and you know how to show it, those laughs confirm a superior decision with which you wanted to nail me taut and be the first to claim me by spitting, ay, to melt my frigid flames like a collision with the situation, no, not to look for me anymore among your sheets nor in any stain on the page, nor in any eye you've seen or touched after me, nor even some reverie brimming with the sheen of that heart your heart i ended up turning to shit lo escupo así pelado y sin pelos en la lengua, quién dijo miedo atrás de un palo, se los dejo ir así nomás porque ya no iba a soportar ningún encierro, ni alegrón de burro, humillación es una melodía que ya no me gusta, shic, shicsabros, xicsabrosdelicios, shicsabrosdeliciosquisit, qué xic, ay qué shique, qué shic tu mic, xic tu cul, shic tu pus, tu cuc mamit, shic tu chich, ay, mi shumita de oro me llamaste, remedabas mi habla, lengua torciéndose en ampollas cuando intenta tu Castilla, me soplaste a la oreja tantos avernos y sueros alcohólicos, risa y risa, puras burlas sos, la pura gana de chingarme, típico mal del hijo del sol, Tonatiú pisado, canchón de río, rubio por gusto, sin alcurnia ni linaje ni nobleza ni nada, por eso lo que te gusta es transar, ser amigo de los más malvados y peludos, xic, así andás mostrando el sombrero o el grillo de coca y ese es todo el orgullo que va a poder nacerte de tu enfermedad, sombrerudo mierda, shic decís, shictuchich decís con baba escurriendo en mi espalda y mis sentaderas, xicsabros y pura baba, te reís, remedás mi hablado, te cagan de risa los ancestros en mi sangre, shictumic, purO burla le das a mis decires, mi mala Castilla, shicdelicios, pero ahí te gusta estar, ahí bien apunuscado entre mi pusite xicsabros y los pelos, el aroma a camarón, sí, te sentís gallito por tus cuates, maldición del monte, pero conmigo sos otra cosa, por ratos te portás manso, mientras voy olvidando todo lo que perdí en la aldea, desde los animales hasta los aparecidos, hasta los desaparecidos con los que sigo hablando, sí, me siento valiente por ratos, shic, por ratos sí y por ratos no, pero tengo más huevos que vos, canchito pisado, shictuculmamit, xicsabros, y la metías bien duro, trababas los ojos como yegua y pateaste todo el recuerdo de mi familia, ay, no te dan vergüenza esos dientes, tan shucos, amarillos, amazorcados y llenos de hoyo, es que ya ni planta de cuque tenés, ya no sos el soldadito mamado que conocí en el Parque Central, adonde andabas cazando, adonde me agarrarías en un día buena onda, porque los días que andabas mala onda con tus cuates se ponían a violar, se decían "juguemos trompo" y la onda era jalar a las indias y hacerlas dar vuelta sin el corte, a varias muchachas les tocó su shictucul masivo, las subían a un pick-up y hacías fila, me contaste, bolo, apestoso a cerveza, hacían fila y los excitaban los alaridos de angustia más el sudor de tu escuadra, ni el humor a guaro te hizo la idea de que eso no me lo tenías que contar a mí, en tu borrachera pensaste que risa me iba a dar, pero ya vas, para mí ya no valés nada, cuero malo y ladino, ya no me eriza el recuerdo de tu boina roja y tu emblema guerrero, ya ni siquiera le dan alegría a mi corazón los pensamientos con tu carita de chucho colorado, perro hambriento que moría encima de mí, te vi por un lado sacando la lengua, puro chucho, perro de la calle, shictucul, xictumic, shicsabrosdelicios, shictupusmamit

money order: sent november 25, 2007, delivery and knife, please

spitting the cat out of the bag nude like that no cat's got my tongue, who's afraid with a club in the hand, i let them go just like that because i wasn't going to take being locked up anymore, nor donkey joy, "humiliation" is a melody i don't like anymore, chic, chicscrump, xicscrumpdelicio, chicscrumpdeliciodelect, how xic, oh how shique, how chic your slit, xic your rump, chic your pus, your ump mamita, chic your tit, ay, "my little golden squaw" you called me, you aped my speech, tongue twisting into blisters as it attempts your Castile so many seeya's and alcoholic serums you blew into my ear, laughing and laughing, mere jeers you, mere desire to screw me over, typical evil of the child of the sun, Tonatiú full of shit, big blonde redneck, blonde for the pleasure of it, with neither pedigree nor lineage nor nobility nor nothing, that's why what you like is to compromise, to be amigos with the baddest and the hairiest, xic, that's how you roll showing your hat or your dime bag of coke and that's all the pride your sickness is going to be able to make in you, hat-sporting shit, chic y'say, chicyertit y'say with drool running down my back and my haunches, xicscrump and mere drool, you laugh, you ape my speaking, you die laughing at the ancestors in my blood, chicyerslit, meer jeers you make at my speeches, my bad Castilian, chicdelish, but there's where you like to be, there good and snuggled between my pussite xicscrump and my hair, the scent of shrimp, yes, you feel like a little rooster in the midst of your posse, curse of the mount, but with me you're something else, once in a while you act tame, while I forget everything I lost in town, from the animals to the appeared people, to the disappeared people I continue to talk to, yes, I feel brave once in a while, chic, once in a while yes and once in a while no, but I'm more ballsy than you are, shit-for-brains little blond boy, chicyerumpmamita, xicscrump, and you stick it in good and hard, you were rolling your eyes like a mare and you kicked the entire memory of my family, ay, aren't you ashamed of those teeth, so filthy, yellow, corncobbed and full of holes, it's just that now you don't even act like a soldier, now you're not the well-built little soldier boy i met in the Parque Central, where were you going hunting, where would you grab me one day feeling cool, because the days you weren't feeling so cool with your pals you'd start to rape, you'd all say "let's play spinning tops" and the cool thing was to pull at the *indias* and make them spin without their skirts, a number of chicks got their turn at a massive chicyerump, they'd gather them all in a pick-up and you'd get in line, you told me, fool, reeking of beer, they'd get in line and the anxious howls excited them plus the sweat of your squad, not even the smell of booze gave you the sense that you didn't have to be telling me this, in your drunkenness you thought it would make me laugh, but get out now, for me you're not worth anything now, with your bad half-breed skin, now the memory of your red beret and your warrior emblem doesn't make me hard, now not even the thoughts of your little colorful doggie face make my heart happy, starving stray that was dying on top of me, i saw you off to the side sticking your tongue out, total stray, street dog, chicyerump, xicyerslit, chicscrumpdelish, chicyerpusmamita

Aclaraciones:

NOTA 1

mientras lee esto Ud., cierto, va a ir percibiendo la Farsa y se dará cuenta que poesía nada que ver, pues, esta onda puro rollo, pura Farsa, pero ahí viene lo bonito, sí, que entonces Ud. tiene que empezar a imaginar la salida, sí, su salida de este sitio infernal y aquí se le da una su ayudita:

UNA ESCALERA EN LAS ARENAS DEL MAR

NOTA 2

mientras lee esto hay un artista fabricándose su escalera y Ud., cierto, también es ese artista...

NOTA 3

vaya con el chisme a donde más se necesite y empiece a construir o enseñe a fabricar escaleras en los barrios y tugurios o asentamientos, ahí donde tanta mugre se come a los niñoscomeniños, sí, porque así la ciudad se irá transformando en un tremendo océano adonde irán dirigidas todas nuestras escaleras y así el dolor ya no:

podríamos pensar que se sube de la Atlántida pero no es así

NOTA 5

cuando vaya en algún bus urbano y de repente note que una pandilla de niños ultraja a alguna señora de lindas carnes, detenga, métase, defienda, o simplemente constrúyales una escalera a los 4, pues todos la necesitan, luego hacen una reunión en el mar y reflexionan.

Clarifications

NOTE 1

as you read this, surely, you will perceive the use of Farce and you will realize this has nothing to do with poetry, really, this thing merely a rant, merely a Farse, but that's where things get good, yes, so then you will have to imagine an exit, yes, your exit from this hellish site and here's one to provide you with a little help:

A STAIRCASE ON THE SANDS BY THE SEA

NOTE 2

as you read this there is an artist constructing a staircase and you, surely, are also that artist...

NOTE 3

go and take that gossip to where it's most needed and begin to build or teach the construction of staircases in the barrios and shantytowns or camps, there where the kidseatingkids are eaten by so much filth, yes, because the city will thus be transformed into an enormous ocean where all our staircases will lead, and thus pain no longer:

might we think that it rises from Atlantis but it's not like that

NOTE 5

when you are riding some city bus, and you suddenly notice that a gang of kids is raping some lady with a great bod, stop, get involved, defend, or simply build all four of them a staircase, since all of them need it, and later meet up by the sea and ponder.

Feverfew

Phil Cordelli

1-14

Passing on the inoculant,
one that fell between two like.
This soporific, sickness that brought his head,
promised next to comfort him,
and live thereafter with him.

After all this trouble to secure a throat,
as if you could move any air with it.
Anyway, it becomes host.
The contractions come irregularly
and cannot be choked down.

I've been a bombardier,
floral bursts of juice, thick liquid
of organs, your sacs of air, which heat and respire.

You wish to parse waking from sleeping,
organ from animal, and yourself
from both, permanently.

So you take on water again
instead of dreaming. You are a shape
trying to become a color, a kitten
made of string, loosely formed,
and walking somehow. Also
somehow made by you.

And you must make it move
but do not wish to, do not care to even know
how to do so. So you crouch under it,
with those flatter-winged pigeons,
vague-eyed and stupid, wondering
who crowded the skies in your absence.

In a fit of bursting, the various factions rise
in turn to play at rebellion and grow sickly
in turn, red and tender, a consequence of excess blood.

Your organs no longer seem to digest,
only to chew your own interior
to get drills through.

Half fade for tickling, big fellow.
The walls have speaking parts tonight.
The news from your left side is not good,
it died. Face down behind an ice cream parlor
counter.

2-2

There is a fish which I have heard also breathes
with its ears. And cats are not allowed in here,
but they come one by one to the door. They command
but do not give.

The great inclusion will survive the succumbing.
Lawrence rolls out of Arabia with bowling scores
in his sidecar, draped in ever-newer rags.

They have the stores with the cigarettes,
the money-changers and launderers, lower light fixtures,
dogs running through alleys, hills half chopped away.

A vague citrus slant, drunk from postcards.
The softer parts maturing, and hardening.

FROM Looking for the Object that Is Ballast in My Head

Corina Copp

I. (ARE)

Men are comfortable. What is, is COMFORTABLE, apparently.
Bedbugs ARE. Girls grouped on the lawn ARE.
Cocktails containing grenadine ARE.
Money saving emotional Ducky
from desperate moves. If enough tea-cakes, ok.
If not, she will pounce
on your man and her object will heat up
like the rapid wings of a bird.
Oh, it got the fountain you want, Duck.

The roses have very straw,
across a thousand miles
Roses, very kindly,
the roses have very straw
clothes and are supposed to
sit up straight in them
for morning tea. Most men still
look perfectly NORMAL
in the Victorian setting
despite an unabling smirk
dissolves upon one
got quite red in the face,
a cricket, his doomed shirt
unfurling,
though perfectly normal.
Heavy shoes ARE chiefly
minding,
Trousers ARE.
Porch swings,
to match your mood, can go on being,
for a ballast

the center of my head...held
handiwork, Sir. Do not
make that face.

I like men and I want to respect
mesh and lace, left uncomfortable
all the year round
to be COMFORTABLE,
but we have changing times to cope with,
say the ailing. Stiff collars ARE.
Ah, that's the point. NO.
See the mesh and lace white tops are near
the fountain in the absinthe courtyard,
absinthe droplet
courtyard, my grayish courtyard,
Ducky, splayed around
Tops.

Grab them (or don't) and
abide by ACE rental service.
Straight chairs for us there
in a lead fluorescent register
and the soft, yielding couches for us too
under a warm glow.
But wants better skin. Picnicking
at the request of an author of an article
on Men's Clothes, angelic
girls group on the lawn
and pintuck and pincurl and punch.
Of a maypole in their life span
never heard, but one gets very cherry
in the face, somehow.

(...)

III. (THE PETROL STATION)

Am I to provide a set of straight chairs for my male guests?
Or pretty soon A Tart, A Lady, A Whow, A Southern
Belle, and Mae West will shake their heads
(because they have never known what comfort is).
Their spines will have frozen into their correctly tailored
suits and pardon, we're used to having them around.
NO. The men must change their clothes
as we all like men. Without their clothes,
it would be hard to identify them, wouldn't it?
Perhaps some man will read this piece
and tear off his own collar and vest. Such a man
might hang upside-down at the petrol station
while us ducks talk
to each other very kindly about matters
most picketed. N says now! In the next century I expect!
A majority of women will be ABLE
to give me the cold shivers; who is left? I speak thus glibly
for my whole sex because our eyelids
are smeared and heavy and I know a majority
of women simply won't *do* anything about it?
Just prefer to be footing.

(...)

V. (WHO DID WHAT, WHERE, WHEN AND TO OR WITH WHOM?)

Don't bend to form an arch
over me you captured
red droplets!
Newborns complete
window earthwork
to loosen its silver threads
and golden
needles. So everyone in this town
has friends but me,
and imagine among
white vans deindustrialized
cow soaps strain to hear
bel canto black walnuts
falling from her ears

Geometry, what did she do
wrong, was she unfaithful,
like knocking off
pull cooperatively
on baked apples, everyone
screaming near in their
carefree...near the end
of my breath, I knew I had
little faith yay sun flowers

Three Poems

Matt Reeck

The Shop Windows of Eid

I

Shop windows are
showing fall denim

Uncle arrives
bearing presents

Date: *Tue, 16 Oct 2007 13:02:30 +0530*
From: *"Ajay Kumar Shukla"*

Salah is prayed
facing Mecca

Gnarled hands
fondle green ribbons

II

The singer was
wearing ripped denim

To: "Matt Reeck"
Subject: hello

Black and white tiles
betoken the bar

Whiskey will quicken
his heartbeat

The neighbors were
waiting on thresholds

III

The dye ran
throughout the water

At the fair
a centrifugal machine

The idols were burnt
over holidays

hello mattsir
goodafternoon, how r u?

A dust storm descended
on Thursday

IV

i hope that u r very well
i wiss u

Here they're worn
with suave jackets

Leila clasped her
emerald redeemer

It was surely
a wrong-type reason

Cue cards produced
out of order

V

Lightning strikes
the isthmus

A cart's shadow
behind the station

One date was broken
by pleasure

The new moon rose
over the rooftops

HAPPY EID
from ajayshukla lucknow

Ode to /a/

all aardvarks, waltz
  malls, all faults,

falls, nawabs, all
  bods, daubs,

FOBs, all prawn
  mods, mob

lawns, all qualms,
  fawns, locks, all

rocks, straw Bobs,
  all Allahs, all

long odds, all malt
  bars, pompoms,

claws, all hearths,
  alms, balls, all

drawls, all stars,
  dawns, all parks

Ode to /I/

in lyrics, riddles,
  in tin wigs,

fickle thrills, in
  girls, tidbits,

in fish gills,
  krill, dills, in

crisp linen, thin
  bills, trick

limericks, in pimp
  cribs, bling,

in blimps, in
  trim limbs, in

thick licks, hips,
  in silk slips,

guilt, rings, in
  little hills, stills,

in whisk, figs,
  whist, gigs

FROM **in very Variant**

Nathan Austin

hymn • plan

"— then we're lost"
at home in hymn

longer   tto mean
a silent H   Devised for expression
                                        for formal aching

sections with deeply felt
O something!   An end to
thrust, as all in warmth

these and these and some I place
a thing, and sometimes

ruffle • thimble

abrapt or trouber vex
is a roughen not ruffled

ff f in fled – by such barbs
need   , by such
as need trembled in or like

two a a groov ed a
loop   a spliced loop

night • trust

keeping   in eveniving
or f elt time

dawn   dence visible
               an event to taken
                         "to luck."

               O! dune rupts, giving th
ruthfulness of night, *of meters laugh*
       of June. Of care or keeping
       's s as for to re

to rely semble — O! occuracy
in the beginning of hope fall

take • call

t ache   call you want
   of off th trouble to •

            the Birds a
a the Skies old — old and

  he roll off row of figures   sign ls
voice for help as a bird

no e or cry o ge or ry o ge

     hu an cry • he flee
               he home

roads

Elisabeth Whitehead

1.

someone has dropped combs and someone has dropped hair another left unclothed by the road / with their skins and wolves their slowly rounded stones pin-light snow accrues / where you once pressed my hand my hand is quite cool / here you must figure all words by their endings / a sound heard only when no longer there / tan trees in last light / dim takes the eyes ask which days are days I cannot remember / pouring sugar in the wounds / the horn of sleep or newly cast mead / these roads in bone are round / claim capable accounts

2.

for those waylaid / starved the ribs crushed of a cloud / they swallow their copper coins and shine toward the edges / theirs is a falling / in 6 sleeves and particle points / cells as a city and not enough water to sweep out the throat / littered on route a cache / providing all news on twin burial remedy for insect sting / plates of ware / flora a forced jubilee on their / silent waists the wind settles pomp / sunrise 9:19 / sunset after 3

3.

you are more north / a known pike of trees just ahead / the regional pale bee sighted just beyond the next valley / ignore the roads' rough ribbons its new languages of burial / instead keep toward / the clear tubes and cross roads where still / the paths will not collide and where the weather / will not raw / early this morning: the rise: all sugared fabrics and dye

4.

walking can cure headache but sometimes the thread braids back to the neck and thighs / on these days the muscles orbit / roads: bricked cobbled printed and packed / the costumes despite their age will remain white as aspirins / did you find the silk thread in the markets? / to hold the teeth tight in the mouth?

FROM The Putterer's Notebook: An Anti-Memoir

Akilah Oliver

alcoholic, and sedentary in that way, we missed the revolution or more often, the day. but at any rate it wasn't salvation we were looking for, unsure as we were that little ghost was our savior.

We'd been practicing departure through every exit, and then. Difficult though, without any new body parts.

This head talking is not a new body part [I construct a negative limb].

Someone I once know calls, leaves a message on the machine, as if I would be happy to make omelets. I am happy to make omelets.

Again:
What is the primary duty of repair?

Awake, and immediately then nervous.

Softest, most ______________eyes, looking at me.

I had the loneliest parents ____________dissipating strategies,

Using the now unfamiliar tense _____________________

________________thinking how not so bad

No body I am are ____________________no bodies are here tonight

You, my gracious un/other, I come to you as I would proposition though I know in secret I am simple tautology, taunting in my dictionary slang.

Earlier and am thinking.

The window watching, the keys watching, the paranoia, all watching the early morning parade of habits distended,

the wind my ungainly elbows, these winged bones dressed in skin.

As if articles were only parts of speech.

I am going to write that story about the evil nurses one day soon, I'm going to condemn my raced past. I'm going to fight you, my self, my love, my long past destination. Some crossroads arrived at, forgot that song, choke. Sweating like a junkie, like a champion, like a peripausal attempt, and no sleep.

They don't really love you sister.

Is it prophetic or paranoid to say: I know they're going to kill me, I know I won't just die.
X.
I love (unqualified, not minding). All this time later. This romance.

Michael row the boat ashore.

Fucking haunting dirges, all this time later.
In this century, no less. [An imagined Jetson cartoon.]

I didn't know what lint was. Why it swirled in the air like that. Why they called my mamma black. Why the anger was shame. Why a white xmas tree was ridiculed. Why she put on her underwear in the hallway closet. Why the oatmeal was so runny. Why then the predominance of non-colors, black and white. Why it is all not a kind of Mayberry remembrance. A reference uneven in its vacuity.
No time at all it's been.
The calendar, serious optical distraction.

I don't like you, he scribed.
I like you. *You rocking those shoes, baby.* He had to turn away. I would have turned away. All this witnessing with no kryptonite. No assigned roles. No way out.

I would like to dedicate a song or poem to my mother.

It would say, *for my mother.*

The song would say,

I love you. Stay. I love you, stay.

Then off we'd go to Disneyland [not the similacrum, but the Real] sleepy all the drive back.   Every once.

Portrait:
This is the way you talked,
Your system hyperventilating,
Your dreams in a bologna wrap,
Your mortars recently clipped, [chipped]?
Your eyes formally dipping,

,

,

.

how then, the primary duty of
repair?:

Finding myself deposed between parallel borders of
dysmorphic imaginaries,

Graafian follicle, named after Dutch anatomist *de Graaf*
Uteri, compare with *hysteria,* or see, "angry blogs," compare with *hysteric*
Finger, you fingered me, our eidos
Joint, to join, *joindre*
If the sun is masculine, what is masculinity?
Ovariectomy, non-magical incision, the knives are out
"god don't like ugly" mother's logion
Get your footing
Thumb your nose
Armare, arma, armor, arms
If the sea is a woman, what is a woman?
Heart, kindred aria
Lung, compare with *lights*
Cortex, or vortex, *bark* or *eddy*
They're speaking in tongues again

A sensation, hardly bearable,

across
phantasmic geographies

my lovelies, my loves]

What does it mean to be in a new century: to be present, citizen of this Time,
outside, yet still anchored to
the sensibility of a land-based disruption?

Aphasia
Induced by
this yearning for lineage, as if proof of existence depends on cowrie shells bartered in preindustrial markets.

Joey, what happened to you? Did you ever get a life out of this life? Berkeley

when sensitive, when *the wood was dry, but it was still heavy.*

Memory as non-consecutive propositions,
recognized as double performatives

(proposed here as, though not limited to):

MasqueradeApologyI as spectral negotiation

I didn't want you to sit with the body, I wanted you to go to my kid; you remember the baby, I wanted someone to be with him, till I got there, so he could remember. I don't know if I don't still love you, or if this is nostalgia, or if nostalgia is a legitimate expression of affection, this wanting to talk about jimmy hendrix's sister and the low curves of Berkeley, Telegraph ave, Joey and the pot plants, that Nigerian guy who wanted to marry me. Your aunt lived in the front house.

Both of us so shy and I attracted to her translucence on display beneath
chaotic knitted cap offsetting a deadpan sky, what passed for winter,
a screen that made me want to go around saying "Dakota," those clear
consonants holding us dear

I have been loved by women before, some of whom I've loved back.
I have loved women before this simmering [it is not always an equation]

Should I wait, I should make time a pressing thing. Should I want? I should
Want

She wrote me a picture that made a personal pronoun nascent
I wrote her a street in return, a green one with leafy things massing
Her mouth a wet and crawling thing I want in
My anticipatory field is not just any girl
She is many words before I may say an occasion
Having dinner with them was an almost pornographic experience
Has anyone seen my straw?
She eventually began to notate scripture
I learned to run, to gallop
So bright, it is hallucinatory in this room, fear breaking like distant bones
I've somehow navigated this life, somehow on the run

Standing here as I am away from Ave A, styling a kmart coat rabbit fur
lined collar & my afro wig, [writing in pauses] trying to capture the text, the
account in [of] the breaks, that silly tv on, making paralysis seem hip & the
Absolut bottlers on strike

In recalling the details, I may have forgotten the particulars, of say, for
example, rain

In situating the comedians as true, I may have foreclosed the narrowly
attempted scat

In owning her causal lipsticks, I may have written too quickly a word
canceling a form

May I imagine well enough to live forever as this gunner, as this diviner, at
rest at this port

Shame is the lie, & its cousin, collusion, middling to fair.

May I want, again and, then, moisten the language.

Pull out of the closet, my shy mistress, Desire.

Shame a lie though not consistently the most deliberate maker to desensitize gesture, here to touch an other position, the possible nibble.

Forgiveness, this quandary. Why would I forgive it [you], [them] the face that turned away?

Two Poems

Geoffrey Detrani

News Boy

The emissaries' heart
Dries on the platen of the

Printing press
Curing in the cleansing sun.

Crazyhorse alone in the root cellar
Not to succor the blond beast

But to make presentation food
Out of mouthfuls of earth.

Shaped like last minute bunker
Pills storaged between

The gum line and teeth.

Jet Set

Shaft light slots their corridor

Among the darling gray blocks.

All dust jacket
Columned like the narrowest

marrow of window light, sifting
Through tar and salt marred panes.

(a soil dark habit) all damsel eyes adrift.

For these jet set I
Turn half their apocryphal

Glitter to August blond straw.

Two Poems

Sarah Gridley

Intimations

Museum darkness has its natural history. Back in the planetarium, I am pretending closer
to the exotic classes, the blue stragglers in much higher temperatures.

The audience extends from there. A silhouette crop, washed in what looks like television.

I came through my birth a little bit ragged. My feeling comes spacey or faintly populous.
I can't say *souls* and know what I'm saying. Still, Tiffany glass has fumes inside it:
every Sunday's daylight knows this.

I look to the doge enfolding the balcony. *Ummm* goes the Venetian piva.
The lutes like halves of pears have stopped.

That was no game of hangman.

Now what will he put in the sky? A book of all moons. The shadows in Galileo's head.

The body is always being educated. Theater is like this. The planetarium is like this.

The whale is not hurt or in any way ruined. The whale is a great lightness.

Strokes

the comb gave out a different honey
when the farmer went under the fallow acre
and they told his bees with a black cloth flag

1849 — the gizzards of a camp chicken
made gold disclosures
it had been eating gold somewhere where
sunlight changed water to water

{gain}

what survives of a once common prefix
no longer active in compounds —

{say}

the load of hay approaching
is wished upon

the wish to be fulfilled
when the bale is broken open

Vocablos

Yo no era un médico rural y habían venido a
buscarme. No sé si habían venido para que
sanara o para que fuese sanado. *Las sìlabas
levantaban las patas sobre la mesa* y no se
avanzaba un centímetro. No importaba
tampoco avanzar. "Hubo un tiempo en que
las palabras y las cosas..." "Hubo un tiempo
en que el hombre y la naturaleza..." El médico
que había en mí, tomaba el bisturí y cortaba;
el paciente que había en mí, se sometía con
la docilidad de un guante doblado. Arrojaba el guante
a la espera del reto y sólo aparecían vocablos.
Los vocablos no daban en el blanco y
se alejaban como venablos cabizbajos.
Las sílabas doblaron las patas, sujetas
a la caballeriza, pues no había herida
que sanar ni viaje alguno que emprender.

FROM **Hard to Gnaw**

Damaris Calderón

de Duro de roer **Translated by Dolores Dorantes and Jen Hofer**
(Ediciones Las dos Fridas, Santiago de Chile, 1999)

Vocables

I wasn't a country doctor and they had come to
find me. I don't know if they had come so I
might heal or be healed. *The syllables*
put their paws up on the table and there was not
even a centimeter of forward movement. Nor did
forward movement matter. "There was a time when
words and things..." "There was a time
when man and nature..." The doctor
that existed in me picked up the scalpel and cut;
the patient that existed in me submitted
docile like a folded glove. I flung off the glove
expecting a challenge and only vocables appeared.
The vocables didn't hit their target and
withdrew like darts with their heads down.
The syllables folded their paws, subjected
to the stable, as there was no wound
to heal nor any journey to begin.

Las alucinaciones en el metro

Se toma el metro cuando no hay donde ir.
Cuando no se espera nada. Las estaciones
reclusas carcelarias cambian de uniforme.
Se avanza. No se avanza. El oficial golpea
el puño contra la mesa. La velocidad es un método
correctivo. La velocidad *es lo que te saca*
el mundo interior del mundo exterior
del mundo interior. La VE-LO-CI-DAD
demuestra lo que te separa de la flecha
de Zenón de Elea y ... Si alguna vez se
llega a descender no se sabrá nunca por qué
nos atragantamos con el raíl de sangre
como con una frase punzante deslizada en la mesa.

Hallucinations in the Metro

We take the metro when there's nowhere to go.
When we expect nothing. The imprisoned
jailed stations change uniform. We move
forward. We don't move forward. The official pounds
his fists on the table. Velocity is a corrective
measure. Velocity is *what removes*
the interior world from the exterior world
from the interior world for you. VE-LO-CI-TY
demonstrates what separates you from Zeno
of Elea's arrow and... If at some point we
happen to descend it will never be known why
we choke on the rail of blood
as on a piercing sentence slid onto the table.

Él Asesino

Él asesino es un bello animal socrático, pero
al revés. Si Sócrates reprimía sus impulsos,
el asesino, con diafanidad, los saca a la luz.
Él no vela por su alma sino por las nuestras.
Todos los estados saben que las coartadas
del asesino son nuestras coartadas, que él
asume generosamente.
Él asesino es así el elemento estabilizador
de la comunidad, la pieza que nos permite
creer en ese refinamiento supremo de la crueldad:
la cultura (Nietzsche).

Cuando las noticias de la prensa vienen manchadas
de sangre, la mano tiembla, la leche se derrama.
Como tigres alimentados con zanahorias, sentimos que
el asesino redime la especie. Nuestros impulsos,
nuestros apetitos, nuestras latencias, son ejecutadas
por la mano del asesino.

¿Qué sería de nosotros sin el asesino?
Gracias al asesino podemos descansar en paz.
Somos civilizados.
Repudiamos la pena de muerte.

The Murderer

The murderer is a beautiful Socratic animal, but
backwards. If Socrates repressed his impulses,
the murderer, with diaphanousness, brings his to light.
He does not watch over his own soul, but ours.
All the states know that the murderer's
alibis are our alibis, which he
generously assumes.

The murderer is thus the stabilizing element
in the community, the piece that allows us
to believe in that supreme refinement of cruelty:
culture (Nietzsche).

When the news from the dailies comes stained
with blood, our hand trembles, our milk spills.
Like tigers fed on carrots, we feel that
the murderer redeems the species. Our impulses,
our appetites, our latencies, are fulfilled
by the murderer's hand.

What would become of us without the murderer?
Thanks to the murderer we can rest in peace.
We are civilized.
We repudiate the death penalty.

Lengua y verdugo

Entre el verdugo y la lengua hay una serie
de relaciones. Entre la lengua, natural, y
el verdugo, antinatural, existe, como en la sangre,
un sistema de vasos comunicantes.

La lengua, como el verdugo, no es homogénea ni unitaria
(un verdugo está hecho de todos los pedazos de sus
víctimas, además de los suyos). En ambos, fatalmente,
no hay solución de continuidad. Por razones obvias,
el verdugo prefiere siempre las lenguas muertas,
aunque en los restos de las lenguas habladas (y las
reconstruidas) es posible encontrar la misma ceniza
que en la ropa del verdugo.

En lo que se refiere a su brutalidad, el verdugo
no es un sistema, sino un conjunto de sistemas,
opera siempre por selección, prefiriendo la
expresividad a la comunicación y es anónimo,
como la mejor literatura.

El hecho (la hipótesis) de la existencia de una
lengua madre, de cuyas ramas se derivaría
un tronco común, sólo facilita, (qué duda cabe)
la tarea del verdugo.

Tongue and Executioner

Between the executioner and the tongue there is a series
of relationships. Between the tongue, which is natural, and
the executioner, which is anti-natural, there exists, as with blood
a system of communicating vessels.

The tongue, like the executioner, is neither homogenous nor unitary
(an executioner is made of all the pieces of his
victims, in addition to his own). In both, fatally,
there is no resolve into continuity. For obvious reasons,
the executioner always prefers dead tongues,
although in the remains of spoken tongues (and
reconstructed ones) it is possible to find the same ash
there is in the executioner's clothes.

In reference to his brutality, the executioner
is not a system, but a set of systems,
operating always by selection, preferring
expressivity to communication, and he is anonymous,
like the best literature.

The fact (the hypothesis) of the existence of a
mother tongue, from the branches of which might be
derived a common trunk, is only facilitated (beyond any doubt)
by the task of the executioner.

Four Poems

Laura Sims

Yellow Cord — A Golden Earring — and A Surge

That lit me up and led me

To the center of

The quiet & unmeaning

Shadow of the Gator Bowl —

The mind, erased,

Became

a million thin veneers — a snake — a feast of plastic forms — a giant

Ruling twilight, making

Riot in the earth and I

Endured a spasm and began

The spaceships above them

Like stars

They fell

To pieces —

Hands in one country, heads in another, organs, arms

They wanted

Their bodies to be handled boldly, as they'd boldly handled

The bodies

On water or land

They carried

Their fear of the living

Assured

Into crawlspaces, lighted with singular bulbs

In plain words I think I am a worm.

— Bill Heirens

I
Think

Words
Am I

In
I Think

A
I think

Worm
I

Think
Am

I think
Words

I think
Worm

In a field in a

field in a field in a field in a field in a
field in a field in a field in a field in a
field in a field in a field in a field in a
field in a field in a field in a field in a
field in a field in a field in a field in a
field in a field in a field in a field in a
field   in a field in a field in a
field   a body   in a field in a field in a
field   in a field in a field in a
field in a field in a field in a field in a
field in a field in a field in a field in a
field in a field in a field in a field in a

body sparkled in a diamond field
body dampened a fire field body
clamored in a nation field body
tumbled in a battle field body spent
in a cash field body greased in a rifle
field body caught in a force field
body ends in a body field

We found a body in a burned field.

Now a wet field. A sooty field. A

wet-because-it's-dawn field. What is

also a mine field. And is often a

playing field. Once any but a body

field.

He feels
a body is a   somebody

She feels
a body is a   nobody

They feel   with their
soles or knees or bare feet or palms
or sharpened sticks

                              and the body

                         softly

               responds

as a body in a field

is a body is a body is a body is a
body is a body is a body is a body is
a body is a

                              field

Three Poems

Tyrone Williams

Farm Stock & Crop Data

worth in the hand
worthplus in the heads$^{\text{cabbage lettuce Holsteins}}$ $_{\infty}$

pluperfect in the bushels
"of building after building"

after building after building

public domains
common goods
+
good commons
equals ∫ condensed$^{\text{milk bottles ships}}$

bottled-up
market correction$_{\text{tape over}}$
$_{\text{[-al-]}}$obsolescent contradictions

Occam's co-ops
co-opt headless chickens flapping frantically to catch the coop
dot
ville

the take takes
[put your wings in the air like your wings in the air]

bit-cum-halter
bite declensions

"rapid strides"
round the ∂

@newsstand
confectionery ”not the row” of bar-cum-post

office—“the idea of vegetables
under glass”

cedes to a chair ode to an ode
“On the Chicago Board of Trade” winds strapped to the chant

Village Population & Occupations Etc.

At Eleven

11 "colored people" of no significant or unusual occupation (a future the middle classes disappear into...)

11 percent (almost), slightly higher than the then national percentage, a liberal interpretation (of the village), a "free" translation (of the "new" non-Africans...)

11 an upright equal sign or freeze frame

11 months better than 51 weeks (Woodson had to begin time before it was time)

11 names property of imposed lineages, pre-eubonic ubiquitous y cuttings across the field, yoking together plant, plantain, plantation

11 parallel tribes (ideality of the name) that nonetheless intersect at some indeterminate moment in the future or in the eubonic y, letter as effect or mark/scar of the "lost" tribe—or "Geology and Chronology"

11 minus cul-de-sac equals self marked Roman via aqueduct column et alia

11=9:02 a.m.

11 cul-de-sac: disbelief trademarked

11 "went into w nter [sic] quarters," "lived in small log huts or wigwams." Errata not cited, this description of "Aboriginees" [sic] concerns their "moderate reflective faculties, bat [sic?] prominent perceptives, especially locality, which gave them the ability to travel in the woods and retain the point of compass."

11 parallel disciples (ideality of the integer) that nonetheless intersect at some indeterminate moment in the future or in the Semitic x, number as effect or mark/scar of the "lost" disciple—or Godel's Theorem

Between Midnight and Noon

This year collapses into a day,
an address

system bouncing off the eye candy.

The string theories slide into sections, aftward.

The new p.c.zar of under B.O.O.P.
o.o.f.

Having rammed the feewalls, warehoused lifeboats.

Orange badges demand an open kimono

["Please floor?"]

Courts gronk.

This much for the zero-bug release of Livingston Village,
vaporware development.

Blue badges packing parachutes crouch at the bleeding edge,
prime-rated (no points) to leap into reality-distortion fields.

This vocabulary will self-toast in so five minutes ago.

Evidence or Sign

Rachel Levitsky

It seems needless to say we did not believe in miracles nor care so much about alien occurrences, even as they affected us. They profoundly affected us. We were especially sensitive to loud noise and random violence perpetrated by the State on unprotected urban bodies because they were or we imagined them to be our bodies. The sudden and specific military or police helicopters, the magical anticipation suggested by the police barricades which appeared each time we joined each other in a social group on the street, the shooting and neck braces we expected from the police if we did not appreciate their dominating presence in our midst.

These remained both constant and alien, and despite their presence, which did in fact blur our vision, we often perceived things that indeed looked like evidence of the increment we sought but in moments which pass as quickly as they reveal themselves, like turning your head to confirm to yourself that you saw a little girl on the sidewalk gliding past you two feet above the ground without the aid of a machine... by the time you see her face to face she is back on the ground smiling at you and all you have for a fact is that of your confidence or its lack. These moments pass quickly and because of this very fleeting aspect, don't hold up well, if at all, in the telling. How one knows or thinks they are attending such a window in time and space does itself feel somewhere between impression and intuition, both are suspicious even to we who like such things and are prone to resist the chill of scientific inquiry. Although I do feel strongly that being able to give images toward this thread would help, I find that when I reach for one I am back to relying on the categories which such revelatory moments of incremental alteration transcend, for it is not that men are not acting like men, nor the rich or famous bearing no affect of reflected projection, but rather that one witnesses an opening in which the terms are expired into the dust they were born to become, when the accumulated anxieties of past experience melt because the stern-looking teacher posted firmly beside you making you more than a little nervous with impressive stature emanating from macho bearing and muscular heft asks, before explaining to you that which you don't yet know, but need to know in order to complete the task to which you've been assigned, "tell me first, how is it you learn best?"

Two Poems

Tim Peterson

Bobadyllo

The reporter poses a question:
We're sitting beneath a translucent shell that's
suddenly lifted, to reveal a guilt furnace
internecine arras. Moebius shadows
we let down our locks within
circle children, reduced to them, canvassing
the murk I am delivering to you, kilts and curls,
the damages or dampers we enlist.
Everything courts dusk, doodlee doodlee doodlee
doo — even the prescient chorus
who handles our introductory rate
encroached upon the plaza with cardboard signs.
The mistaken idea of the glamor in the
protest that hurts us, affirms this.
Consistently attached like a decal at the site,
a passive persistence of activism tongues
can pry lids. Yet somewhere a fist is pumped
for information, punishing the documentary film
and the gown that surrounds it, the oxygen.

Content

More piles are driven into the ground, the gravel
inevitable, down to, without reaching bedrock, gavel
encasing us in machines, to save us
from the technical loophole in the machine.
Letting in light, air, and greenery,
one ether I chose to be selected, flowing
through spaces, unassigned, living
between bricks, removing support
materials. Found myself among an assembly
line, shouting new substitutions
upon the inability to name our confinement
with the same tools. Let's level the streets with mind
bears further examination. I put on a
painter's cap, a newsboy's finish,
to relieve a pinch of the distance
between my talk and my identified
unalienable objects. Aerosol winds along the
sidestreets were safe, tagged walls
the brackish markings of an advanced future
civilization, unclocked, anonymous,
fearless. Our project management continued.
It slept while our looms itched
books no one would hear, to abrade words
no one would mistake for change.

Memory From a Bone Sample

Xochiquetzal Candelaria

Flags in the winter sky,
you at the pillars

with your tongue in a glass box,
ashes settling on carts and props.

Or mammal carcasses hauled on board,
the subcutaneous fat spread around.

I finger a piece of your vestment
in the checkpoint basement.

Sparks in the dark, blue flicker of
book-filled cisterns: summer crops.

Frases que dijiste en un jardín botánico.

Palabras para nombrar un cactus.
Palabras para nombrar un camaleón.

Palabras para bautizar plantas con la palabra "abuelito."

Palabras dentro de una catedral.
Palabras de tus dedos sobre mi frente.

Un núcleo de cristal en medio de una canción.

Frases que aparecen otra vez en mi teléfono celular.
Palabras para decir más palabras.

Un núcleo dorado.

Palabras que nombran los nuevos sabores de la nieve.
Palabras aquí.

Allá pétalos para hacer papel.

Palabras como dibujos sobre madera.
Destellos de lonas rosas al final de la calle.

Un callejón tapizado de pétalos.

Palabras de madrugada que regresan de día.
Destellos de vetas.

Un núcleo.
Palabras para describir una semilla.

The Bougainvilleas

Inti García

<u>Las buganvilias</u> **Translated by Román Luján and Brian Whitener**

Phrases you said in a botanical garden.

Words to name a cactus.
Words to name a chameleon.

Words to baptize plants with the word "grandpa."

Words inside a cathedral.
Words of your fingers on my forehead.

A crystal nucleus in the middle of a song.

Phrases that appear again in my cell phone.
Words to say more words.

A golden nucleus.

Words that name the new flavors of snow.
Words here.

There petals to make paper.

Words like drawings on wood.
Flashes of pink tarps at the end of the street.

An alley papered with petals.

Words at dawn that return in the day.
Flashes of streaks.

A nucleus.
Words to describe a seed.

Destellos de números para decir más palabras.

Un resplandor de frío en las luces de la ciudad.

Palabras para conocer un caballo de madera.
Palabras para leer.

Un resplandor de frío.

Una noche que termina,
más o menos, termina.

Una noche regresa
como un halcón
al brillo de unos ojos.

Palabras para describir las cintas sobre un cuerpo.

Un halcón de electricidad.

Un circuito de frases para proteger tu nombre.
Un circuito de números.

Flashes of numbers to say more words.

A glare of cold in the city lights.

Words to know a wooden horse.
Words to read.

A glare of cold.

A night that ends,
more or less, ends.

A night returns
like a falcon
to the sparkle of a pair of eyes.

Words to describe the ribbons over a body.

A falcon of electricity.

A circuit of phrases to protect your name.
A circuit of numbers.

inmóvil por más de tres semanas
la mano

cierto tipo de escritura
como la nieve

como la fabricación de flechas
el presente de cada color

acumula cielos
registros de lugares

hablarán de nuestro corazón sin haber hidratado
sus cuadernos de notas

inmóvil por más de tres semanas
el lugar del pronombre

hablarán de nosotros sin venirnos abajo
cayendo como la nieve

immobile for more than three weeks
the hand

a certain kind of writing
like snow

like the fabrication of arrows
the present of each color

accumulates skies
records of places

they will speak of our heart without having hydrated
their notebooks

immobile for more than three weeks
the place of the pronoun

they will speak of us without overthrowing us
falling like snow

ante el muro donde se borra la palabra "hermética"
una mano sobre la cabeza que duerme

lengua materna
yo sé que tienes sueño

yo sé que puede ser monótono decir
mano ciudad fábrica

cuando cocinamos manzana con piloncillo
o pollo con cebolla

lejos de la máquina
cerca de la mano que duerme con nosotros

cerca de la mano que pintó sobre el bastidor
la más perfecta tarde para las alas de los gansos

y les recuerdo

un poema se hace
un poema se deshace

y les recuerdo

se derrite la nieve

before the wall where the word “hermetic” is erased
a hand on the head that sleeps

mother tongue
I know you are tired

I know it might be monotonous to say
hand city factory

when we cook apples with piloncillo
or chicken with onion

far from the machine
near the hand that sleeps with us

near the hand that painted on the frame
the most perfect afternoon for the wings of geese

and I remind you

a poem is made
a poem is unmade

and I remind you

snow melts

la mano tendida para llegar hasta aquí
da vacas

el crepúsculo sobre el pasto de la ribera
precisamente

una mancha de tinta
bajo un cielo lleno de borreguitos

a los siete años
pasto de la ribera leída con sílabas cortas

cortadas recortadas en el cuaderno de dibujo

la maestra wendy
da vacas

bajo un cielo lleno de borreguitos
la mano la nube el corazón para llegar hasta aquí

al atardecer
después de nadar

esas vacas que dices

the hand outstretched to reach over here
gives cows

the twilight on the grass of the bank
precisely

an ink stain
under a sky full of little sheep

at age seven
grass of the bank read with short syllables

cut cut out in the sketch pad

teacher wendy
gives cows

under a sky full of little sheep
the hand the cloud the heart to reach over here

at evening
after swimming

those cows that you say

todavía presente
una mariposa en el lomo de la vaca

la montaña predica
rocas donde

era verdad la nieve

en una gama de 25 semitonos
da su música

obra común
hace escuchar

entre las ramas de los frailes
una misa de estructuras fantasmas

still present
a butterfly on the back of the cow

the mountain preaches
rocks where

the snow was true

in a scale of 25 semitones
gives its music

common work
makes one listen

between the friars' branches
a Mass of ghostly structures

al pelícano parado sobre la piedra
lo he visto

parado sobre el bote que cruza a la isla
lo vi tras el atardecer

también vi

erizos incrustados en las rocas
donde el pez vaquita se esconde del depredador

escondido con ella
recorrimos doce kilómetros en bicicleta por la costa

tomamos rumbo
asesorados por una galleta de la suerte

y el rumbo fue

the pelican perched on the rock
I have seen

perched on the boat that goes out to the island
I saw it behind the setting sun

also I saw

sea urchins encrusted in stones
where the little cowfish hides from the predator

hidden with her
we traveled twelve kilometers by bike along the coast

we took the route
advised by a fortune cookie

and the route was

Two Poems

Paula Koneazny

Prehistoric fable

In our era, we were percussive, timed to the minute. Instead of subtlety, we were given explosion. Our parents, stunned by antiquity and the villaesqueness of the setting, became disconsolate. We tried gourmandise, then alert repose, to recapture their attention. Ravenous at take-out windows, we kissed the corpse, sniffing for a pulse. But after decades of flattening to the diction, the bluest fragments wouldn't fit. When objects, bruited about, were called upon to make themselves available, they stared back at us with regret. Even our extra leap-second had been spent. The youngest among us shouted from atop the tower-relics, "It's so damn bootleg!" while deep within the subterranean, their siblings muttered, "Coherence is a lie." In self-defense, our parents dismantled our cracker box to buttress their plea. They tried touching our temples to calm us down. After centuries of excessive fascination, we lay down to sleep it off.

Ahistoric fable

She factors the spindle, the gate. when she toes the threshold, it tips. this is how she enters the weaving room. her arm's off but she means no discourtesy. there is reluctance. one-handed, she splices her diffidence. splits the thread till the dye stains. her nails. her mouth. it's after. it's ruined. storm of lint through an occluded window.

Setting gears. oiling hinges. she works the rumor mill. guards the dent. it's after. it's warned. the kill for perfection. automatons marching. stop marching. she inventories the glamour. sears the divides. exquisite begins to radiate. landfill is the largest object.

She flicks the portraits. the preference for whiteness. the turbid lens. a boy spits in the dirt; beads of mud desiccate to dust. a girl staples a wage to her bodice. her eye's off but she means no incivility. there is obstruction. one-eyed, she sutures her reticence. it's after. it's marketed. time severs the pane.

She braces the whine. slips a risk. yarn dyes. she shakes out the boards. it's her job to needle the brood. without a stipend the template is the knuckle. the template is the nape. it's after. it's paid. she sews up the discards. they din. they pleat. they wrap their digits around.

The color is terra. iron is the choker. the color is ebony. burnt morning-glory incandesces the filament. this is how she louvers the door. when she requisitions the factory, her miter scants the seam. it's foreshadowed. it's before. she joints the reels. clocks are about to run. nighthawk is the stroke.

carromato

ruina rara entre fresno y cerca

un charco, unas botas rojas de goma
el niño con el aro camina sobre el agua

carruaje

suena más tolerable el ruido de las gotas
sobre el techo anterior, tiempo de madera

FROM **Book Title Here**

Eduardo Milán

Translated by Garrett Kalleberg and Laura Solórzano

covered wagon

unusual ruin between ash tree and near

a puddle, some red rubber boots
the boy with the hoop walks on the water

carriage

sounds more tolerable, the noise of the drops
on the former roof, time of wood

ciruelas del esbozo

agria, fría, fruta de fruición
a los labios rojos por índice y pulgar
de uñas pintadas de rojo llevadas
la mujer liba

hueco en aquél país tan torturado
cuyo nombre así empieza

cocuyo no es
nombre de fruta que así termina

abandonados, truncos

tronco aserrado todavía huele
los poemas abandonados huelen a cuerpo fresco
cuerpo fresco sin ser amado merma
hay un mar
donde la indiferencia traga

plums of the sketch

sour, cold, fruit of delight
at the red lips by index finger and thumb
of nails painted red, taken,
the woman sips

hollow in that country so tortured
whose name begins like this

firefly is not
name of fruit that ends like this

the abandoned, the truncated

a sawn trunk still smells
the abandoned poems smell like a fresh body
fresh body without being loved diminishes
there's a sea
where indifference devours

Where to Write

Miles Champion

So going around to get
in

The composition, exact
The grouping calmer yet
more precise

a profitable exercise
resting on nothing
wet cups leave blisters
no dice

there is a voice
nearby

suppose it is obtrusive
but we
play
nice

the use of prefabricated senses
restores grip

able to fondle the handle
likeness
brings warmth of attack
its own lips

while the tune is held by
a few assistants

the blotter questions the widening
shape

what balloon famously
lost its speech

white of the cloud
exudation of cumbersome
parts holding tears

the right place
should have cloisters

or at least a home depot

paint some of your chairs
expose others

before that show of colour
a more nervous furniture likes
to prepare

the tune lacks
polish

which closet vegetable says green is wrong

collars, steamed
and in
the dressing room
salad tongs

the potato sweeter
the social
eater
more pale than hurt
asking
why is there no occasion

the stiff, paper plate
moisture cakes
hat season

agreeably stultifying
peace
between two folds
suggests a crust
bolsters

secure a yellow corner
plaster
flake on cigarette end

makes an
opportune
blend

there having been jack
cheese on
everything else

seen cows shaving
with better lather
cream of single
take or leaf

where each double negative answers
both sides make four points
points that squares show
suggestions

that there might be a simple extension
wings
a nausea that medicines can
taste

if they like a magazine
the patients increase circulation
see chart attached
it makes easy reading
certainly
does this change?

I think so
a symbol adjustment to do with dates or figs
pleasure at any rate between curves and outlines
and a suitably cheap
gown that fits

to submit old claims
promptly
alter your birthday
don't forget to sign

as pedestrian clergymen cross
chickens extract meaning
perhaps pecking at a string bean
to be contiguous

later if it isn't dangerous
an asparagus
meets breakfast eggs
mixed up in counter action
with a pan

The Seven Windows

Suzanne Jacob

Les sept fenêtres **Translated by Nathalie Stephens**

I was born afar sheltered from the text
My mother had sniffed out a cargo hull
        to drop me
I was born afar in the earthly ocean
My mother of mother with salted milk
        hadn't a flag to swaddle me
She cast me out of the shelter early
        in the far dawn
        she cast me onto the coast
        where everything is exposed to the text.

I crossed everything I found
If I found a place
        that place stank of text
        and I crossed it
I had no hand in it and for naught
I walked far for a long time
        accumulating my ages
        fleeing always again
        the fatal contagion of the text.

I reached my confines
        in the country of seven windows
        screwed out of their wall
        against the calcified sky.

At the first window
    my weightless gaze
    stole a shadowed prey
    without it raining
I didn't have to pay for my lot
    the inside was outside.

At the second window
    it was noon on the table
They don't talk with their mouths full
    of whole grain bread
They belch with incredulity
    if the sun explodes
Memory needs us all
    to weave its party
    or to hatch its drama
They close the blinds to distrust
    because the outside here is inside
No one saw me
    though the hand of death be nimble
It wasn't noon anymore already.

At the third window
    they held mirrors out to me
    but no reflection formed
They arrested me to resolve their terror
I became myopic
    to escape the targets aimed at me
They let me flee under the sky
    without it raining
    and without having to pay for my lot
In my flight
    I nonetheless picked all the water sewn
    into the folds of the pearl
    because memory wants all of it
    to weave its party or to hatch
    its drama.

At the fourth window
the parasite snickers
in the shade of the strangled tree its dry white
snickers and dares me to be moved
I am filmed
without appearing on the witness screens
My bones fly to pieces in my shoulders
"Go, son of the mother of mother,
whistles the parasite,
you will find better than emptiness
in the throat of the Milky Way."
I leave whistling in turn
for the outside is here inside
"Go, only the daughter of the mother of mother
is born out of the text
and my finger will find better than emptiness
in the throat of the Milky Word you said it!"

At the fifth window
I committed myself without proof
to the din of mined numbers
I flapped in the floating frame
a tatter of shadow torn from the stolen
prey.

At the sixth window
monsieur the officer
his muscle rested on the dresser
touches himself at nap time.

At the seventh window
washed and ridded of its cries
by the laws of a last stinking text
chaos suddenly seduced me
and appeared possible
I saw the role I was playing
The name that my mother
my mother of mother
had branded with a hot iron on my eardrum
resonated in my nerves.

I was born afar
sheltered
without the text
My named is branded with a hot iron
on the slip of my eardrum
I turn in my confines
a brief country
where only seven windows
screwed to the calcified sky
turn on themselves
such that the inside is outside
turn on themselves
such that the outside is inside.

All that I know ignores me.

essays notes reviews

Edited by Julian T. Brolaski

"Thing 03." by Kim Beck

Singing in Cincinnati

Dana Ward

For Kevin Killian

Michelle Williams plays a woman named Cecil Mills in this movie from a year or two back called *The Baxter*. Cecil's a provincial just arrived in Manhattan, & she's temping, & learning her way around the city.

She's determined to be a cabaret singer or something, an aspiration she mostly keeps to herself. To bring us into Cecil's world of frenzied trepidation and big time pie-eyed wonder, Williams modulates her voice as if her cheeks were full of icing & clomps around in big clunky shoes like a satyr-Clydesdale hybrid; she's wise though, & thoughtful, & full of deep feeling. Watching her I got the sense that once organized the daydreams of the conspicuously in-officious will change the world.

So Cecil is dating this guy named Dan, & our protagonist Elliot, he's engaged to Caroline Swann. Elliot secretly loves the quirky Cecil but he's a cautious, nerdy sort unwilling to risk life with someone so whimsical. He's found conventional fulfillment with Ms. Swann, a Connecticut-bred WASP-y blonde sprung straight from the fountain of preppy beau-ideals. Elliot & Caroline nearly marry but don't. The thing ends as you'd expect — with Elliot & Cecil coupled up & in love.

At one point before they've finally hooked up Cecil announces to Elliot that she's moving to Cincinnati with Dan. If Elliot is to marry Caroline then there's nothing in Manhattan for her anymore. Elliot's distraught.

He twists up his features in eager desperation — "can't lose her, can't lose her" — we see his heart's breathless demand blow through his face.

"But I thought you didn't really love Dan," he tries that, certainly she'd rather be alone than live a lie. "Something is better than nothing," she responds, "It's better than being alone." Fuck, what now?

He's completely freaking out. "What about your singing, that's something, a reason to stay." "They have singing in Cincinnati," she responds.

> When you're sick of your body
> You wanna trade with somebody
> Wouldn't that be nice

They fix it so Cecil is a fairy-tale blue-jay escaping our sleepy-eyed convent of a city. She would never hear Matt Shelton's voice. The plot becomes beautiful here. Elliot arrives to confess his love for Cecil both late & at this so-exquisite moment. He'd not managed to set himself free before she left, but now, at the instant love's will has possessed him, Cecil's returned to New York. She arrives at her apartment just in time to find him waiting. "Remember when I said they had singing in Cincinnati? I lied."

The New Prehistory: Kevin Davies' *The Golden Age of Paraphernalia*

Jasper Bernes

The Golden Age of Paraphernalia **by Kevin Davies**
Aerial / Edge Books 2008
ISBN: 978-1-890311-28-5 $18.00 US

The vaunted liquidity of the modern world — where money and information, people and warplanes circulate at ever-increasing speeds — rests upon bedrock that is as inert and refractory as the activities it supports are mercurial. Call it infrastructure or, as HBO's series *The Wire* does, institutions: container ships that cross the oceans at a mere 30 miles per hour; machinery for oil extraction and refining that takes decades to build and billions of dollars to finance; suburbs arranged according to the logic of cheap and abundant oil. These structures contradict the impression we get from our keyboards and screens that the world is a fundamentally fluid and fungible thing. In Kevin Davies' new book, *The Golden Age of Paraphernalia* (Edge, 2008), the contours and textures of a world both immovable *and* fluxive stand forth. No poet has taken as clear a measure of our "unexpectedly / depressing millennium," which now even the cheerleaders of the new economy agree, as they stuff their mattresses with cash, has been "a real letdown after the frisky ad campaign." For letdown, read collapse. And in the collapse of the American empire's deluded self-presentation (whatever the happy, hopeful face Obama applies) it's easier to glimpse those solid foundations upon which the bread and circuses of the 00s have foundered, easier to read their weak points, the places where they might yield to human action, where they might be cleared away and society established on a new basis.

As the final installment of Davies' "trilogy of error," the new book follows the earlier *Pause Button* (Tsunami, 1992) and *Comp.* (Edge, 2000), careening through these transitional spaces where, to quote Antonio Gramsci's justly famous characterization, "the crisis consists precisely in the fact that the old is dying and the new cannot be born; in this interregnum a great variety of morbid symptoms appear." The sense of being between things — between people, between untenable political alternatives, historical periods, poetic modes — permeates the book, and indeed constitutes its basic formal principle. Of its five long poems, the first three "'Floater,'" "Remnants of Wilma," and "One-Eyed Seller of Garlic" form an English braid, their mutual interruptions announced by the different symbols — bullets for

"'Floater,'" numbers for "Remnants of Wilma" and vertical lines for "One-Eyed Seller of Garlic" — which Davies uses to connect individual strophes in the manner of mathematical operators. Here's a sample page:

collide
With protocurrency • [Only the skeletons
go to
heaven, youngster.] • Red, red, red,

can be looked up
to | A fairy princess
In-a-box, A + B
cannot buy enough to propel the economy
into a renaissance of Ruskinian objects appreciated on days
off

(*Golden Age*, 131)

Since the individual poems are themselves formed through accretion and interruption, it's rather easy to read these three as a single work running from pages 1-36 and 110-142 of the book, a series of parenthesized parentheses themselves interrupted by the two stand-alone poems in the book — "Lateral Argument," previously a chapbook from Barretta Books (2003), and "Duckwalking a Perimeter." Every moment in the book thus comes wedged between two adjacent, and yet non-continuous, moments. Perimeters abound and the feeling that comes through these rhythms, these peri-meters, is that of being inserted into structures and matters the exact measure of which can't be taken. In a way, the parenthetical composition of the book follows from his work in the middle section of *Pause Button*, in which words come together not only as parsable units of grammar but as members of a vast data set:

{reminiscent} {chronology} {response}
{in time for} {space}

{the}
{fiery}
{subway}
{silence}
{elliptical} {repression}
{rational} {tattoo breeze}

{gathered} {bourgeois} {wool}

(*Pause Button*, 37)

Unlike other visually conspicuous arrangements, the relations between these words, it seems, are less spatial than operational, dependent less on adjacency than relations of inclusion and exclusion, inside and outside, between and around, voiced by speakers who recall "coming of age between musical generations / waiting around outside the rink."

It's this liminal positioning that makes Davies so insightful about the world we live in now. Sometimes the people most capable of pointing out the salient features of a historical period are those who occupy a position slightly outside the centers where things are changing the fastest, close enough to observe the changes but far away enough to compare them with something else. This is the case with Karl Marx's insights about British capitalism, and Theodor Adorno's about the American culture industry, and it is why, according to Ronald Meek, the most cogent theoretical articulations of early capitalism were produced in Scotland, by people like Adam Smith, rather than in England. This concept of "uneven development" may also be why two of the most interesting poets of recent years hail from Vancouver. Obviously, Canada can't be compared, in its relationship to the US, with the relationship of the Scottish Highlands to the Lowlands. But the neoliberal revolution that has swept the US since the early 80s — the great wave of privatization, deregulation, union-busting and hypertrophied financial institutions — must have stood in stark contrast to the comparatively welfarist Canadian state, even if the disease was, as Lisa Robertson makes clear in the preface to *Occasional Work and Seven Walks from the Office for Soft Architecture*, written during the turn of the millennium, quickly spreading under the bloodied banner of NAFTA: "The Office for Soft Architecture came into being as I watched the city of Vancouver dissolve in the fluid called money."

Davies' standpoint on the uneven ground of history has to be understood as both spatial — or geographical — and temporal. Davies stands not only both inside and outside of neoliberalism — in other words, on its edges — but both inside and outside the cultural moments of the baby boomer generation immediately preceding his, where the moves, procedures and perspectives we associate with, say, Language poetry, are present but at the same time superseded by a sensibility that seems other to this generation. Whereas writers like Silliman engage in what they imagine as a frontal negation of American society — Ron Silliman's seminal book *Tjanting* begins with the phrase "Not this" — for Davies (and here I borrow from Chris Nealon's characterization of his work) such a head-on attack is no longer an option. He has to go around, along the perimeters, resorting to sidelong, lateral critiques. As he writes in "Lateral Argument," negating the negation of Silliman's opening salvo: "Not not this." All roads feed you onto the Roman beltway, around and around. Downtown is closed:

because

they wanted

to | Because | it was there

what I've watched • I AM THE
GLOBAL POSITIONING SYSTEM,
ME • In
the older days a big part
of the job involved speeding up and slowing down
the machine in order to approximate
reality, but that is
no longer necessary.

(34)

Late capitalism, then, is a circle whose center is everywhere and whose circumference is nowhere. It promises that everyone is the center of the universe. As *Time Magazine* announced in 2006, the Person of the Year is "You." Of course, Davies knows this is utter mystification, and part of the point of this book is to satirize such claims. In fact, despite his claims that an older mode of representation based upon the speeding up and slowing down of machinery has been displaced, those lines describe in rather excellent terms his (disavowed) writing strategy, where interpenetrating and syncopated forms of language articulate the spatial adjacency of successive historical periods, leaping from the Neolithic to the Information Age in the blink of a phrase:

This is a good cave — not much
to brag about at the reunion but it keeps our things
Dry and provides shelter from hungry beasts.
You'd laugh at the things we believed back then.
That our cats *cared for us*.
That Belgium existed.
That we couldn't fight city hall
because it kept running off.
But we didn't have your advantage of logarithmic
detachment and spunk. We in fact had little spunk —
It seemed to dry up even as it was squirting from our ears,
and food preparation was a lot more involved than subsequently.
Eye-recognition software was in its early stages
and we feared death horribly because it seemed so
trivial.

(56)

To be clear, there is no sense here that these successive periods — and the corresponding ways of living and working — constitute "progress." Modernity in its full realization is nothing less than cave-dwelling with eye-recognition software in the place of stone tools. Or rather, it's *worse* than cave dwelling. The world that he describes seems less a *regression* to some original Hobbesian state of nature than the production of such a state. In capitalism, technology and its violent manipulations make us into the animals that we never were:

Koko
  the gorilla expresses pain
Manufacturing a sense
  of healing and then
The sense in which
  your dreams are chosen
Doesn't matter
  to the hegemon
This stapler
  in the same universe
The factories, intense heat
  needed to produce an adjective
    on any continent

(4)

I know that it is customary, a part of reviewing etiquette, to flag some objectionable moment or thought, some structural lapse, in the text under discussion. But I can't do that here. The book is a flawless *tour de force* from start to finish. "Lateral Argument," in particular, may be the finest long poem written in this century. If I have any reservations they must be referred not to Davies' writing but to the world it circumscribes, a world that permits the critical imagination no way *through*, only a way *around*. As a testament to the feebleness of revolt in the face of the calculated madness that followed 9/11, it is without parallel: "This is our heritage, little bits / of burnt paper float over Brooklyn." All of the properly apocalyptic elements are here — joblessness and dispossession, a toxic environment, increasingly brutal political domination:

    The great privatization scam
Indentured workers making bricks, ages 3 to 70+

(42)

(. . .)

    The clerks grown in vats near Johns Hopkins
A tectonic sense of the ends of banter

(45)

(. . .)

A wondrous feeling of emptiness engulfs the extras
Who are everyone not currently engaged in a real-estate transaction. . .

(50)

(. . .)

The young graphic artists and web designers stand on street corners
hoping for day labor, next to hookers slugging forties.
Most of the crops look bad, the reservoirs are severely
depleted, and a huge brown

cloud hangs over south Asia

(61)

But importantly, alongside these visions of catastrophe, Davies offers a savvy gloss of the technological mediation that comes to displace or ameliorate the above political crisis, that hawks, in place of this absolute exclusion

. . .the great work of a young-adult global
civilization, a metaliterate culture with time on its
prosthetic tentacles, at this point slightly more silicon
than carbon, blinking vulnerably in the light of its own
radiant connectedness.

(58)

Alongside the fluid and false connectedness that squeezes through the pores of a brutal exclusion, Davies' continual shifts, swerves, syncopations and interruptions counterpose a parenthetical stance that refuses any determinate connectivity, that stands between, snipping the wires:

But all collapses before one's bloodshot eye, the load-
bearing walls composed of particles
that prefer not to, who strike against the conditions,
who saw nothing and ain't talking,
refuse even to sweep themselves up.

(46)

Like that perennial touchstone of resistance, Melville's Bartleby, the collapsing walls here, in their active passivity, would *prefer not to*. Bartleby, let us remember, is a knowledge worker, someone who produces and reproduces the great flows of legal language that make 19th-century capitalism possible. Today's scriveners have taken various stances with regard to the radiant connectivity of our hyper-mediated world, and much of the poetry of the 00s will no doubt be seen as fleshing out these positions — from those who celebrate these mediations, to those who make fun of them, to those who pretend they don't exist. Davies' Bartlebyan stance is one of the more promising, neither excepting himself from a world of fake relationality nor affirming it, neither pretending to the pure autonomy of the outsider nor, thankfully, greeting us with the unctuous alacrity of the knowing insider. This knight's move will, I suspect, serve us well in the coming period.

Si c'était moi, j'aurais préféré n'avoir jamais écrit cela,
je l'aurais aussitôt brûlé.

— Jacques Derrida

Vous dire mon hésitation. Vous faire *l'aveu* de ma maladresse. De mon émoi.

Ouvrir à l'endroit de la faille, où *je* défaille*nt*, où l'émoi s'empare de moi pour se faire émeute : loups, charognes et brasiers.

Hésiter devant vous, cette ville enflammée, où vous et moi sommes, serions, ces brasiers.

L'émoi parfois trop vif, insupportable, l'émotion provoquée par l'accueil dans ce lieu qui m'échappe et m'appelle, l'écueil incité par l'éclat du moi dit singulier en plusieurs moi à la fois, les moi éparpillés imprudemment devant vous cette nuit, écartés, voire écartelés, entre les voix transmuées, transmutantes de Nathalie, Nathanaël, détournées aux frontières de je ne sais quelles syntaxes, de je ne sais quels passages déclarés ou non, l'émeute survenue à l'endroit où les littératures fuient l'historicité, où elles meurent de n'avoir, de ne s'être, pas assez *tuées*.

Tueries dont nous avons la hantise, et l'avidité, meurtres dont nous sommes indéniablement habitées, habituées; meurtres que nous sommes, et que nous sommons.

Émue, je vous dis, avec et sans e muet, devant le risque et la volonté qu'ont dû engager le choix d'un livre dont le titre guillotiné pressait déjà l'oblitération d'une conception de la littérature, de l'écriture, honteusement accablées de désistements.

Mue par cette morsure de Pierre Alain Buhler, par une fin de chapitre achevé-inachevé qui me conviait, j'anticipais, sans le savoir, en ponctuant le début du livre par sa fin, *une fin infinissant*[1], une question qui me posait : « Que fais-tu quand la minuterie s'arrête? Je »

J'anticipais cette joncture catégorique, c'est-à-dire que je l'ouvrais en la fermant, c'est-à-dire avant tout qu'*elle* me reconnaissait à la façon dont je, c'est-

1 Jean-Luc Nancy.

Untitled

Nathalie Stephens (Nathanaël)

> If it were me, I would have preferred never to have written that,
> I would have burned it immediately.
>
> — **Jacques Derrida**

Speak to you of my hesitation. *Admit* to my awkwardness. To my emotion.

Open along the fault line, where *I* falter, where emotion takes hold of me, severally, becomes riotous: wolves, carrion and flames.

Hesitate before you, this enflamed city, where you and I are, might be, those flames.

The emotion, at times too forceful, unsupportable, the emotion provoked by the welcoming in this place which calls and escapes me, the hazard impelled by the outburst of the self said to be singular into several selves all at once, selves scattered carelessly before you tonight, divergent, or divested, between the transmuted, transmutant voices of Nathalie, Nathanaël, turned back at the borders of I don't know what syntax, of I don't know what declared or undeclared passages, the riot surfacing at the place where literatures flee historicity, where they die for not having sufficiently *killed themselves*.

Killings which haunt us, and incite our avidity, murders by which we are undeniably inhabited, habituated, murders, which we are, and which summon us.

Emotion, I say to you, with and without a silent (sh)e, before the risk and the will that must have entailed the choice of a book whose guillotined title already impressed a concept of literature, of writing, shamefully burdened with desistances.

Moved by this morsel of Pierre Alain Buhler's, by a complete-incomplete end of chapter that solicited me, I anticipated, without knowing it, while punctuating the beginning of the book by its end, *une fin infinissant*[3], a question that asked me: "Que fais-tu quand la minuterie s'arrête? Je"[4]

I was anticipating that categorical juncture, which is to say that I was opening it while closing it, which is to say most of all that *it* recognized me

---

3 Jean-Luc Nancy — an end unending.

4 What do you do when the timer stops? I

à-dire les moi, se débattaient et m'en a fait le rappel sidérant. Car *...s'arrête? Je* est un livre qui se relève avec peine de *L'injure*.

Il aurait fallu à nos littératures qu'elles puissent se survivre.

Mais survivre, c'est d'abord mourir, et mourir, c'est tuer. *Inavouablement.*[2]

2 Texte prononcé à l'occasion de la remise du prix Alain-Grandbois le 17 septembre 2008 pour son livre,... *s'arrête? Je*, publié à l'Hexagone.

by the way in which I, which is to say my selves[5] were grappling with one another and were a staggering reminder. For ...*s'arrête? Je* is a book that rises with difficulty from *L'injure*[6].

It would have been necessary for our literatures to be able to survive themselves.

But to survive, is first to die, and to die, is to kill. *Unavowably.*[7]

---

5 les moi, meaning "the selves," is a homonym of l'émoi, "emotion"; with which émeute (riot) shares etymological referents.

6 L'Hexagone, 2004. Finalist, Prix Alain-Grandbois and Prix Trillium.

7 Text read on the occasion of receiving the prix Alain-Grandbois, September 17, 2008, awarded by the Académie des lettres du Québec, for... *s'arrête? Je*, published by l'Hexagone (2007).

Batman That One

Paolo Javier

the Joker is here/A.D./Bat symbol swoop into death building/a bank window a building window explodes/market collapse insane plunge rooftop to rooftop/ BANG!/ Camera i n place with music action/research how you enter safe

*

why does manager have a shotgun in/his office/vigilanteeism/Gotham in disrepair/Where did you/this is a mob bank

*

what doesnt kill you simply makes you/ stronger/Q U E E R /bigfoot

*

Who Shot Ya/an artist a martial artist/will the real DK show up/LOITER/INTIMIDATE

*

dont point that thing at me/ hes bleeding/I dont need help/ the difference duality/hockey pants/under that make-up/lipstick /on a/pig

*

oh so fly under the rubble/know your limits/its my fathers only wish/Batman fathered all of them/Male in China??/buy American/fuck this D.A./lynching irradiated bills/Kaiser SMITH/i n China in China

*

you want to be able to form your bad/hello Mike Keaton/someone like you one final vinegar with my pals...../cut to/criminals gathering/the bad guys are non - WHITE/or/-WASP

*

a guy like me/FREAK/ CHINAMAN is a squealer/lets not blow this out of proportion / the camera circle/the good guys/slippery point of view

*

Batman Hong Kong/Helen referred to Batman shrine/and then/made his own/ how about writing your own/MACROSS movie/did research of CIA
use conspiracy threads

*

Batman has limits/Why so serious/Father/Fathers/BATMAN is insane
CHINAMAN/is an object

*

Italian/Eastern European/leader of crime syndicate/ will/the real/BATMAN/ please stand/up?/Joker Joker /I m a man of my word/Sun as Wayne suggests Death/it all goes to/hell/from here/I dentity/I dentity/I dentity/J o ker/ WHITE FACE/an undertone of /critique of white society/ THUG/All dark culture

*

BATMAN/consume blackness/to fight/the Darkness/blackness/Dark Knight/ Joker disrupts an All White Party/all the money makers in Gotham/ WHITE/I hated my father

*

Watch the world burn/two sides of the same coin/WHITE MAN caped crusader/ WHITE MAN serial killer/The rat is a LATINA cop/A critique of the White Man/The Dark Knight / is / the White Man

*

Batman can make the choice/I am the Batman/I am the Batman/ I am the Batman/Like the Mothman, a harbinger/You make your own luck/LYRIC OPERA / S l a u g h t e r is the/Best Medicine/the workers/on break/get to see/a rich mans/toy emerge from/a car that they/historically may/have built

*

What would I do/what/ you/You complete me/to them / youre just a freak / like me / Its a bad joke/Only as good as the world allows them/to be

*

Joker doesnt bleed/That guy was in Seinfeld/He sees his reflection/in the/gasoline/the Chinaman is a coward/Why should I hide/Who I am

*

Wheres the Italian? /THE TRUE IDENTITY OF BATMAN REVEALED/THIS town/tell your men/they wont work for a freak Everything burns / Ive had a change of heart/Lets give someone a chance

*

the nurse/the night nurse/your men your plan/Im a dog chasing cars/ I just do things/I try to show the schemers/how pathetic/ their attempts to control schemes/are/Nobody panics/when a gangbanger is shot

*

Its all part of/the plan/Lipstick on a/ Im an agent of chaos/ Not Anarchy/NIHILISM/FEAR/EMERGENCY/Death/Joker in drag/ AMBULANCE

*

Joker is a white man in whiteface/we cannot MISIDENTIFY/ his race/ BOMB BLAST LEVELS /DOUBT Fires/BATMAN sign in next scene/“Beautiful .”/This istoo much power/sonartapping

*

I want whomever let go/of the/let him off/the leash/you get to know the real person/moments before they die/IDENTITY OF GOTHAMS PUBLIC/criminal & civilian/Harvey has his limits/murdering white civilians/decide on whos criminal/in THEIR society

*

SONAR POV/Perception in the/dark/the big bad black prisoner/stares down the white officer/ w/ mutton/ and offers to person better/and here we go/and/here/we/go

*

It all boils down to/decision of/white men/we are still/Goths/at their mercy/whiteface staring down midnight/youre alone/I cant rely on anyone these days upside down/camera/moves upside down/unstoppable fiend/meets/immovable object/truly/ incorruptible/I think I/Till their spirit breaks completely

*

I took Gothams/White Knight/and brought him/ down to our / level/ madness / like / gravity / a little push

*

the winner is / Gordons blonde / blue eyed / son / someone / whom Harvey Dent / once was / there is no escape from this / whats fair

*

the world is cruel / only morality / is chance / combined

unprejudiced / fair / because you were the best of us /

like I lied / Lie / its going to be alright, son

*

see yourself / become / the villain / I killed these people /
Batman / Batman / because we have to chase him

*

the hero Gotham deserves / but doesnt need / right now

Virility, A Close Shave?

Catherine Mavrikakis

Translated from the French by Nathalie Stephens

King Kong Théorie by Virginie Despentes
Grasset 2006
ISBN: 978-2246686118

In *King Kong Théorie*, Virginie Despentes warns us against blaming women for the current "devirilization" of men. According to Despentes, women are the object of a systematic campaign which would have them be responsible for the crisis of masculinity and its consequences. If we are to believe social discourse, it is the fault of women if men are reduced to playing the madman on the Jacques Cartier bridge[1], to beating their wives after a day's work where an ambitious and hysterical female boss reigns, or even to massacring their family by rifle shot. This would suggest men's violence toward women is something new... Women would have castrated men with their delirious ideas of equality: they should feel shame in the face of masculine despair. They should pay for all of that and especially find a way to give back to men what is theirs by rights... their virility. Current feminist thought, which fancies itself guilty, has become an enterprise for the reparation of masculine identity in crisis, a machine of *mea culpa*, of public avowal and disavowal. Women give in to voicing themselves with shame and can't stop apologizing and setting themselves limits... They are henceforth the allies of their own victimization, and feel obliged to keep saying (while continuing the struggle, of which there is no lack): "We went too far..." and to comfort men in their identity by helping them to reach a dignified place.

1 In order to obtain custody of his children, a man stood on the Jacques Cartier bridge in Montréal, blocking traffic. He was apparently a member of Fathers 4 Justice.

You must be dreaming...

In her manifesto-book, Virginie Despentes opts for a radical feminism which must not let itself be impressed by the so-called crisis in western virility.

It seems important to me to analyze what Despentes is denouncing: the role of women and of feminism in its alliance with a "revirilization" of society. For me, in keeping with Despentes, it is clear that current "soft" feminism, steeped in feelings of guilt toward men, must think of itself in the West as the space of a new white masculinity and a barely latent global and "feminist" racism. In the American Democratic Party, the presidency's stakes are posed in precisely these terms: is it better to have as president a black man, such as Barack Obama, or a white woman like Hillary Rodham Clinton? What kind of alliance with the "weak" must a white leftist American man consent to? What demands will allow him to remain "virile" and maintain his power?

What I want to show here is how banal feminism, the one that is alive and well in our institutions, functions with the revirilization of white men (and women) and with the global feminization of all alterity.

La Pucelle of the South

On April 24, 2007, an American soldier, *Private First Class* Jessica Dwan Lynch, prisoner of war of the Iraqi army in 2003, admits before American Congress that she never fought ferociously against the enemy, as she was required to do as a soldier or as the American media had amply reported by making her into a heroine. On the contrary, Lynch never even had time to use her weapon before losing consciousness during an accident that led her directly to the hospital where she awoke without even having fought for the American cause and American honor.

She who was affectionately dubbed the "Rambo of West Virginia," she who was the object of a film entitled *Saving Jessica Lynch* which was broadcast by NBC, she who received war honors and medals, was in fact but an instrument of American war propaganda in Iraq. At 19 years old, in a curious role reversal, Jessica Lynch was what can only seem ironic: the symbol of American resistance in the face of Iraqi violence. There are certainly no lack of war heroes in 2003, but why was it necessary at that time for George Bush's government to create from scratch a Joan of Arc of the South? Why was it necessary for a very young woman to become the symbol of military virtue and virility, if not precisely in order to erase the brutality of the American invasion of Iraq, if not to expose the savagery of Iraqis, if not to make Lynch into an Antigone made in the U.S.A., or even the Athena of a white America, bearer of law and justice? The military media's strategy was very simple: while an American (male) soldier would always receive bad press in the world and might always recall a certain imperialism and recent defeats, Jessica Lynch carried an admissible and, in our day, acceptable virility (from *vir*, Latin for "man"). She embodied a feminine masculinity capable of making us forget the very origins of violence. Jessica Lynch, the courageous young girl, was able nonetheless to appear as the bearer of a certain weakness, which called upon the protection, the tenacity and the strength of the American army, while humanizing this army, and while calling for the vengeance of such mistreated women. In effect, in order to liberate Lynch who was ostensibly brutally raped, and anally to boot (which was of course proof positive of the barbarism of Iraq and demonstrated the need for every invasion on the part of the United States which does not tolerate such things...), the American Special Forces seized a hospital (where there was in reality not a single Iraqi soldier) and filmed an entrance worthy of Sylvester Stallone before handing the video of the soldier's rescue over to the media. The video-hoax of this spectacular attack demonstrated the courage of the United States Army, but it especially legitimated the virile violence of American soldiers who could but come to the rescue of one of their own. Thus was it possible to justify the war in Iraq.

The fuzzy reasons for this war were forgotten. It became a matter only of defending "our" victims. Many black women and women less white than Lynch were taken prisoner or killed in Iraq during the same period, but it was of course the image of a young, very young WASP from a good family in the hands of the bloody and perverse Iraqis which best served the American cause. Apparently Lynch later confided that she was never raped by enemy soldiers and that, on the contrary, the Iraqi doctors saved her life.

Clean-shaven

Masculinity which is considered acceptable these days can no longer, of course, be directly embodied by American soldiers, Rambos or Terminators, and to a degree, not even on American televised news. Uniformed soldiers that parade by in single file on CNN or that are even exhibited in the Canadian *Globe and Mail*, are for the most part dead and thereby become victims of war. The images of pure virility in which boys brandish weapons and fists are henceforth associated with ideas of murderous madness, carnage in the schools, uncontrollable massacres. The military masculinity represented by Jessica Lynch must show itself to be both courageous and vulnerable, and in the end, allow men to exert their true force with impunity, and with goodness and honor, in order to save white virgins. Lynch, in her virile position as a soldier to whom the media attributed courage and in her position as a woman raped by the nasty, moustached, enemy soldiers enables the clean-shaven American male soldier to regain virility beyond all suspicion, to buy back his warrior virginity and to give himself a good and noble cause. Of Jessica Lynch, there remain photographs of her naked which Larry Flynt, the owner of *Hustler* keeps in a safe. Lynch is after all but a woman; she remains a simple Eve, a girl like so many others who can be undressed in America, at the front, and who now spits on the military, like only disappointed women know how...

If masculinity can no longer exist these days brutally or manifestly, it remains no less violent in its most hypocritical manifestations. Virile man is of course experiencing a definite crisis in his representation. But henceforth, we must take heed, masculinity knows how to travesty itself, take on other disguises, use other fetishes. It must remain colorless and lackluster, wear the suit of anonymity. If we poked fun in the West at Saddam Hussein's moustache, and bearded Muslim men, and if Borat's body hair provokes unanimous uncontrollable hilarity in movie theatres, it is because the lesson of our side of the world has been well assimilated: the masculine must learn deceit, it must find other strategies of representation of its power and not resort to too-feminine ostentation. From now on, Magnum PI must shave off his moustache, and if Nietzsche, Claude Gauvreau[2] or Freddy Mercury wear a growth of hair, it is because they were crazy, philosophers, poets or homosexuals. Domesticated hair, and hair growth of three days or more, is good for Latinos, Ginos, "chrome-plated" foreigners, Third-World flunkeys ready to slit "our" throats and who especially crave demonstrating what it is to be a man.

One must never understimate race and social class considerations in the construction of western virility which presents itself both as more civilized and less hairy than what is to be found in the sexual and "shabby" parade of the rest of the planet.

---

2 Québécois poet.

White Feminism

The modern American man must play his virility shaven and invest his money in Gillette and beauty products. The masculinity which has learned perversion (false gentleness, false kindness, false femininity) remains no less terribly formidable because it has become of particulary bad faith and claims never to be where it is. "I am not remotely virile," it might swear... And yet, "woman, your feminism is outmoded. Take heed."

Current feminism is in the image of the soldier Lynndie England. In the prisons of Abu Ghraib, in 2004, England mistreats Iraqi men by submitting them to acts of torture and degrading scenarios, aided in her games by her profesionally warring boyfriends who giggle with her over photographs of the horrors imposed on the "enemies." The perverse white dominatrix humiliating Iraqis and leading American men to reconstruct a strong identity with homosexually connotative scenes, performed against their will by men of another "race," provides food for thought. These images which made their way around the world allowed us to say that women in positions of power are "worse than men." It is what needed to be demonstrated and what women love to prove and to say. But what is at play for me here, is Western racism in the face of what it perceives to be a virility which must at all cost be humiliated and destroyed. Current feminism, in its most anodyne, and most underhanded forms, works hand in hand with the whitest possible Western supremacy, to revirilize the "humiliated" white man. It is up to women to show men a new virility which must go through the hatred and disdain for other planetary representations of masculinity.

Lynddie England, in her great savagery, and despite her having been briefly condemned to imprisonment, represents the possibility for Western men to "find their virility again" alongside feminist women who show them the way while retrieving their own ancestral identity as bitches... Women are carriers of an excessive masculinity which will be reprimanded and "shaven," but which will nonetheless return virility to American masculine troops in the face of Iraqi and other enemies.

It is this virility anchored both in feminism and misogyny which establishes itself little by little in our so very white and so very masculine globalization. Let us not be fooled.

Virility these past years (and I am pointing to much more than simply the American army but all of "our" instances of power) has been willing to accept its share of feminity to better keep up with the fashion of whiteness, and that white is not the white of peace...

Notes for erica While Reading *Civilization Day* and *Censory Impulse*

Alan Davies

Civilization Day by erica kaufman
Open 24 Hours 2007

Censory Impulse by erica kaufman
Big Game Books 2006

Civilization Day

The words stutter toward an utterance — they conclude closely.

The totality of a verse (can we still say that — and not mean its ob-verse?) is a silent null void — nothing left over (to chance) — as it should be (here — I think).

Speech is a kind of cataract — writing its obverse implosion (over time) (i.e. a waterfall of words not falling) — that (that) you grasp.

My entire life has its idea, *and all my minutes work toward creating it.*

— Stéphane Mallarmé, 1866 letter

To have grasped that is to have grasped (almost) too much. In a certain sense there is (only) too (too) much (too much). Otherwise — no verse.

erica doesn't waste words — and yet she doesn't hold them back.

And always the "other" — the *she* (as it should be).

To think otherwise would be to be less than bold. To be otherwise — (more than) ditto.

And the (sad) humor of the daily humdrum (these days) — *because only paranoia / creates eye contact.* As if it could have us in it — and that it does.

There're days.

The language seems to be speaking itself (not always the case) — battering back at itself (seldom the case). It has its own grit in its own teeth.

This language is a kind of religion (really) — a spirit(edness) — in that it bakes itself into a kind of compactness — (which it then inhabits). The vestment. It is its own vestment.

And yet then the work (the language) backs us — and has plenty of room for us in it. In fact (in a curious sense) we are (are (we are)) it. That / this — it. The language is beholden to us — so it makes room for us (in it) — and that's where we sit (when we read this).

love poem

sometimes her eye
follows me. and I want
to be re-taught the verb
"to be." all dreams of
magnetic surfaces and
prepositional speech.
this postmodern sense
of vulnerability. basic
binary code language.
take me. all receptor
and consequence.
the process of becoming
physical like I take
pictures for a reason.

And we're always spliced into it / into that — (as the willing participant). It's a grace to be such a reader — to be so felt.

And always that *she* — a kind of measure in-and-of itself (of what is of this moment in being here). This (this) *she*.

There is always space for another word. Except in poetry. That is where the question arises.

Eagerness. That's the word. These poems are eager.

Censory Impulse

Is this the impulse to not (not (to not)) write? — the impulse against (against) (back (is it back?) against) writing? Perhaps so. And perhaps it is precisely that impulse that is the (is (that is the)) impulse to write.

Little do we know.

We are the mistake that writing makes.

Its license.

Language is a whole lot of bother (really). For those of us who write — it is what we bother ourselves about. And it bothers all about us — and that's what we're all about.

These are the sorts of things that this writing makes clear.

These are fourteen-line poems. That doesn't matter — but that a form has been chosen (and is being used) — that (that) does (that does) matter. Form is an implied presence — and it implies our presence in it (as it?).

erica's impulse is to write — to make the words conform to a pattern that they then find themselves to have implicit within them. This is no mean feat (feet).

There's always an obtrusive sameness — by obtrusive I mean that it's felt (gladly (and firmly) felt) — and by sameness I mean that the words are contained (in what they are as they contain them). Neither of these are meant to be / as a "bad" thing. The words shimmy down into their own presence.

6.72

perhaps because the Monday
passed able to pen public
june rain june door
physical factors empty
i indulge it not
because of capture
weather or game

the question is how
long an altar obstacle
how many decline
to see I'm talking
of an intimate relationship
an establishing shot
a hunger for shame

Trying to find the right word. That's what it's all about. And it's never apparent — if it were... then no trying. And no right word — (in a singularly odd sense) no right word.

Studying *Studying Hunger*

Kimberly Lyons

I took a nap before studying *Studying Hunger* and dreamt the sentence *Call me Ishmael*. In Melville's sea crate everything that follows, the mess of it, comes out of the impossibility of a singular literary identity. *Studying Hunger* (hereafter *SH*) finds out just the opposite: a difficult, and different you/I has to undergo a hellish struggle of differentiation so that by analyzing, discarding and wholly ingesting the you, the I may start to begin again. From *SH*: *I'm you...I'm a history...sea crate full of junk & language twisting....That's what opened the question of who is the you* (9).

By dint of Mayer's explicitly familial linkages, *SH* is a descendant text of Melville's, although she asserts: *Clark Coolidge is my father*. But a reader is never on stable ground with Mayer's lineages — later along, she states: *Shakespeare and I made Clark*.

What I hope to propose about *SH*, which was published in 1975, is that it's a pivotal departure from *Memory*, the book that preceded *SH*. She writes: *If the language must resort to analyses to "keep going" then let it be closer to that than to accumulate data* (7). *SH* is an attempt to enact an internalized process of relationship in writing rather than to record thoughts and sensations in time, as she did in *Memory*. Mayer is trying to extricate herself from a disastrous set of internalized self and other representations/ghosts/parasitic attachments that haunt and entangle her writings in their sea nets: *I will come out of hiding it's time...I know you better than myself, been inside you...*(47).

The writing of SH allows Mayer to advance: to move out of the conceptual rule-based writing projects, the accumulation of data and on to the fuller spectrum of writings that she subsequently produces. These prodigious psychic, spiritual and literary tasks produce a humongous and marvelous text. There are several areas of critical consideration that may further open *SH*, including how it is situated within the avant-garde writing practices of Mayer's poet and artist peers (as Nada Gordon's 1986 thesis, "Forms of Life: An Exploration of the Work of Bernadette Mayer," available online, reads her work). Additionally, Leslie Scalapino's essay: "transcription — (or lineage) as visual" in *R-hu*, (Atelos, 2000) examines aspects of SH as "experiment": "looking intensely at the mind's present" (111).

I also find the psychoanalytic theories of the British Object Relations School a particularly illuminating and useful filter for understanding much of the content, relational communications and flow of utterances within *SH*. The

British Object Relations School, in particular Melanie Klein, Donald Winnicott and Ronald Fairbairn, proposes a complex and voluminous set of theories on how a cohesive self in relation to others is developed via an integration of mental representations of other and self. According to their theories, internal representations of sensations of "good" and "bad" sensory and relational experience is imprinted on the infantile mind as "part-objects" — the famous "good breast" of the responsive caretaker and "bad breast" of the withholding caretaker. Klein, in particular, describes infant and childhood development via stages of schizoid paranoia, depression, and reparation. The developing self tries to protect its ego and self-concept from overwhelming anxiety, dissolution and loss of omnipotence in the realization of its separateness from the needed other by using mechanisms of incorporation and projection. In the British Object Relations view, an intrinsic, biologically driven goal of human development is to integrate fragments of polarized representations of oneself — and others — into a homeostasis of self, tolerant of ambivalence, that can love, attach to others and bear separateness.

Mayer writes out the internalized utterances of these part-objects in *SH*, the drift of remembered, fragmented and recast communications, incompletely formed. By giving herself permission (perhaps with Stein's and Melville's models of writing as a guide) to give over to the incompleteness and disorganization of this writing process, without regard to normative narrative or consistently normative grammar, emotional reactions and disassociated states of mind finally cohere. In *SH*'s raw agitated flux of disclosures, multiple narratives spill over to make a newly open and unbounded writing.

The book begins with a list of intentions and constraints, vestiges of the data collecting and experiment mode of *Memory*. As Mayer delves, a deeper core dilemma emerges, a central knot of an unbearable symbiosis: *I have to stop addressing you…why am I writing for you…I am hurt pushed into you, where I belong, I am keeping a secret I am not speaking…in the confusion of yous for you I must make magic, I must stop, I've got to stop and make magic, magic to feel to work on you…but since I am you now, a part of the fusing, the condition of possible yous…I am starved…I am the scapist, the stalker, the shafter* (70). With the admission *I am starved*, she shows us the complication: hunger is desire, unfulfilled and frustrated by inconsistent or absent attention and feeding, only satisfied by the persistent internalized memory traces of "you." The antidote is incorporation, a kind of compromise action that joins "you" with the narrator so as to ward off awareness of a state of aloneness.

She writes: *I couldn't swallow & hated them parents…then I thought they would die…nobody knows the trouble I've seen with my own two I's* (55). One of the sustaining conflicts within *SH* is the terrifying probability that with the overpowering of the *you*, a cessation of life within the matrix might occur: *[y]ou are the energy which forces me to tell, and to tell you the greatest envy of them all – to their envy – to tell you that kind of love that sustains the enemy I've imposed on you is impossible anymore so I must kill you* (56).

It seems as if *you* is fighting the writer for life. To work this out, Mayer constructs a dimensionless realm of haunted echoes and resonances: *am I this surface...of equilibrium, a void in which where am I fall endlessly into.* The text swells with various floating presences, demons, captured in consciousness *to get in touch with someone beyond.* No ground is offered, there are only floating pedestals of transaction (Leslie Scalapino's essay brings a Buddhist phenomenology to bear on this condition of *SH*). *SH* is animated by a vast horde of formations, a literal flood of millennial predictions and transformative occurrences: *dynamite the iron, my heart of iron simply to use it, fiercely, to create something, mine it, out of you, in the most human way* (56). Ever the literary scientist, Mayer emerges from the depths of this trance to figure its uses within a global trans-historical project of writing: *the difficulties of story & transforming information into terms of human adaptability are manifold, open like paper, like prints, like books* (41).

However useful British Object Relations School concepts are for mapping the processes at work in *SH*, I find that I have to give up my intention to harness its symptoms within theory. It seems that no psychoanalytic theory and framework could encompass, analyze, and explain *SH*'s range of writing. Perhaps I am daunted by its thick, sometimes hermeneutic, texture and am compelled to either stand aside as its ruminative, propulsion floods by, or to be flooded by it — a transferential reaction formation (per Anna Freud's naming of this defense) against engulfment by this melancholy, manic and cannibalistic text.

In order to arrive at explanations and find metaphors that would encompass *SH*, I turn to an understanding of it as alchemy — *will iron burn? The mix with you ally, to make an indestructible alloy....you are the black ash...a bed for hundreds of years of black work emerging...*(64) — then to mediumship as an explanation for the wild penetration of the text by outside voices, and, finally, to poetry. One is left with an exhilarated, albeit exhausted, realization that only in poetry anything may and will be written. *SH* had, in fact, *planned the disappearance of my desire* (7). It's a massive book, and scholars might consider these threads:

1) How the ecology movement of the 1970s informs *SH* in its intimation of disaster: *whole chunks of ice melted downtown to destroy, and they will destroy the whole graphical and ecological set up of the whole world* (66).
2) References to ethnopoetic terms and practices, perhaps known to Mayer through her reading of the texts in circulation in the 1970s.
3) Incestuous familial relations and the coda of keeping secrets: *I must get out of the code beyond the secret code.*

4) Uses of lists of food representing plenitude and surfeit, of hunger and emptiness.
5) The textual functions of the named figures of Ed, Marie, and David.

SH might be summarized in this way: Mayer in the 70s is drastically impeded by trauma. Threaded throughout *SH* is the narrative of the sudden deaths of the author's parents when she was a young adolescent, followed by the deaths of a care-taking grandfather and then uncle. The text alludes to an ongoing incestuous situation and also describes the author's observation of a hit-and-run death (these biographical details are also explicated in Mayer's later works). The narrator is hungry and cannot eat, to do so would assert her will to thrive and kill/starve the mourned-for, incorporated, part-object. Through the process of writing *SH* and some kind of simultaneous internal process, all of the floating object voices are *released into the clean white sheet of my surface in the room* (51). In the narrative's ending climactic sacramental cannibalism, the *you* that has so symbiotically attached itself to the *I*, is saturated in the author's awareness and finally digested. As *SH* concludes, battering utterances finally are becalmed, formed into strands of self and a differentiated other with a history. The flow is less agitated, the strands of its voices read more distinctly. I don't read *SH* this way to valorize individuation and integration as an objective for all of writing but to say that for Mayer, this process opened up her future work and at least partially resolved compulsions and constraining frameworks that had impeded past writing.

Made more whole, an integrated self allows the writer to proceed: *I am alone, I am all one & you are free to visit me whenever you please, as a matter of fact I give you the key, we are so serious we play...the room is mine and your life would be yours to be left alone...*

"Your life to be left alone" is surely the most hard fought-for achievement of *SH*. Although her subsequent writings will work and rework these knots and recapitulate the nature of separation and solitude, the traumas that inhabit this work — and the writer's life — are never again so harrowingly brought to the surface. In the writing out — and through — Mayer finds this communion: *poetry where you all find something maybe I could find something to eat there.* Her work going forward will be sustained by what is to be found there.

NOTE

A version of this essay was first presented at "The Poetry of the 1970s" Conference at the University of Maine, Orono, Maine, in June 2008. Thank you to Steve Evans, Jonathan Skinner, Lee Ann Brown, Julian T. Brolaski, Vyt Bakaitis — and Bernadette Mayer.

The Cosmopolitan

Noah Eli Gordon

The Cosmopolitan by **Donna Stonecipher**
Coffee House Press 2008
ISBN: 978-56689-221-6 $16.00 US

One hundred and fifty years ago, the Baudelairean flâneur's sidewalk botany birthed the prose poem's first foray into capturing urban life. But things have changed. Just as the city, with economy, industry, culture, and all of its various erstwhile insularity propelled into a matrix of exchange, is no longer tethered to geography, so the prose poem of observation and allegory is no longer its form *par excellence*. Donna Stonecipher's new collection, selected by John Yau as a recent winner of the National Poetry Series, comes as something of a corrective. She replaces the sauntering flâneur, content to peer in from the wings, with the cosmopolitan, one who takes to the stage, orchestrating interaction and reportage: "'Ideally, I'd like to look like a Spaniard, fuck like a Serb, and make money hand over fist like an American,' said the cosmopolitan sitting in Hong Kong drinking a caipirinha."

Among the international cast of pronouns and personages populating these prose poems, one finds a theoretical architect, a Russian exile harboring "an indeterminate accent when speaking English, and an English accent when speaking indeterminately," Austrian Anglophiles, hungover tourists, and any number of locals and foreigners, all of whom exchange nomenclature as quickly as the poems shift from city to city. Stonecipher, who has lived in Tehran, Paris, New York, and Prague, and now divides her time between Berlin and Athens, Georgia, brilliantly investigates the implicates of name and place: "The American man who was living in Tanzania was an expatriate, but the Tanzanian man who was living in North America was an immigrant."

While everything here is rife with a metropolitan largess, from memorials to shopping malls and museums, airports to alleyways, there is always the presence of the simulacra we use to take the unfathomable down a few notches: viewfinders, snow globes, and architectural miniatures. This mastery of scale allows the poems to stand in complete reverence before famous works of art and still ask what empire and imperialism might have to do with our understanding of beauty.

Each of the book's near two dozen poems carries the title "Inlay," followed by the parenthetical inclusion of the author's name, who, at some point within the poem's sequence, lends a free-floating quotation. Stonecipher notes this as her attempt to manufacture a kind of inlaid furniture which might account for what she calls her "generation's relationship to quotation and collage." Although Thomas Mann, Zaha Hadid, Kafka, Sontag, Emerson, Benjamin, Elaine Scarry, and a dozen others haunt the periphery of these poems, their presence is a mere inexplicably opened door or the distant rattling of a few phantasmagorical chains. Far more enchanting is Stonecipher's method of playing snippets of narrative against pulpy aphorisms, stirring the cityscapes and citizens of each poem into a constant, surprising flux.

After Cissexual[1] Poetry: Thinking Trans Figures and Feminist Poetics Now

Trish Salah

When I think of feminist poetics today, I find it difficult to do so without recourse to the advent of queer theory, and the privileged, or at least, central, figuration of transgender within queer rhetorics and poetries. Writing transgender "after queer theory," invokes it as displacement, or deferral (or reiteration), of a certain reworked languaging of sexual difference, of a feminine (or feminist) subject-in-process, an avant-garde écriture feminine. Looking backwards through the lens of 90s queer theory, "writing (in) the feminine," "writing (on) the body," possessed a force that was no less radical for literalizing and misprising what the discourse meant to be about. All the things gender performativity could be made to mean only sweetened the deal. Figures for gender, its crossing or undoing, the ephemera and collectibles of a sex, and the eroticism of becoming, became staples of the poetry of everyday life, and not only for those who change sex. Otherwise how could we know to take so literally Kate Bornstein's half-joking dictum, "Never be anyone you wouldn't want to fuck" — "Never fuck anyone you wouldn't want to be"?[2]

---

1 The terms "cissexual" and "cisgender" name non-transsexual and non-transgender persons respectively. Their analytic and political force obviously resides in writing in the usually unmarked embodiment, subjectivity and social entitlement of non-trans persons. Julia Serano describes cissexism as, "the belief that transsexuals' identified genders are inferior to, or less authentic than, those of cissexuals." Julia Serano, *Whipping Girl: A Transsexual Woman on Sexism and the Scapegoating of Femininity* (Emeryville: Seal Press, 2007), p.12. Transsexual and transgender have been, and continue in some measure to be, contested terms. Here I use "transsexual" to refer to persons who work to transition, i.e. to align, their physical embodiment and social identity with their "unconscious sex," or gender identity, using some combination of hormonal, surgical and social technologies (legal name change, social presentation and vestment). In its current use a much broader term, "transgender" refers to all those who express gender at odds with societal expectations of their physical sex; it is broadly inclusive of cross-dressers, genderqueers, butch lesbians, drag queens and drag kings, intersex and transsexual folks, both those moving in the direction of male to female (mtf) and female to male (ftm). Arguing in their cases that gender is not at issue so much as sex, many intersex and transsexual activists have eschewed "inclusion" under the "transgender umbrella." "Trans" also sometimes serves as both shorthand and an overall rubric for gender-variant/transgender folks.

2 *Too Tall Blondes in Love*, written and performed by Kate Bornstein and Barbara Carrellas, directed by Rebecca Patterson. Boston Centre for the Arts: Black Box Theatre (31 May-16 June, 2001).

In feminist and poststructuralist discourses there has been for some time an interest in the figuration, écriture, and/or representation of transgender, whether as evidence for the constructedness of sex and/or gender;[3] to celebrate "transvestitism" as liberation from, or carnivalesque reversal of, gender (and other) hierarchies;[4] and, to mark both the constraints and the necessary subversion of "sexual difference."[5] The figure of transgender, and its psychoanalytic prehistory, similarly animates projects of "becoming-woman" as "the first quantum, or molecular segment" in an anti-identitarian line of flight,[6] and subtends the reading of transgressive gender codes as transformations of genre (from readerly to writerly texts).[7]

In a less libratory vein, for some feminists transsexuality has long figured the violence of masculinist appropriation, indeed the rape of women's bodies and subjectivities. Paradigmatically, in her book, *The Transsexual Empire: The Making of the She-Male*, Janice Raymond figures transsexuals as the objects of a patriarchal medical establishment, and as its agents, male creatures who by both action and being violate women. Raymond locates transsexuality within a more general critique of masculine medical hubris, and of patriarchal science's assault upon sexual difference and women's reproductive autonomy. Like her

3 Examples are too numerous to list, but recall Virginia Woolf, *Orlando: A Biography* (London: Harcourt, 1928), Herculine Barbin, *Herculine Barbin: Being the Recently Discovered Memoirs of a Nineteenth-century French Hermaphrodite*, introd. Michel Foucault, trans. Richard McDougall (New York: Pantheon Books, 1980), and Harold Garfinkel, "Passing and the Managed Achievement of Sex Status in an 'Intersexed Person'" in *The Transgender Studies Reader*. Stryker, Susan & Stephen Whittle, eds. (New York: Routledge, 2006), (58-93). As these examples suggest, at the level of figure, the bodies of intersex and transsexual persons are often confounded and transposed.

4 Immediately preceding, and during the early years of enthusiasm for queer theory (the late 1980s and early 1990s), there was a proliferation of writing concerned with gender ambiguity and (feminist) cross-dressing in Shakespeare's comedies. Exemplary and influential texts include: Jean Howard, "Crossdressing, the Theatre, and Gender Struggle in Early Modern England," *Shakespeare Quarterly*. 1988 (39): 418-440; Stephen Orgel, "'Nobody's Perfect': Or Why Did the English Stage Take Boys for Women?" *South Atlantic Quarterly* 88.1 (1989): 7-30; Marjorie Garber, *Vested Interests: Cross-Dressing and Cultural Anxiety* (London: Routledge, 1992); Valerie Traub, *Desire and Anxiety: Circulations of Sexuality in Shakespearean Drama* (London: Routledge, 1992).

5 Judith Butler, *Gender Trouble: Feminism and the Subversion of Identity*. (New York: Routledge, 1990) and *Bodies That Matter: On the Discursive Limits of "Sex"* (New York: Routledge,1993).

6 Deleuze and Guattari, *A Thousand Plateaus: Capitalism and Schizophrenia*, trans. Brian Massumi (London: The Athlone Press, 1988), p. 279.

7 Roland Barthes, *S/Z: An Essay*, trans. Richard Miller (London: Jonathan Cape, 1975).

mentor, Mary Daly,[8] Raymond positions transsexuality along with cloning, in vitro fertilization and other technologies as the latest attempt to seize from Woman her reproductive powers, attempts which are, in turn, local instances as patriarchy's ongoing metaphysical struggle to quash and control women's creative energy (xx).[9] Comparably, Rita Felski notes in *The Transparency of Evil*, Jean Baudrillard laments our passage from the authenticity of a history in which the world was organized around the "once stable polarities of male and female,"[10] into a posthistorical "undifferentiated circulation of the signs of sex"[11] in which "playing with the commutability of the signs of sex...we are all transsexuals."[12]

Of course it is usually awkward when someone you've been talking about walks in on you. If one wanted to locate a moment when cissexual feminists, leftists, queers, began to have their conversations about "the transgendered" interrupted, one could do worse than point to Sandy Stone's "Post-Transsexual Manifesto."[13] Stone's "Manifesto" spoke back to feminism's then dominant position on transsexuality, one that hoped to "morally mandate [us] out of existence."[14]

---

8 Though *The Transsexual Empire* only appeared in book format in 1979, as Raymond notes in her acknowledgements, it had its genesis in a conference paper delivered at the New England Academy of Religion Meeting in 1972, had a second life as a doctoral dissertation completed at Boston College in 1977 under the supervision of Mary Daly; and, again, judging by the acknowledgements page, the text was critically supported by, and circulated among leading 70s feminists such as Andrea Dworkin, Michelle Cliff, Robin Morgan and Adrienne Rich, among others. Daly's characterization of transsexuals, as Frankensteinian monsters and "a necrophilic invasion of women's space" were published in book form in 1978 in *Gyn/ecology: The Meta-Ethics of Radical Feminism* (Boston: Beacon Press, 1978, pp. 69-72). Though it is clear from Raymond's earlier work, correspondence between Daly and Raymond, as well as from stories and letters published in the Daughter of Bilitis' newsletter, *The Lesbian Tide* and Robin Morgan's denunciation of transsexuals at the 1972 Los Angeles Lesbian Conference, that these positions were developing over the course of the previous decade in lesbian feminist communities and discursive networks. For more on lesbian feminist debates on transsexuality in the community press of this period, see Henry Rubin's *Self-Made Men: Identity and Embodiment Among Transsexual Men* (Nashville: Vanderbilt University Press, 2003).

9 "All transsexuals rape women's bodies by reducing the female form to an artifact, appropriating this body for themselves...." Janice Raymond, *The Transsexual Empire: The Making of the She-Male* (Boston: Beacon Press, 1979), p. 104.

10 Rita Felski, "Fin De Siècle, Fin De Sexe," in *Doing Time: Feminist Theory and Postmodern Culture* (New York: New York University Press, 2000), p.138.

11 Jean Baudrillard quoted in Felski, ibid. p.139.

12 Jean Baudrillard quoted in Felski, ibid. p.138.

13 Sandy Stone, "The Empire Strikes Back: A Posttranssexual Manifesto" in *Body Guards: The Cultural Politics of Gender Ambiguity*, Julia Epstein and Kristina Straub (eds.) (New York and London: Routledge, 1991), pp. 280-304.

14 The full line reads, "I contend that the problem of transsexualism would be best served by morally mandating it out of existence." Janice Raymond, ibid. 178.

It can be difficult to call people *out*, when you are, or appear to be, the only one. You don't want to be too angry, humorless, to appear hysterical, or worse, to look like an asshole, a man. One's credentials should be in order. And in my reading, Stone's rebuttal to a then normative feminist transphobia is marked by such general and specific representational pressures. This may be one reason why Stone's "talking back" to feminism also concedes considerable ground to an avowedly anti-transsexual analytic. Alongside her rebuttal to Raymond, Stone offers in her manifesto a critique that also functioned as an "insider report" on the normativity of the dominant form of transsexual discourse, an autobiographical genre she castigated for being unduly conventional, even essentialist, politically regressive and embarrassingly, kitsch. At the same time, Stone hopefully gestures towards, that is to say, performs, the first moves of what she first calls post-transsexuality, but later terms "transgender." Her post-transsexual, or transgender, performance eschews attachment to gender identity, preferring to imagine and invoke new "trans-genres": "a set of embodied texts whose potential for productive disruption of structured sexualities and spectra of desire has yet to be explored" (296). Effectively it re-reads and re-inscribes (post) transsexuality as a potentially feminist poiesis of the self, a radical esthetic praxis.

Somewhere between this utopian, gender-deconstructive, manifesto and the burlesque "female impersonator's" classic reveal, lies much of the pedagogical, queerly themed "trans-genre" performance art, and fragmentary, postmodern, transgender autobiography of the late 20th and early 21st-century.[15] Most famously, with her theatrical performances, personal essays, and postmodern memoir, *Gender Outlaw*, Kate Bornstein brings together fragmentary, at times scintillatingly pedagogical assemblages combining autobiographical vignettes of experienced transphobia and transition, Butlerian gender theory, gender radical polemic, with showgirl charm and a liberal dose of self-help speak. Spoiling Butler's distinctions between performance and performativity, in ways not atypical of early 90s misreadings of *Gender Trouble*, Bornstein productively misreads queer theory to literalize, vitalize and expand its transgender metaphor into a *trans-genre* form.

15 Kate Bornstein, *Gender Outlaw: On Men, Women and the Rest of Us* (New York, Vintage, 1994), and *My Gender Workbook: How to Become a Real Man, A Real Woman, the Real You or Something Else Entirely* (London: Routledge, 1998). Other texts in this genre include Jill St. Jacques, "Embodying a Transsexual Alphabet," in *Queer Frontiers: Millennial Geographies, Genders, and Generations*, J. Boone et al. eds. (Madison, WI: University of Wisconsin Press, 2000), Susan Stryker's "My Words to Victor Frankenstein Above the Village of Chamounix — Performing Transgender Rage," in *GLQ* 1(3): 227-254. 1994 and Susan Stryker, "The Surgeon Haunts My Dreams," originally published under the title "Pre-Operative" in *TNT*, Spring 1996, Riki Anne Wilchins, *Read My Lips: Sexual Subversion and the End of Gender*. (Ann Arbor: Firebrand Books, 1997).

For instance, in a play that dramatically stages and conjugates the philosophical appropriation of trans (actually intersex) figures, specifically the "19th-century Hermaphrodite," Herculine Barbin, with the voyeuristic gaze mobilized around the surgical "sex change" theatre, Bornstein responds to naturalized societal transphobia, in a parodic double gesture, one that critiques the socially imposed limits of, but still affirms, both her own and Barbin's "life-plots."[16] As she camps, "I'm real glad I had my surgery and I'd do it again, just for the comfort I now feel with a constructed vagina. I *like* that thang!"[17] Bornstein draws upon and reinvents feminist critiques of patriarchal science, as well as feminist performance art idioms, to talk the (transsexual) body, gender oppression and to speak against and through the terms of their socially imposed unintelligibility. Her mixed genre, polemical-affective interventions play both live and "on the page."

The question of women's writing, of feminist writing, has seldom been posed without recourse, implicit or otherwise, to the matter of how women have been written, which is to say against their interest, or alternately, written out, erased. Janine Marchessault offers a timely analysis of the problematics of feminist avant-garde authorship:

> The equation of avant-garde and experimental forms with the 'feminine' foregrounds a disturbing problematic: if, in the post-structuralist scheme an author is a man in his purest expression, then the dead author is indeed a woman — a 'fluid' phantom, 'unfixed' and 'multiply' existing always in the elsewhere. Specificity is doubly lost in this instance since there is no apparent difference between a female and a male avant-garde; all avant-garde practices are simply feminine — though women seem to be the less apt practitioners.[18]

While Marchessault here addresses specifically the challenges to North American feminisms posed by the theories of male poststructuralist thinkers, she also argues the impasses and limits of feminine economies of language in the works of Cixous and Irigaray, as prescribing "the task of inventing an entirely new language by means of [a] negation [that] denies women the possibility of engaging in the public sphere...[and that is] completely determined and inflected by a phallic order which excludes women" (85). As Rosi Braidotti and others

16 Jay Prosser employs the term "life-plot" to describe the performativity of "citable" transsexual and transgender autobiographical narratives in securing sexed subjectivity, and viable embodiment in the face of bodily and societal alienation. Prosser, ibid. pp.103-107.

17 Kate Bornstein, "Hidden, A Gender: A Play in Two Acts," in *Gender Outlaw*, pp.119-120.

18 Janine Marchessault, "Is the Dead Author a Woman? Some Thoughts on Feminist Authorship..." *Open Letter*, 8:4 (Summer, 1992), p.86.

observe, the philosophical and figural inflation of the idea of the feminine quite routinely proceeds in tandem with the "discarding" of women.

In a similar vein, transsexual and transgender critics have drawn critical attention to postmodern, feminist and queer theoretical rhetorics that specifically image the deconstruction of binary gender relations through figures of transvestitism, gender blending and bending, and transsexuality. Trans scholars Jay Prosser and Viviane Namaste take issue with the deployment of transgender in the work of Judith Butler, Marjorie Garber and Eve Sedgwick, suggesting that "in what are now considered its foundational texts, queer studies can be seen to have been crucially dependent upon the transgender figure,"[19] such that "transgendered people are reduced to the merely figural: rhetorical tropes and discursive levers invoked to talk about social relations of gender, nation, or class, that preempt the very possibility of transsexual bodies, identities, and lives."[20] From this vantage then, queerly trans-genre writing seems to imply, alarmingly, rather than the writing of trans subjects, a writing that mobilizes trans figures in the same gesture that erases the capacity of trans people to be speaking, writing, indeed living, subjects.[21]

Prosser and Namaste are undoubtedly correct in calling into question the anti-transsexual effects of a certain class of trans figures, and are correct as well in their critical assessment of cissexual appropriation of representational resources from a highly marginalized community with limited access to self-representation. At the same time, it is clear that queer theory's investment in trans figures has helped leverage discursive and social (lesbian, gay, feminist) space for at least certain trans subjects to appear as speaking subjects, even as it implicitly regulates the range of what may be spoken.

Further, as Rita Felski observes, while a critical relation between esthetic and political imperatives is certainly necessary, much of what gives the esthetic its specificity and its power is lost when that relation is constructed in such a way that determinedly subordinates the esthetic to the political. Poetic writing troubles the idea of woman's experience and of identity per se: "writing undermines, even as it rehearses at its most glaring, the very model of sexual

---

19 Jay Prosser, *Second Skins: The Body Narratives of Transsexuality* (New York: Columbia University Press, 1998), p. 21.

20 Viviane Namaste, *Invisible Lives: The Erasure of Transsexual and Transgendered People* (Chicago: University of Chicago Press, 2000), p.52.

21 Obviously this discursive mode of erasure operates in tandem with material, societal and institutional factors that have also functioned to pre-empt transsexual self-representation (pervasive discrimination in housing, employment, access to social services, including healthcare, individual and state violence, poverty, criminalization, etc.). For a detailed sociological account of the situation of transsexuals in Canada, see *Namaste*, ibid., chapters 6-9.

difference itself."[22] Clearly *trans-genre* writing, particularly as Stone evokes it, is not indifferent to this conception of writing.

In the spirit of Sandy Stone's "Manifesto," by the mid-90s several (post) transsexual, or transgender, writers set out precisely to "disrupt structured sexualities" and "explore new spectra of desire" in works that thematized, queered, and reinscribed the available discourses on transsexuality. In this section of the paper I want to look at three *trans-genre* texts which took up Stone's invitation, albeit in different directions and to differing effects: *Boys Like Her* by Taste This (Press Gang 1998), *All Boy* by Nathalie Stephens (Nathanaël) (House Press 2001), and *iduna* by kari edwards (O Books 2003).

> My Body is a map
> I am the cartographer.
> Desire, my language.
> Sometimes I get lost.[23]

Taste This' collection *Boys Like Her* is subtitled *Transfictions*, and it is an early example of what Butler calls the "New Gender Politics," as well as of what I am here describing as trans-genre writing. Self-describing as a collective of four women[24], Taste This performs its politics through an identity poetics of transgression and as collaborative performance that is genre-crossing in several ways.

As they announce in their introduction, "We didn't set out to write a book. [Taste This began]...quite by accident in November 1995, [in] one show, a spoken word, storytelling, boot-stomping, fiddle-playing experiment in a small theatre in East Vancouver."[25] The show became a cross-country tour and Taste This were encouraged by Persimmon Blackbridge, founding member of the feminist artist collective, Kiss & Tell, to envision their show for the page. Taste This' performances were generic hybrids then, drawing upon performance monologue, music, storytelling and theatre, while *Boys Like Her,* like Kiss & Tell's earlier texts *Drawing the Line* and *Her Tongue on My Theory,* functions both as bookwork in its

22 Jacqueline Rose, *Sexuality in the Field of Vision* (London: Verso, 1986), p. 121, quoted in Rita Felski, *Doing Time: Feminist Theory and Postmodern Culture* (New York, New York University Press, 2000), p. 182.

23 Anna Camilleri "Rush," in Taste This, *Boys Like Her: Transfictions*. Foreword by Kate Bornstein (Vancouver: Press Gang Publishers, 1998), p. 209

24 Taste This is comprised of the writer, Anna Camilleri, storyteller Ivan E. Coyote, actor Zoë Eakle, and musician, Lyndell Montgomery. Additionally the book, *Boys Like Her*, employs the photography of Tala Brandeis, Chloe Brushwood-Rose and Tricia McDonald.

25 *Taste This*, ibid., p. 12

own right and as documentation. The work of translation, of making a book out of performance, entails its own transgressions, disappearances and losses, its own productivity. Most obviously, the book *Boys Like Her* lacks fiddle music and audible/embodied voice in performance, though those lacks make pronounced and visible impressions within the work.

The book is a visual work as well as written, and there is a kind of grammar to its image repertoire. In their introduction, Taste This describe the inclusion of photographs as a way to "capture the performance energy" (14), though the photos are by no means limited to representing the troupe's live performances. Rather the photos, and their process of selection, possess their own productivities. Taste This describe the process as a "give and take, back and forth collaborative process...[i]n some cases the images inspired us to write more" (14). The photographs also function citationally in and across the text, as a sequencing of "talking pictures" and visual signs, indices to the phenomenal-perceptual world as well as its languaged organizations: "...the period, the breath, the continuation of a much longer conversation" (14). Images illustrate accompanying text, repeat and anticipate themselves in blow-ups and incised picture elements from larger tableaux, some palimpsest (are palimpsested by) text, and each section of the book *(bound, sick, bent, wet)* overlays its titular, iconic word with an image. In these full page compositions, the relation between the two registers stages their ekphrastic incommensurability, which doubles the visual register's libidinal excess. *Sick* opens with a blow-up[26] of the small of a woman's back: her hands dominate the upper half of the image as she undoes her bra, and throws shadow over the image centre, where the word "sick" appears in white outlined font; below, her body is actually written on, tattooed with a stylized Eye of Thoth in an inverted pyramid. The visual sign on the body, with its evocation of the lunar, as well of s/m, lesbian, and punk cultures, doubles and speaks in tandem with the fullness and activity of the body. How this is *sick* is a question that opens up the meaning and authority of the categorization.

In these photographs both the body and desire have their distinct if overlapping economies, in and out of what these image-texts can signify. The photos stage erotic *mise-en-scène* in which the performers seduce, arouse and fuck one another, pleasure themselves, and appear in less definitive erotic tableaux. The masculinity of Ivan, Lyndell and at times Zoe draw upon, and out, the presence of gender-transgressive, masculine identifications and desires in queer women's erotic repertoire. As such they also queer the relation between desire, identification, erotic practice and female embodiment. Chloe

26 The image is from a photograph by Chloe Brushwood-Rose, of Camilleri straddling another member of the group, which appears later in the text, on pages 208-209.

Brushwood-Rose's photograph of Lyndell Montgomery, from the waist down, shows corduroy pants with a hint of tenting at the crotch, heavy boots, her bow and fiddle depending from loosely held hands. Images of Montgomery's fiddle recur frequently throughout the text, open and close it, even appearing in ink across a woman's back, which Montgomery is playing with her bow. An explicit, if not heavy-handed, metaphor for (a queerly phallic) erotic competence, it also evokes in the text the present absence of music and live performance as a mode of seductive performance.

At the same time, it is the explicitly high femme Anna Camilleri who, in several of these images, holds a blade. One is also inked into her upper arm. Zoë Eakle, who narrates fluid shifts in gender presentation, between a lesbian boyishness and high femme, wields lipstick. Phallic Femininity is willfully incarnated through the gendered eroticism of diesel Femme identity performance.

The transition from stage to page is also complex, and demanding, at the level of writing. While the imaging of *Boys Like Her* embeds the book's written discourse with a rich supplementarity, the cross-genre, and gender-confounding movement of the writing stages itself a kind of collaborative threshold play, wherein autobiographical anecdote spills into storytelling, verse forms interrupt and fill out prose, and the theatrical backdrop of "the original performance(s)" haunts its transmission into print.

The edge this writing plays upon most consistently limns gender with sexuality, sexuality with gender. It inverts outsiderness into queer pleasure, stages becoming other to oneself as becoming one's self. For example, an erotic trialogue, "Sweet Boy," stages a femme's seduction of her boy(s) in a call and response, wherein Camilleri's speech evokes responses from two different(ly masculine) lovers (Montgomery and Coyote). This play in three voices opens with Camilleri's words followed by Montgomery's, then Coyote's, returning then to Camilleri's, which initiate another sequence.

> *Anna:* Sweet Boy. You came to me with your calloused hands stuffed into your pockets and your eyes unable to hold my gaze...

While each is speaking back to Camilleri, differently, the contrast and juxtaposition of their doubled, if not parallel, responses also communicates a relation:

> *Ivan:* She called herself a femme. It was a matter left up to her to decide, for her to let me know that she was one of my kind. I had made it safe for her because of how I looked. This is the dilemma of the gentle-butch...

> *Lyndell: Sweet.* The word rolled off her tongue and lodged itself in my heart, cunt and ass. It slit my flesh and slid its five letters into my veins...

While Coyote's narrative interweaves gender theory with personal history, Montgomery's words are less committed to story, seeming to dwell more fully where a language of desire collides with sensual body. At one point, Coyote's text breaks the trialogic structure, seeming to speak back to Montgomery's text, distinguishing modes and temporalities of female masculinity as they are playing out within the piece. Here and elsewhere, in its identity work Taste This' collaboration involves the negotiating some fine and shifting distinctions, and it is in that identity work that *Boys Like Her* seems most to break its own form, and to surprise itself.

The narrative of a hostile encounter with Canadian customs agents is told four times throughout the book, by each member of the group, foregrounding that transgression carries its meaning in relation to the law, and occupies multiple registers, including violation. In Zoë Eakle's words:

> To cross the U.S./Canada border without incident it is best to look and act as though you never have and never would think of crossing any border, metaphoric or otherwise, without the express permission of someone very official with a government issued badge and uniform. Either that or you actually have to own the border outright. If you do not own it, transgressions are not allowed. (113)

Their varying perspectives on the event, carrying differing degrees of rage at the routine, if targeted harassment, and fear of further violence, sketches differences between gender transgressive subject positions while evoking residual attachments to the clichéd nationalist expectations of a kinder, gentler Canada. The stories' repetitions both cohere the group and text; narrative contradictions and inconsistencies underscore their multiplicities.

At the same time, these transfictions do perform trans as a kind of performance of a pre-given, if differently inhabited, female body, and draw upon an economy of dyke desire as a cissexual phenomenon that can accommodate gender transgression, and transgenderism to varying degrees, but leaves transsexuality as largely figural. There are two key exceptions, an "authorizing" and authenticating preface, by Kate Bornstein, and a loving if brief anecdote about Coyote's surrogate dad, who used to be a lesbian; otherwise transsexuality appears largely as a phantom ghosting the text's outside.

In ways both like and unlike *Boys Like Her*, the poems in Nathalie Stephens (Nathanaël)'s chapbook *All Boy* writes gender through the figural possibilities of sexuality, rendering inscription as acts of taking/making up a sex in a linguistic theatre of transformation. Stephens plays quite knowingly with the condensation of theoretical and literary figures for desire in language (desiring language) while staying close to the vernacular and romantic poetry of bodies fucking and breaking/making themselves against one another.

Formally, *All Boy* is comprised of fragmentary, yet narratively linked erotic lyrics, arranged in longer and shorter free verse lines, separated and joined by the spacing that largely replaces punctuation — though Stephens still has some use for question marks and possessive apostrophes. The possessive, and possession is actually quite important to this work. As is Stephens' use of spacing: with borders of white space segmenting lines into grammatical, and smaller semic and sub-semic units, the text cuts away at and towards the linear flow of reading, proliferating enjambment, but also the long pause within fragments of sense, image, sound, signifying inscription. As with the genre crossing of *Taste This*, Stephens' association of sex changing with a poetics of translation, intervenes into established sexed metaphorics of language.

Again we are not too distant from the realm of identity poetics. While Stephens' work has long been associated with experimental lesbian and queer women's writing, *All Boy* seems to be sketching out a decidedly different economy of desire. There are Sapphic echoes here, perhaps a suggestion of Anne Carson's well-known translation of fragment 31 and her discourse on eros, "the limb loosener." Yet, if in Sappho, in Carson, what is staged is desire's capacity to animate identification across sex, to triangulate and transpose desiring positions, in Stephens' work desire goes further. Desire changes the body's sex in ways that displace questions of sexuality as they are usually configured through "homo-hetero, male-female dichotomies."[27] Rather, the poems in *All Boy* give us a (at least one) *he* and a (at least one) *she*, and an *I* that may fold into or flit away from either of those positions; what seems relevant is that *she* is the one with the cock, though *he* or *I* might have one as well, it seems less pressing to know. Of course just what a cock is, is another question.

> she grabs hold of her cock and lifts her   glass a toast   with a shiver
> nipples hard under her shirt
>   at what speed must a body fall against water in order to
> break   (as against a wall or roadside   something fast and hard) he   is
> fucking her   cock with his mouth saying fall for me   ~~in winter~~
>   in winter
>
> ("synapse," 5)

"Synapse" is the chapbook's opening poem: notice, *her cock* first appears in a phrase, that enjambed with the next, suggests and quickly subordinates (if not rules out) a "straightforward" lesbian reading of the text, wherein *her* might

27 TDR: Profile Nathalie Stephens (Nathanaël): Interview with Nathalie Stephens by Nathaniel G. Moore. *The Danforth Review*. Toronto, 2006. http://www.danforthreview.com/features/interviews/stephens.htm. Accessed on June 11, 2008.

signify another woman, or a feminine pronominal reference back to cock in a way that might detach it (her) from the body of the initial she: in the latter reading *her cock* is detachable, a dildo, a lesbian phallus.[28] But it is her glass she lifts, and soon it is *he* "fucking her." Again the white space border enjambs phrases on a single line, with consequences for sex, gender, our ability to make a distinction between them. Initially, we are floated the possibility of a heterosexual moment, one with stereotypical associations of gendered sexual agency: "hard) he is/fucking her," though perhaps our initial *she* has become *he* through lifting *her cock*, complicating the reading somewhat. On the other side of the white space, there is a turn: "fucking her cock with his mouth saying fall for me" *he* is still agentive, after a fashion, giving a blow job and speaking a demand for love, so close together. But it is *her cock*, and one assumes it is doing some fucking as well.

The title poem, *All Boy*, which immediately follows "synapse," suggests that these shifts in sexed embodiment, though they enter the domain of sexuality, are not exclusive to it. And curiously they are animated by gendered discourse:

> Want me she said I have read Sylvia Plath I know how to die
> she is pushing sharp poems under skin inviting bone to snap thin bone I
> did this once before and my hand grew stronger my fingers wider
> [...]
> to him she said follow me
> pushing his hand deeper in saying see how hard I am we are both
> hard biting his lip
> bone against bone don't stop just yet with her ass raised she is all boy
> wide hands
> and stubble
>
> ("All Boy," 6)

Here again the pronominal play suggests mobility between either multiple sexual partners, of differing sexes, or chronotopic shifts in the sexed position of one or more subjects within the poem: in the opening stanza a narrative I

28 Within classic psychoanalytic theory, one comes to have a sex, to be one, through one's orientation towards castration anxiety or penis envy respectively; in Lacanian parlance this is a distinction between being and having the phallus. Of course, for Lacan no man actually possesses the phallus, they are merely aligned with the possibility by virtue of its metonymic relation to the penis. Noting the similarities between the symbolic overvaluation of the penis as placeholder for the phallus and the overvaluation of phallic substitutes characteristic of fetishism, Judith Butler argues, "the displacement of the phallus, its capacity to symbolize in relation to other body parts or other body-like things, opens the way for the lesbian phallus, an otherwise contradictory formulation" (84, 85). This in turn implies the ubiquity of cross-gendered desiring subjectivities. Judith Butler, "The Lesbian Phallus and the Morphological Imaginary," in *Bodies That Matter* (New York: Routlege, 1993), pp. 57–91.

observes *she* "pushing sharp poems under skin inviting bones to snap" and recalling how taking such poetic language into *his body* masculinized it. Does this imply *she* is on a similar path, or does incorporating different languages sex us in various ways?

In any case, the poem is giving us markers of embodied shifts, those that accompany the injection of testosterone, even as it attributes them to the agency of poetry. At the level of narrative then, this is a transsexual poem. Recalling the question raised in the last poem, *All Boy* might be read as suggesting a relationship to the phallus that is again, neither lesbian, nor conventionally heterosexual: "pushing his hand deeper in saying see how hard I am we are both/ hard." With "bone against bone" *he* and *she* and Stephens seem to fashion trans-sexes that matter in intimately enabling ways, even while leaving "another/ gender broken" ("Text," 12).

For Stephens it seems that writing trans-genre encompasses many forms of transgendering, including a transsexual poetics that finds its specific radicality in writing out of not only the vicissitudes of cross-gender identification, or gender dysphoric relation to one's embodiment, both of which may play out in a range of transgender writing, but in relation to an itinerary of transition between sexes, whether it be social, surgical, hormonal and/or psychical in character. Which is not to claim that Stephens is transsexual.

In a blog entry ruminating on the death and life of poet, kari edwards, Ron Silliman recalls, "kari didn't like you to use pronouns except to refer to yourself, because pronouns in English invariably register gender and kari's position as a gender activist...was that there was no way to go about this that wasn't wrong. Others tended to use the feminine..."[29] Underlining some of the difficulties elided in this account, Tim Peterson reflects in another memorial blog entry, on the contradictions kari edwards "lived through, of wanting to see and write without gender but wanting also to pass as a woman, of wanting to coalesce into a new identity without that identity actually being stated and thereby commodified."[30]

It is the tension between, or rather the varying and contradictory imperatives of, esthetic-political critiques of identity categorization, the identity-poetic project of coming to voice from places of social abjection, and the "business" of living in the world as a minority subject that edwards attempted to think through in hir essay, "a narrative of resistance":

29 Ron Silliman, "Silliman's Blog: A Weblog Focused On Contemporary Poetry and Poetics," Monday, December 4, 2006. http://ronsilliman.blogspot.com/2006/12/kari-edwards-died-of-heart-failure-on.html. Accessed on May 23, 2008.

30 Tim Peterson, "My kari edwards (written for and presented at the NYC kari edwards memorial, 6/24/07)." Mappemunde: Tim Peterson's Blog: June 25, 2007. http://mappemunde.typepad.com/mappemunde/2007/06/index.html. Accessed May 23, 2008.

> recently I went to a 'I am a __________(fill in the blank) and I am beautiful and sexy and I am okay with who I am no matter what you say' performance. the fill in the blank in this case could be any word that describes a category or any groups of nouns that describe a category that is recognizable within the repeatable patterns of situated narratives. this is not a judgment. the 'I am this __________(fill in the blank)?' is a first step in seeing one's self as other than formlessness situated in social shame. But should this be the stopping point? [31]

edwards needn't here be read as speaking specifically about sexual minorities, though sie does take a shot at the particular conditions consolidating transsexuality in medical terms and homosexuality economically: "one becomes a target for new markets. or one becomes a member of a group locked into the diagnostic and statistical manual of mental disorders (DSM-IV)" (267). Nonetheless, what edwards is describing is the performance of "coming out," whether it be as Latina-Laguna mixed-race fag, or working-class (white) transgender disabled dyke; sie is not negating the value or necessity of such performances, sie is merely marking out their probable trajectory if one makes it beyond survival, through affirmation/mirrored recognition from whatever locally passes as normal, into the commodification of difference/identity and narcissistic, consumer citizenship. Of course when you're still working at survival this kind of thinking seems an effect of inordinate privilege or reactionary commitments. But as Wendy Brown points out, our sense of woundedness at social exclusion and oppression often exceeds their material duration.[32] edwards is not unclear on that point, and hence hir question: "should this be the stopping point?"

Even if one is familiar with edwards' stance on such matters, the persistent linkage of the figures of sexual instability, gender transgression, and the fluidity and mutability of our sexed beings to transgender and transsexual subjects creates a discursive environment in which the easiest way to read edwards' admittedly quite difficult trans-genre poetics is through referential recourse to personal autobiography. This would be a mistake, but a not uncommon one.[33] Thus Ron Silliman's reflection on edwards' "November 28th's carrier pigeon": "On one level, these are identarian (sic) texts that remind [one] of first-generation gay liberation pamphlets produced by such poets as Judy

---

31 kari edwards, "a narrative of resistance" in *Biting the Error: Writers Explore Narrative*, Mary Burger, Robert Glück, Camille Roy, Gail Scott (eds.), (Toronto: Coach House Books, 2004), p. 266.

32 Wendy Brown, "Wounded Attachments" in *States of Injury* (Princeton: Princeton University Press, 1995), pp. 52-76.

33 Viviane Namaste has suggested that "autobiography is the only discourse in which transsexuals are permitted to speak." (*Invisible Lives*, 273)

Grahn or Aaron Shurin. On another, however, these are identarian texts for an identity totally up for negotiation."[34] Here is the poem.

I am a man being a woman
I am a woman being a man
I am a homosexual man being a straight woman being a
homosexual man —
I am a homosexual woman being a straight man being a
Homosexual woman —

I am a tree in disguise
        with an edge predicament
I am a young boy being a young girl being
Whatever for gazing elder eyes
I am licking an envelope over and over and over

I am the new wholesale neither nor nightwear
        plural narrative
        a succubus and an incubus rolled into one
        here to remove organ functions

I am a penny dreadful with a legion of
electrical teeth and gritty eyes
angels and hermaphrodites are my
children and playthings
I pre-check my own in-flight devices
And riddle oedipus to shame
        I am I

a shadow that becomes
  the coffin of your dreams

inspired by:
Brigid Bropley (sic) — *in transit*
Natalie Barney — *the one who is legion, or a.d.'s after-life*

While Silliman's reading of the first stanza does not reduce the poem to biography, recognizing in it a genetic inheritance from lesbian and gay radical

34 Ron Silliman, "Silliman's Blog: A Weblog focused on Contemporary Poetry and Poetics." Wednesday, February 4, 2004. http://ronsilliman.blogspot.com/2004/02/q-how-does-one-pronounce-title-of-kari.html. Accessed June 30, 2008.

poetries, it also "discovers" in edwards' poem the naïveté of a kind of coming out gesture, though that quickly gives way to the deconstruction of any sexed location one could come out from or to, which Silliman also highlights and delights in. Still, even then it is as if the undecidability of gender then asserts itself as the new truth of the speaker's (author's) sex.

My own first readings of the poem followed a similar tack, finding in the first stanza a densely coded and quite witty unpacking of phobic medical and societal diagnoses of transsexuality, and I went so far as to speculate the poem's first stanza was a scathing commentary on the psychoanalytic theory of transsexuality as a symptom of pathologically repressed homosexuality. That only gets us as far as the end of the first stanza. The error however, that both Silliman and I made was in assuming the poem was in some sense about transsexuality, about edwards. That is not to say it is not, but rather to understand what is obscured when autobiographical comment is the first, and all too often last, word.

After all, *iduna*'s opening pages carry two citations that between them offer a guide to reading: "do violence to your body or give way to the beauty of the dawn" (Catherine Clement: *Syncope: The Philosophy of Rapture*), and rotated 90 degrees to the left, and running the upper left hand corner of the page: "Continuous variation/constitutes the becoming minoritarian of everybody, as opposed to the Majoritarian fact of Nobody." (Gilles Deleuze and Felix Guattari, *A Thousand Plateaus: Capitalism and Schizophrenia*). The latter provides an obvious cue to how to read through the arboreal allusion of "a tree in disguise/with an edge predicament" as well as "the riddle of Oedipus" and the assertion, "I am I." The irony with which edwards writes those words is emphatically an effect of the way this seemingly "me narrative" piece, liberally palimpsests and cites its source texts: Brigid Brophy's *in transit* and Natalie Barney's *the one who is legion, or a.d.'s afterlife*. In *in transit,* a concrete novel set in an airport, the protagonist loses language and hence the ability to situate her or himself in terms of gender and sex; bereft of a symbolic orientation, the protagonist becomes increasingly subject to the vagaries and vicissitudes of a world structured like a language. There is a kind of transsexual in edwards' poem, or rather a trans figure, but s/he comes from somewhere else: her/his origin and ongoing sexual ambiguity is precisely a linguistic, and literary effect. Likewise, edwards' lines bear the traces of Natalie Barney and her cross-dressing lover, the painter Romaine Brooks, who provided the images for Barney's only novel, *the one who is legion, or a.d.'s afterlife*. Brooks and Barney's polyamorous lesbian lives, at the heart of literary and gay Paris between the wars, provide a model of queer sexual freedom that remains startling given its context. Brooks and Barney's lives and art could also be an early inspiration for the frankly seductive and trangressive ethos and esthetics of both *Boys Like Her* and *All Boy*.

This then is one answer to the question edwards poses in "a narrative of resistance" as to how one writes one, without falling into "the 'me' theme in personal 'I' narratives" (266). For edwards the desire for recognition, though understandable, necessary even, leads to a dead end, a mirror game. In the poem above, the success of its ruse underscores our desire for reflection as it is manifest in our usual inability to read past our esthetic and political commitments. For edwards, perhaps echoing Stone, but imaging a broader field of social engagement, what is called for is a politics and poetics of alliance across (against?) identity lines: collaboration with stranger friends, cultivated deviance, ethical migration, queerness (if it is still possible without simply inflating the ego ambitions of homosexuality); "seeking out multiple connections to create new systems that take us into communities where we might not otherwise go." (268).

The Hunger Patient

Margaret Ronda

The oldest story: mother as aversion and desire, daughter as darker, dispossessed, as tender and tended to, as tether. The mother all symmetries, the daughter forged improvidently. A borrowed dress, a forgery. Daughter a watcher, mother the turret or tower, impenetrable.

I wanted to eat all day. To become all body, dense and substantial, to take the entire world in. Never been so famished. I devoured her untouched trays of food, meals from the cafeteria, chocolates and oranges the nurses would cadge for me. I refused nothing. Perhaps I wanted, like Ugolino's sons, to offer myself as food: *thou didst us clothe, now in return this wretched flesh receive*. If she would eat, we could remove the feeding tube, the tube of black bile draining from her nose, yellow tubes and red.

S loved God and abhorred her body.

Read her a series of nostalgic stories. The words on my tongue — *Once there were four children whose names were* — stale nourishment. Always she was tired, stoical, she wanted sleep, a stream of words to half-hear, or nothing. Held the plastic cup to her lips as she drank, wearily. Hours of her sleeping, oceanic suck and thrum. To be shelter and succor for one who wants not.

As a child, S was convinced her mother's milk had poisoned her. *C'est pourquoi je suis tellement ratée.*

My mother, all her life, desired to forget herself. So many barriers to vision. To be free from hunger and thirst, excessive desire for material goods, to dwell in a light that radiates effortlessly, a lucid state that is sufficiency itself. Wanted to see clearly, to see beyond sight.

S refused the couple's offer of fresh bread and milk, homemade cheese. She often spoke of Krishna instead of Christ or God. Her great desire: to remove herself from the indecency, the indiscretion, of the "I." Her hands were often swollen and painful, and it was difficult to write.

As a child, much was forbidden her. No swimming, no movies, no playing cards, no pants or shorts, no reading certain novels, no speaking out of turn. Her parents believed in a fierce God, a God of iron law, wrath and retribution. My mother learned to regard the world as an obstacle. Loathed the imposition of power over another. She turned from her mother's God, cutting her hair short, falling in love with women, protesting injustice in Nicaragua, El Salvador, Palestine, Iraq. Followed Weil's mantra: *In this world, purity is the only force.*

Three pills in a cup augured morning, glass of water mistrusting her fingers. I deadheaded the roses and weeded the hawksbeard. A month tallied in ribcage peals, a shying away from the unwearied wheel. The machine slipped inside her and found itself irresistable there. I lay by her bed and tried to keep still.

S's favorite childhood story: Marie in gold and Marie in tar. One is punished for one's earthly wants. Two girls asked S, Were you born in a cabbage or a rose? She answered, I was born in my mother's belly. She worked at a milling machine for months, attempting to achieve an "uninterrupted rhythm."

She is as it were deprived of every feeling, and even if she would, she could not think of any single thing. Thus she needs to employ no artifice in order to arrest the use of her understanding: it remains so stricken with inactivity that she neither knows what she loves, nor in what manner she loves, nor what she wills. In short, she is utterly dead to the things of the world and lives solely in God.

In her vision, she beheld a great tree, suffused with sunlight. "And we are the leaves."

I scraped away snail shells and trimmed the sedges. Flurry of nurses going silent in the jubilee garden, a row of sympathetic eyes. She says, I haven't seen myself for weeks. Pale to white-handed hope, another hour slumped in the tidied air. Her body was all mine, but her face was missing.

There is much speculation that S's mother, a doting, neurotic woman, was the primary cause of her inability, or unwillingness, to eat. "To wrest herself from maternal control," goes the theory. Or she hoped to identify more strictly with those who suffer, to mortify the flesh in order to salve the spirit. Her favorite poem, by George Herbert, ends: *You must sit down, sayes Love, and taste my meat. / So I did sit and eat.*

She dwelled in this presence from that moment forward. She often said she could feel Christ "just beyond her sight," dwelling in unseen corners. In my child's mind: a gently fathomed bird, green shirt of wind in the churchyard. A murmur in the hedge. She called herself his "seeker and servant." She called him her "bread."

S decided, when unable to find employment, to survive on three francs and fifty centimes a day. In practical terms this meant starvation. She wrote, *Slavery has made me completely lose the feeling of having rights.* One morning, a man knocked on her door, but she refused or was unable to answer.

Stripped now to animal humiliations. All body. Crushed birdskull curled in a white box. Little hermit sphinx with bloodied organ swinging above its head. Sallow cleanplucked hen. Gaunt and guttural, moan and claw. Hated her sour breath, black sores on her mouth, fouled and rank. Her skin stitched haphazardly, spittle and heaving bile. Yet I did nurse her close to my breast, timorous beastie, o creaturely life.

S's "shipwreck of beauty": a burden systematically destroyed. Her hunger to be effaced. The poet wrote of her: "A kind of bodyless bird, withdrawn inside itself, in a large black cloak down to her ankles that she never took off, still, silent...."

Mostly she waited.

My mother's goal: to consume less. Pinned on her wall, a quote from Thoreau: "Our lives are frittered away by detail. Simplify, simplify. Instead of three meals a day, if it be necessary eat but one; instead of a hundred dishes, five; and reduce other things in proportion."

I grew in her unseen, a skinny shadow. At the verge of absence — "run and play" as she lifts me into the grass. And so I ran, borrowing her gait. With an eye on her faraway patience. A difficult child, always underfoot, jealous, hungry for attention, acquisitive. I learned to read by reading her gaze, reflected in a hundred unwanted objects.

A child does not stop crying if we tell him there is no bread...he goes on crying all the same. The danger, for the soul, is not to doubt whether there is any bread, but to persuade itself, through lying, that it is not hungry.

S contemplated a method of sustaining human life on sunlight and minerals alone, without taking in any food. In the factory, S stood in front of the furnace, inserting and extracting metal bobbins with a hook. She wrote, "Why imagine it is better elsewhere? I have seen some of these elsewheres."

She was for many years a pastor. Her vestments: a long white robe and a wooden cross from Guatemala. Believe what you must, she told me. After turning from the ministry, she had trouble finding work, ended up cleaning houses. Tasteful homes in the foothills. For her, all labor makes one an instrument. And in this way, all work is God's work, a reminder that we are not free. Some of them belonged to classmates of mine.

Cancer appeared first as a loss of appetite, a listlessness. But the doctors failed to read the signs — "eat more," they urged.

Near the end, she contemplated the "chance" connecting her with others, fragility and finitude. In *La Pesanteur et la Grâce*, S writes, "The woman who wishes for a child white as snow and red as blood gets it, but she dies and the child is given over to a stepmother."

In later years, a sterner withdrawal. My father called it her "great lapse into silence." The long pauses on the phone. The sense that she was looking through you when you spoke. Not the body but what it holds, the secret kernel. She was immune to flattery, disinterested in points of view, unfailingly kind. Now I see she was, in Weil's terms, "emptying herself of the world." And how did she love? With luminous distance.

Let nothing remain of me, forever, except this rending itself, or else nothingness.

I poured the water down the drain, kept the story to myself. Watered the flowers, nursed the blackened roots. I poured the story from my mouth into her sleeping eyes. Watered the roots and nursed the worn furrows. I poured out my hunger into the drain. I mended nothing, made nothing appear, my labors amounted to nothing.

Hunger: one imagines foods, but the hunger itself is real: seize it. The presence of the person lost is imaginary, but the absence is real enough; it is from now on that person's way of appearing.

The last words S spoke to her mother: "If I had several lives, I'd have dedicated one to you, but I only have one life."

An old story: the baby wants to be fed but the mother keeps sleeping. The baby needs a new language. In expressible cries. And the mother, whose sleep is the central fact, whose breathing devours the room and its walls. In her sleep she erases all matter, refuses time and air and the mouth, laboring. Every word a supplication, willing her back to the self. Hush now. The mother's eyes are open but she is sleeping. Finding a truer darkness inside form. And in the empty space her arms make —

NOTE

Italics and quotes are from Simone Weil's *Gravity and Grace and The Notebooks of Simone Weil*, and from Saint Teresa's *The Interior Castle*. The essay also draws on biographical information from Simone Petremont's *Simone Weil: A Life*.

"Thing 02." by Kim Beck

Contributors' Notes

NATHAN AUSTIN's publications include *Tie an O* (Burning Press, 1998), *(glost)* (Handwritten Books, 2002), and *Survey Says!* (Black Maze Books, 2009). He holds a Ph.D. from SUNY Buffalo's Poetics Program and currently teaches English in New York City.

ARI BANIAS lives in Brooklyn, New York, and sometimes teaches literature and creative writing. Recent poems have appeared in *Literary Imagination, The Cincinnati Review, FIELD, Mid-American Review, MiPOesias*, and elsewhere. He curates and hosts the monthly series Uncalled-For Readings, also in Brooklyn.

JASPER BERNES is the author of *Starsdown* and *Desequencer*. He lives in Albany, CA.

DAMARIS CALDERÓN was born in Havana, Cuba, in 1967 and currently lives in Santiago de Chile. Her published books include *Con el terror del equilibrista, Duras aguas del trópico*, and *El arte de aprender a despedirse* (all on Ediciones Matanzas, Matanzas, Cuba), *Se adivina un país* (Ediciones UNEAC, Havana, Cuba), *Duro de roer* (Ediciones Las Dos Fridas, Santiago de Chile), *Sílabas. Ecce Homo* (Ediciones Editorial Universitaria, Santiago de Chile), *La extranjera* (Ediciones Cauce, Pinar del Río, Cuba), and *Los amores del mal* (Ediciones El Billar de Lucrecia, Mexico City). Her work has been widely anthologized in Latin America, and has been translated into French, English and Serbo-Croatian.

THOMAS CAMPBELL is a translator, editor, writer, and researcher based in Saint Petersburg and South Karelia, Finland. He is the editor of *Chtodelat News* (chtodelat.wordpress.com) and has recently contributed to the journals *Russian Literature, Ante, Mute*, and *Kabinet*. He was also the curator of last year's exhibition of work by the Azeri artist Babi Badalov at the Freud Museum of Dreams in Petersburg.

XOCHIQUETZAL CANDELARIA was raised in San Juan Bautista, California, and holds degrees from the University of California at Berkeley and New York University. Her work has appeared in *The Nation, New England Review, Gulf Coast, Seneca Review*, and other magazines. She currently lives in San Francisco.

MILES CHAMPION's recent books are *Eventually* (The Rest, 2008) and *Providence*, a limited edition artist's book in collaboration with Jane South (Sienese Shredder Editions, 2008). He lives in Brooklyn.

CORINA COPP's recent short play, "A Week of Kindness," was produced in the 2007 Tiny Theater Festival at the Ontological-Hysteric. Recent poems can be found in *Antennae*, *6x6*, *Denver Quarterly*, and *EOAGH*; and she's the author of *Play Air* (Belladonna chaplet, 2005), *Carpeted* (Faux Press e-book, 2004), and *Sometimes Inspired by Marguerite* (Open 24 Hours, 2003). A former Monday Night Reading Series Coordinator at The Poetry Project at St. Mark's Church, she is currently pursuing her MFA in Mac Wellman's playwriting program at Brooklyn College.

PHIL CORDELLI is a poet and gardener newly residing in the Happy Valley of Western Massachusetts. More poems of his can be seen in *Cannibal*, *Octopus*, *Tuesday*, *Zoland*, and other publications.

ALAN DAVIES was born in Canada, and has lived for over half his life in New York City. Alan is the author of *RAVE* (Roof), *NAME* (This), *CANDOR* (O Books), and *SIGNAGE* (Roof), and an untitled collaboration with photographer M. M. Winterford (Zasterle Press). Recent publications include *BOOK 5*, (Katalanché); *BOOK 6* (House Press); *Odes* (Faux Press); and *a token is a think upon a tongue* (Sonaweb). *BOOK 1* is forthcoming from Harry Tankoos Press. More information is available at:
http://en.wikipedia.org/wiki/Alan_Davies_%28poet%29
http://epc.buffalo.edu/authors/davies/
http://writing.upenn.edu/pennsound/x/Davies-Alan.html
Alan can be contacted at canadianluddite@yahoo.com.

GEOFFREY DETRANI is a visual artist and writer. His artist's books are in the collection of the Museum of Modern Art, the Brooklyn Museum of Art, and the San Francisco Museum of Modern Art. His writing has appeared in *Crowd*, *New Orleans Review*, *New Delta Review*, *Massachusetts Review*, *First Intensity*, *Epiphany*, *Fourteen Hills*, *Parthenon West Review*, *Black Warrior Review*, *6x6*, *Fence*, *The Canary*, *Tarpaulin Sky*, and *Eleven Bulls*, among other publications, and will be included in a "best of" *Fence* anthology. His artwork recently appeared on the cover of the *New England Review* and is featured in the current issue of *Cutbank*.

DOLORES DORANTES' books include *sexoPUROsexoVELOZ* (Lapzus and Oráculo, 2004), *Lola* (cartas cortas) (Fondo Editorial Tierra Adentro, CONACULTA, 2002), *Para Bernardo: un eco* (MUB editoraz, 2000) and *Poemas para niños* (Ediciones El Tucán de Virginia, 1999). Her op-ed pieces, criticism and investigative texts have been published in numerous Mexican newspapers. Jen Hofer's translations of her poems into English have been published in various periodicals, as a Seeing Eye chapbook, and in the anthology *Sin puertas visibles* (ed. and trans. Jen Hofer, University of Pittsburgh and Ediciones Sin Nombre, 2003). *sexoPUROsexoVELOZ* and *Septiembre*, a bilingual edition of books two and three of *Dolores Dorantes* by Dolores Dorantes was co-published in early 2008 by Counterpath Press and Kenning Editions. She lives in Ciudad Juárez, where she is founding director of the border arts collective Compañía Frugal and teaches through a nonprofit women's advocacy and education organization.

THOMAS EPSTEIN translates and writes on contemporary and modern Russian and French literatures, especially their "unofficial" variants. He is an Assistant Professor at Boston College.

ELENA FANAILOVA, a poet and journalist, was born in Voronezh in 1962. She is a graduate of the Voronezh Medical Institute and the Voronezh State University, where she majored in linguistics. Fanailova has worked as a doctor and an educator. Currently, Fanailova is a host of the radio program *Far from Moscow* for Radio Liberty. Fanailova's poems have been anthologized in *Contemporary Russian Poetry* (Dalkey Archive, 2008), *The Anthology of Contemporary Russian Women Poets* (University of Iowa, 2005) and *Crossing Centuries: the New Generation of Russian Poetry* (Talisman, 2000). Fanailova is the author of four books of poetry in Russian, and a volume of selected poems in English translation, *The Russian Version* (Ugly Duckling Presse, 2009). She has received the Andrey Bely Award (1999) and the Moskovsky Schyot (Moscow Score) Award (2003). She lives in Moscow.

KEITH GESSEN is a founding editor of *n+1* and the author of *All the Sad Young Literary Men* (Viking). His translation, with Anna Summers, of Ludmilla Petrushevskaya's scary fairy tales will be published this fall.

PETER GOLUB is a Moscow-born poet and translator. He has published translations of Russian poetry in various journals, and edited "New Russian Poetry" published by *Jacket Magazine*. In 2007 a bilingual edition of his poems, *My Imagined Funeral*, was published in Russia. He currently teaches at the University of Utah, Salt Lake City.

DMITRY GOLYNKO, born in 1969 in Leningrad, is the author of three books of poems in Russian — *Homo Scribens, Directory* and *Concrete Doves* — and one volume of selected poems in English translation, *As It Turned Out* (Ugly Duckling Presse, 2008). Golynko has been nominated for the Andrey Bely Prize. He is the author of numerous critical essays on contemporary art, cinema and literature, and is currently writing a critical book on Dmitri Prigov. His poems and essays have been translated and published in English, German, French, Finnish, Swedish, and Italian. He has taught in South Korea, has been a participant of CEC Artslink's

Open World Cultural Leaders Program, and was a writer-in-residence at the Literarischer Colloqium in Berlin. He holds a research position at the Russian Institute of Art History and is a member of the editorial board for the *Moscow Art Magazine*. He lives in Petersburg.

LINOR GORALIK, a poet, prose writer, and critic, was born in 1975 in Dnepropetrovsk. She graduated from Beer-Sheva University (Israel) with a degree in computer science, and worked in the hi-tech sector. In 2001 she returned to live and work in Moscow. She is the co-author of two novels: *Nyet* (No), written with Segey Kuznetsov, and *Polovina Neba* (Half the Sky), written with Stanislav Lvovsky. She has published two collections of short prose and poetry, a nonfiction book about the Barbie doll, several anthologies of translations from Hebrew and English, a comic book, and several children's books. She is a frequent contributor to *Teorii Mody* (Theories of Fashion), *Novoe Literaturnoe Obozrenie* (The New Literary Observer), the online project *Snob*, the business newspaper *Vedomosti*, and other periodicals.

NOAH ELI GORDON is the author of several collections, including *Novel Pictorial Noise*, which was selected by John Ashbery for the 2006 National Poetry Series, and subsequently chosen by Sesshu Foster for the 2007 San Francisco State University Poetry Center Book Award. His recent essays, reviews, poetry, creative nonfiction and other itinerant writings can be found in *Bookforum*, *Review of Contemporary Fiction*, *Boston Review*, *Denver Quarterly*, *Fence*, and elsewhere. He pens a quarterly column on chapbook culture for *Rain Taxi: Review of Books*, and is an Assistant Professor of English at the University of Colorado – Boulder.

INTI GARCÍA SANTAMARÍA has published: *Corazoncito* (Compañía, Mexico City, 2004) and *Recuento al final del verano* (NarrArte, Mexico City, 2000). He edits the artist's book imprint Compañía and directs the internet video channel AutismoProducciones.

SARAH GRIDLEY is a Lecturer in Creative Writing at Case Western Reserve University in Cleveland, Ohio. She received an MFA in poetry from the University of Montana in 2000. The University of California Press published her book, *Weather Eye Open*, in 2005. Her poems have recently appeared or are forthcoming in *Fourteen Hills*, *NEO*, *Harp and Altar*, *Crazy Horse*, *jubilat*, *Denver Quarterly*, *New American Writing*, and *Chicago Review*. A new book of poems, *Green Transistor*, will be published by University of California Press in 2010.

DAVID HOCK received his bachelor's degree in Comparative Literature and Slavic Studies from Brown University in May 2009 and plans on continuing his studies as a Ph.D. candidate in Slavic Languages and Literatures at Princeton University. This is his first published translation.

JEN HOFER's recent publications include *The Route*, a collaboration with Patrick Durgin (Atelos, 2008), *sexoPUROsexoVELOZ* and *Septiembre*, a translation from *Dolores Dorantes* by Dolores Dorantes (Counterpath Press and Kenning Editions, 2008), and *lip wolf*, a translation of Laura Solórzano's *lobo de labio* (Action Books, 2007). Her forthcoming books are *from the valley of death* (Ponzipo), *Laws* (Dusie Books), *one* (Palm Press), and a translation of Guatemalan poet Alan Mills' *Síncopes* (Piedra Santa). She currently teaches at Pomona College, at Goddard College, and in the MFA Writing Program at CalArts.

YULIA IDLIS is a poet, critic, and editor. She is a recipient of the Debut award for criticism and was shortlisted for the Debut award in poetry. Her poetry is published in various online and print periodicals, and translations of her poems can be found in *Jacket* magazine's "New Russian Poetry" anthology (issue 36). She lives in Moscow.

A major voice in Québec literature, SUZANNE JACOB has twice won the Governor-General's Award, once for fiction and once for poetry. She is the author of seven novels and three novellas, and has written short fiction, poetry and essays. In 2001, she was inducted to the Académie des lettres du Québec. In 2008, she was awarded the prestigious Prix Athanase-David to honor the body of her work. She lives in Montréal.

PAOLO JAVIER is the author of *LMFAO* (OMG Press), *Goldfish Kisses* (Sona Books), *60 lv bo(e)mbs* (O Books), and *the time at the end of this writing* (Ahadada). He publishes 2nd Ave Poetry, and lives in New York.

GARRETT KALLEBERG's books include *Some Mantic Daemons* (Futurepoem Books), *Psychological Corporations* (Spuyten Duyvil), *Limbic Odes* (Heart Hammer), and the forthcoming *Malilenas* (Ugly Duckling Presse). His writings have appeared in *Brooklyn Rail*, *The Canary*, *Crowd*, *Damn the Caesars*, *Denver Quarterly*, *Sulfur*, *Mandorla*, and elsewhere. Garrett lives in Guadalajara, Mexico.

PAULA KONEAZNY lives in Sebastopol, California, with numerous rose bushes and four cameras and earns her living as a tax consultant. Her poetry has appeared most recently in *Volt: The War Issue* and is forthcoming in *Pool*. Her reviews are published periodically in *American Book Review* and have appeared in *Rain Taxi* and *Verse*. She has a chapbook, *The Year I Was Alive*, out from dpress.

SERGEY KRUGLOV was born in 1966 in Krasnoyarsk, Siberia. In the early 1990s, he published through the Vavilon Union of Young Poets. In 1996 he received a baptism and then took the cloth, ceasing his literary activities. In 2006, his work began to appear in print once more. In addition to magazine and online publications, Kruglov has published several books of poetry, most recently *Prinoshenie (The Sacrifice)* and *Perepishchik (The Copyist)*. A book of early poems *(Sniatie zmiia so kresta)* was shortlisted for the Andrey Bely Award in 2003. Sergey Kruglov lives in Minusinsk, in the Krasnoyarsk region, where he serves as a priest of the Russian Orthodox Church.

DMITRI KUZMIN was born in 1968. He is a poet, publisher, editor, curator, educator, and translator. In 1989 he founded the Vavilon Union of Young Poets, which was the organizational hub for Moscow's experimental poetry scene. Since 1993, he has been Editor-in-Chief of ARGO-RISK (which publishes about 20 titles of contemporary Russian poetry yearly). Since 1996 he has been editing the Vavilon Internet project (www.vavilon.ru), an anthology of contemporary Russian writing, with about 200 authors currently. He is Editor-in-Chief of *Vozdukh (Air)*, a quarterly poetry magazine. He is a recipient of the Andrei Bely Award of Merit in Literature (2002), and the Moskovsky Schyot (Moscow Score) Award for the best debut poetry collection for his selected poems and translations, *Horosho byt' zhivym / It's fine to be alive* (2008). He has taught literature and literary translation, and has translated poetry from French, Ukrainian, and English (Auden, cummings, Stevens, and Ashbery, among others). His poems have appeared in translation in England, France, Poland, China, Italy, and the US.

RACHEL LEVITSKY's second long poem, *NEIGHBOR*, was published by Ugly Duckling Presse in 2009. Some of this work can be found translated into Icelandic in the anthology *131.839 Slög Med Bilum*, edited and translated by Eiríkur Örn Nordahl. Online poetry and critical essays can be found on such sites as *Delirious Hem*, *Narrativity*, *Duration Press*, *How2*, and *Web Conjunctions*. She is the founder and co-director of Belladonna*, an event and publication series of feminist avant-garde poetics.

ROMÁN LUJÁN currently lives in Los Angeles, where he is studying for his Ph.D. in Hispanoamerican Literature at University of California – Los Angeles. His books include *Deshuesadero* (Fondo Editorial Tierra Adentro, 2006), *Aspa Viento* (in collaboration with the artist Jordi Boldó, Fondo Nacional para la Cultura y las Artes, 2003), and *Instrucciones para hacerse el valiente* (Consejo Nacional para el Arte y la Cultura and Centro Cultural Tijuana, 2000). With Luis Alberto Arellano, he edited an anthology of poetry from Querétaro titled *Esos que no hablan pero están* (Fondo Estatal de Querétaro, 2003).

KIMBERLY LYONS is a clinical social worker in private practice in New York City. She is the author of several collections of poems including *Phototherapique* (Portable Press, Katalanche Press, 2008), *Saline* (Instance Press, 2005), *Abracadabra* (2000) and *Mettle* (a 1996 limited edition collaboration with artist Ed Eppling), both published by Granary Books. Her poems, reviews and critical writing can be found in the anthologies *New (American) Poets* (Talisman), *The Boog Lit Reader* and *Not for Mothers Only* (Fence, 2008), and recently in the journals *Critiphoria*, *Satellite Telephone*, *The Poetry Project Newsletter* and *The Recluse*. She curated the Zinc Bar Reading Series from Fall 2008 through Winter 2009. She is starting a new small press, Lunar Chandelier.

CHRISTOPHER MATTISON graduated with an M.F.A. in Literary Translation from the University of Iowa and is currently a senior editor at Zephyr Press, co-director of the series Adventures in Poetry and translation editor for the *Zoland Poetry* annuals. His books of translation include Dmitri Prigov's *50 Drops of Blood in an Absorbent Medium* (Ugly Duckling Presse) and the forthcoming *Eccentric Circles: Selected Prose of Venedikt Erofeev* (Twisted Spoon Press). Mattison has also edited Bei Dao's first two books of essays, *Blue House* (Zephyr Press) and *Midnight's Gate* (New Directions).

CATHERINE MAVRIKAKIS teaches literature and creative writing at University of Montreal. Among her numerous publications are four novels and a play, as well as a book-length essay, *Condamner à mort* (Presses de l'Université de Montréal).

EDUARDO MILÁN has moved to Mexico City in 1979 for political reasons and has lived there ever since. He was on the editorial board of the magazine *Vuelta* and has worked with the Sistema Nacional de Creadores de Arte. He has published numerous books of poetry and critical prose, including most recently *Acción que en un momento creí gracia* (Igitur, Tarragona, Spain, 2005), *Indice al sistema del arrase* (Baile del Sol, Tenerife, Canary Islands, 2007), *Sobre la capacidad de dar sombra de ciertos signos como un sauce* (Fondo de Cultura Económica, Mexico City, 2007), and *Hechos polvo* (with illustrations by Gabriela Gutiérrez, Escuela Superior de Arte de Mérida, España, 2008).

ALAN MILLS currently lives in São Paulo, Brazil, where he is writer-in-residence at the Casa das Rosas-Espaço Haroldo de Campos de Poesia. His books include *Testamentofuturo* (www.librosminimos.org, 2007) and *Síncopes* (Perú: Zignos, 2007; México: Literal, 2007; Bolivia: Mandrágora Cartonera, 2007), forthcoming in trilingual edition (French, Portuguese, Spanish; Brazil: Demónio Negro) and in bilingual edition (English-Spanish; Guatemala: Piedra Santa).

MAX NEMTSOV was born in Vladivostok, where he majored in English Literature at university, graduating with honors. He has worked as a captain's mate, a newspaper editor, and a press attaché for the US Consul General in Vladivostok. In 1986, he co-founded DVR, an underground journal of alternative culture. In 1996 he created the electronic library *Speaking in Tongues: A Journal of Non-Literal Translation*. From 2001 to the present he has worked as an editor and translator in Moscow and Saint Petersburg. In 2002, he was named "Editor of the Year" by the newspaper *Knizhnoe Obozrenie (The Book Review)*. He lives in Moscow.

AKILAH OLIVER is the author of *A Toast in the House of Friends* (Coffee House Press, 2008) and *the she said dialogues: flesh memory* (Smokeproof/Erudite Fangs, 1999, Winner of the PEN Beyond Margins Award), a book of experimental prose-poetry. Her chapbooks include: *a (A)ugust* (Yo-Yo Labs, 2007), *The Putterer's Notebook* (Belladona, 2006), and *An Arriving Guard of Angels, Thusly Coming to Greet*, which was published by Farfalla Press (2005) in a text and performance CD edition. She currently makes her home in Brooklyn, NY.

EUGENE OSTASHEVSKY is a Russian-born American poet and translator. He is the author of several books of poetry, including *Iterature* (Ugly Duckling Presse, 2005) and *The Life and Opinions of DJ Spinoza* (Ugly Duckling Presse, 2008). Eugene's poems have appeared in *Best American Poetry 2005*, *Jubilat*, *Fence*, *Boston Review* and other magazines. Ostashevsky edited and co-translated *OBERIU: An Anthology of Russian Absurdism* (Nortwestern University Press, 2006), containing work by Alexander Vvedensky, Daniil Kharms, and others. He teaches the humanities at New York University.

TIM PETERSON is a poet and critic living in Brooklyn, New York. Peterson is the editor of *EOAGH: A Journal of the Arts* and curator of the Tendencies talk series at CUNY Graduate Center. Peterson's most recent book is *Since I Moved In* (Chax Press). A new chapbook, *Violet Speech*, is forthcoming from 2nd Avenue Poetry in late 2009.

NATASHA RANDALL is an American writer and translator living in London. She is the author of new translations of Yevgeny Zamyatin's *We* (Random House) and Mikhail Lermontov's *A Hero of Our Time* (Penguin Classics). Her work has appeared in *A Public Space*, *The Los Angeles Times Book Review*, *The Moscow Times*, *Bookforum*, *The New York Times*, *HALI Magazine*, *The Strad Magazine*, *The St. Petersburg Times* (FL), and on National Public Radio. Her translations of Osip Mandelstam have appeared in *Jubilat* and in the chapbook *Osip Mandelstam: New*

Translations (Ugly Duckling Presse). She has also translated letters by Arkadii Dragomoshchenko and short fiction by Olga Zondberg.

MATT REECK lives in Brooklyn. His poems have appeared or will soon appear in magazines including *Brooklyn Review, Circumference, Conjunctions, Denver Quarterly, They Are Flying Planes, Tight,* and *Upstairs at Duroc.* His two chapbooks were published in 2009, *Love Songs and Laments* by MIPOesias and *Sieve* by Other Rooms Press. His translations can be read online at *Jacket* and the *Annual of Urdu Studies.*

MARGARET RONDA's poetry has most recently appeared in *Pool, Xantippe, Portland Review,* and *Gulf Coast.* She is a doctoral candidate in English at the University of California – Berkeley, writing on the esthetics of labor in American poetry. She lives in Portland, Oregon.

TRISH SALAH is a Montreal-based writer, activist and teacher at Concordia and Bishop's Universities. Her writing addresses questions of desire, identity and the precarity of belonging. She has been politically active in grassroots, campus-based and labor organizations on issues of Palestinian solidarity, anti-capitalism, sex workers' rights, anti-racism, queer and trans rights. Her first book of poetry *Wanting in Arabic* was published by TSAR in 2002 and her recent writing appears in the journals *Open Letter, Atlantis, No More Potlucks,* and *West Coast Line.*

SIMONA SCHNEIDER is a writer and photographer until recently based in Tangier, Morocco, whose work has appeared in *The New Yorker, Harper's, Bidoun, A Public Space, Issue One* and other publications. She was a co-translator for *Today I Wrote Nothing: The Selected Works of Daniil Kharms* and *As It Turned Out* by Dmitry Golynko. She will be pursuing a Ph.D. in Comparative Literature and Ethics this Fall at the University of California – Berkeley.

ZACHARY SCHOMBURG is the author of *Scary, No Scary* (Black Ocean, 2009) and *The Man Suit* (Black Ocean, 2007). He co-edits Octopus Books and *Octopus Magazine.* His translations from the Russian can be found in *The Agriculture Reader, Circumference, Jacket, Harp & Altar, Mantis,* and *Peaches and Bats.* He lives in Portland, Oregon.

ANDREI SEN-SENKOV was born in 1968 in Tadjikistan. He is the author of seven books. His work has been translated into Itlaian, English, French, German, Dutch, Estonian, and Albanian. In 2008, he traveled to the US as a participant of CEC Artslink's Open World Cultural Leaders Program. He lives in Moscow where he works as a medical doctor.

LAURA SIMS is the author of two books of poems: *Practice, Restraint*, winner of the 2005 Fence Books Alberta Prize, and *Stranger* (Fence Books, 2009). Her book reviews and essays have appeared in *Boston Review*, *New England Review*, *Rain Taxi*, and *The Review of Contemporary Fiction*, and she has recently published poems in the journals *Denver Quarterly*, *Colorado Review*, *CAB/NET*, and *Crayon*. She lives in Brooklyn, New York, and teaches writing at Baruch College in Manhattan.

ALEKSANDR SKIDAN was born in 1965 in Leningrad. He is a poet, literary critic, essayist, and translator. He has worked as a journalist, a lecturer, and a boiler-room operator, and has served on the selection committee of the Andrei Bely Award and on the editorial boards of several literary journals. Skidan is the author of several books of poetry and literary criticism, including *Delirium* (1993), *A Critical Mass* (1995, nominated for the Small Booker Prize), *In the Re-reading* (1998), *The Resistance to/of Poetry* (2001), *Red Shifting* (2006, Andrei Bely Award) as well as a volume of selected poems in English translation, *Red Shifting* (Ugly Duckling Presse, 2009). His poetry has been translated into English, Estonian, Finnish, French, Hebrew, Italian and Swedish. In 1998, he received Turgenev Award for short prose. He has participated in the International Writing Program at the University of Iowa (1994) and in the CEC Artslink Open World Cultural Leaders Program (2005). He lives in St. Petersburg.

LAURA SOLÓRZANO (Guadalajara, 1961) is the author of *Un rosal para el señor K* (Universidad de Guanajuato, 2006), *Boca perdida* (bonobos, Metepec: 2005), *lobo de labio* (Cuadernos de filodecaballos, Guadalajara: 2001) and *Semilla de Ficus* (Ediciones Rimbaud, Tlaxcala: 1999). Jen Hofer's en face translation of *lobo de labio* was published as *lip wolf* by Action Books in March 2007. Laura is on the editorial board of the literary arts magazine *Tragaluz*, and currently teaches writing at the Centro de Arte Audiovisual in Guadalajara.

MARIA STEPANOVA was born in Moscow in 1972. She is the author of six books of poetry and the recipient of several literary awards, including the Pasternak Prize (2005), the Andrei Bely Award (2005), and the Hubert Burda Preis (Germany, 2006). She has published poems in many literary journals and poetry almanacs, including *Zerkalo (The Mirror)*, *Znamya (The Banner)*, *Kriticheskaja Massa (Critical Mass)*, *Novoe Literaturnoe Obozrenie (The New Literary Observer)*, and *Vavilon (Bablylon)*, and in the online journal TextOnly. Her poems have been translated into several languages, including English, Hebrew, Italian, German, Serbo-Croatian, and Finnish. She is the Editor-in-Chief of the internet portal, OpenSpace.ru.

NATHALIE STEPHENS (NATHANAËL) writes l'entre-genre in English and French. She is the author of sixteen books, including *The Sorrow and the Fast of It* (2007), *L'injure* (2004), and the essay of correspondence *Absence Where As (Claude Cahun and the Unopened Book)* (2009). Her book, *...s'arrête? Je* (2007) was recently awarded the Prix Alain-Grandbois. *Je Nathanaël* (2003) exists in English self-translation with BookThug (2006). Other work exists in Basque and Slovene, with book-length translations in Bulgarian (2007). In addition to translating herself, Stephens has translated Catherine Mavrikakis, Gail Scott, Bhanu Kapil and Édouard Glissant. She is, she thinks, in Chicago.

FRANÇOIS TURCOT has published *miniatures en pays perdu* (2006) and *Derrière les forêts* (2008) with Éditions La Peuplade. He teaches literature, took interest in the œuvre of W. G. Sebald in the context of a Masters at UQÀM and sometimes contributes to journals (*Riveneuve Continents, La Table des Matières (TM03), filling Station, Nor, C'est selon*).

DMITRY VODENNIKOV was born in 1968. He is the leader of a poetic movement, the New Sincerity, and the author of several books of poetry, and a documentary novel. He works at Radio Rossia, the radio station Kultura, and the magazine *Russkaia zhizn (Russian Life)*. He is the creator of several radio programs dedicated to contemporary literature. In 2007 he was named King of Poets. He lives in Moscow.

DANA WARD is the author of *Goodnight Voice* (House Press, 2008), *The Drought* (Open 24HRS, 2009), & *Roseland* (Editions Louis Wain, 2009) He lives in Cincinnati where he edits Cy Press and works as an advocate for adult literacy.

DIANE WARD attended the Corcoran School of Art in Washington, DC and is currently pursuing a degree in Geography/Environmental Studies at University of California – Los Angeles. She has published ten books of poetry including, most recently, *No List (No List)* (Seeing Eye Books). She has been included in numerous anthologies, among them: *MOVING BORDERS: Three Decades of Innovative Writing by Women*, edited by Mary Margaret Sloan (Talisman House) and *OUT OF EVERYWHERE: linguistically innovative poetry by women in North America & the UK* (Reality Street Editions). She is currently working on a text for avant-garde sound performer and musician Emily Hay.

KAREN WEISER is thinking about the culture wars of the 1790s, conspiracies and all.

ELISABETH WHITEHEAD grew up in the Washington, DC area and Japan, and currently lives in the Blue Ridge Mountains of Virginia. She is the co-editor of *Greatcoat* magazine.

BRIAN WHITENER is a writer, researcher, translator, and member of the collective project La Lleca, an artistic-social intervention into the prison system of Mexico City. A translation of *Colectivo Situaciones' Genocida en el barrio* is forthcoming from ChainLinks. He is an editor at Displaced Press (http://displacedpress.blogspot.com). Since 2005 he has undertaken an investigation on new political and artistic movements in Latin America and autonomist political theory.

TYRONE WILLIAMS teaches literature and theory at Xavier University in Cincinnati, Ohio. He is the author of two books of poetry, *c.c.* (Krupskaya Books, 2002) and *On Spec* (Omnidawn Publishing, 2008). He also has several chapbooks out, including AAB (Slack Buddha Press, 2004), *Futures, Elections* (Dos Madres Press, 2004), and *Musique Noir* (Overhere Press, 2006). A new book of poems, *The Hero Project of the Century*, is forthcoming in 2009 from The Backwaters Press. He recently completed a manuscript of poetry commissioned by Atelos Books.

MATVEI YANKELEVICH was born in Moscow in 1973, emigrated to the US in 1977 and grew up in New England. He is the author of *The Present Work* (Palm Press, 2006) and the forthcoming *Boris by the Sea* (Octopus, 2009). His writing has appeared in *Boston Review, Damn the Caesars, Fence, Open City, Tantalum, Zen Monster*, and other journals. His translations have appeared in journals including *Calque, Circumference, Harper's, New American Writing, Poetry*, and *The New Yorker*. He edited and translated *Today I Wrote Nothing: The Selected Writings of Daniil Kharms* (Overlook, 2007; Ardis, 2009); and contributed translations to *OBERIU: An Anthology of Russian Absurdism* (Northwestern Univ., 2006); *Night Wraps the Sky: Writings by and about Mayakovsky* (FSG, 2008); and *Contemporary Russian Poetry* (Dalkey Archive, 2008). Matvei teaches Russian Literature and Language at Hunter College while pursuing a Ph.D. in Comparative Literature at City University of New York. He is a founding member of Ugly Duckling Presse, where he designs and edits various books and runs UDP's Eastern European Poets Series.

SERGEI ZAVYALOV was born in Tsarskoe Selo (near St. Petersburg) in 1958. Educated as a classicist, he is the author of three books of poetry, the *Melik* cycle, recently collected in one volume in Finnish translation. This year, a selection from this series was published in Swedish as *Melik & tal*. His essays have appeared in *Novoe Literaturnoe Obozrenie (The New Literary Observer)*, and English translations of his poems have appeared in *A Public Space*, *St. Petersburg Review*, and the anthology *Crossing Centuries: The New Generation in Russian Poetry* (Talisman House, 2000). The poems included in this issue are from a collection soon to be published under the title *Rechi (Orations)*.

IGOR ZHUKOV was born in 1964 in the city of Kovrov, Vladmirskaya region. He graduated from the Philology Department of the Ivanovsky State University. He is the author of five books of poetry, as well as many books of poetry and fairy-tales for children. He lives in Moscow.

TATIANA ZIMA was born in 1968 in the port of Vanino, Khabarovsky Region, in the Russian Far East. She is the author of an award-winning poetry book, *Skoby (Shackles)*. She edited *Ryby i Pticy (Fish and Birds*, 2006), an anthology of alternative poetry from Vladivostok, where Zima organized many poetry events and workshops for youner poets. In 2007, she traveled to the US as a participant of CEC Artslink's Open World Cultural Leaders Program. Her poems have appeared in many literary journals and almanacs, including *Seraia loshad (Gray Horse)*, *Den i Noch (Day and Night)*, *Rubezh (Boundary)*, *Dalnii Vostok (Far East)*, and *Deti Ra (Ra's Children)*. She lives in Moscow.

OLGA ZONDBERG studied chemistry at Moscow State University. She has written two collections of poetry, including *Seven Hours Two Minutes* (2007), and a book of short stories, *The Winter Company of Year Zero* (2001). In 2006, *A Public Space* published two of her prose poems in English translation.

do you Aufgabe?

Aufgabe #1, edited by E. Tracy Grinnell and Peter Neufeld, with guest editors Norma Cole (covers and content pages of small publications from France) and Leslie Scalapino. (out of print)

Aufgabe #2, edited by E. Tracy Grinnell, with guest editor Rosmarie Waldrop (German poetry in translation).

Aufgabe #3, edited by E. Tracy Grinnell, with guest editor Jen Hofer (Mexican poetry in translation, bilingual). (out of print)

Aufgabe #4, edited by E. Tracy Grinnell, with guest editor Sawako Nakayasu (Japanese poetry in translation).

Aufgabe #5, edited by E. Tracy Grinnell with Mark Tardi and Paul Foster Johnson (special issue dedicated to Norman O. Brown's lecture "John Cage") and guest editors Guy Bennett and Jalal El Hakmaoui (Moroccan poetry in translation). (out of print)

Aufgabe #6, edited by E. Tracy Grinnell, Paul Foster Johnson and Mark Tardi, with guest editor Ray Bianchi (Brazilian poetry in translation).

Aufgabe #7, edited by E. Tracy Grinnell, Paul Foster Johnson, Mark Tardi, and Julian T. Brolaski, with guest editor Jennifer Scappettone (Italian poetry in translation).

WWW.LITMUSPRESS.ORG

Subscriptions are available through the publisher. Back issues may be purchased through Small Press Distribution or as part of our "Full Series Deal" (on our website & only while supplies last). Issues listed as "out of print" are only available through our "Full Series Deal" with a certain number reserved for libraries and other public access collections. Contact us for more information. Does your local library, university, or bookstore carry *Aufgabe*? Ask them to. Anywhere else you'd like to see *Aufgabe*? Let us know!